Dialogue in the Analytic Setting

DISCARDED

WIDENER UNIVERSITY

of related interest

Circular Reflections
Selected Papers on Group Analysis and Psychoanalysis
Malcolm Pines
International Library of Group Analysis 1
ISBN 1 85302 492 9 paperback
ISBN 1 85302 493 7 hardback

Self Experiences in Group
Intersubjective and Self Psychological Pathways to Human Understanding
Edited by Irene Harwood and Malcolm Pines
International Library of Group Analysis 4
ISBN 1 85302 596 8 hardback
ISBN 1 85302 597 6 paperback

Active Analytic Group Therapy for Adolescents
John Evans
International Library of Group Analysis 6
ISBN 1 85302 617 4 hardback
ISBN 1 85302 616 6 paperback

Attachment and Interaction
Mario Marrone and Nicola Diamond
International Library of Group Analysis 3
ISBN 1 85302 587 9 hardback
ISBN 1 85302 586 0 paperback

Dialogue in the Analytic Setting
Selected papers of Louis Zinkin
on Jung and on Group Analysis

Edited by Hindle Zinkin, Rosemary Gordon
and Jane Haynes

Forewords by Malcolm Pines and Rosemary Gordon

Jessica Kingsley Publishers
London and Philadelphia

'Death in Venice – A Jungian View' (1977) *22*,4; 'The Collective and the Personal' (1979) *.24*,3; 'Paradoxes of the Self' (1985) *.30*,1; 'The Klein Connection in the London School' (1991); 'The Hologram as a Model for Analytical Psychology' (1987) *32*,.1; 'The Grail and the Group' (1989) *34*,4 are reproduced here from the Journal of Analytical Psychology by the kind permission of Routledge Ltd, London.

'Person to Person: the Search for the Human Dimension in Psychotherapy' is reproduced from the *British Journal of Medical Psychology* (1978) *51*, 25–34 by the kind permission of the British Psychological Society.

'A Gnostic View of the Therapy Group' (1989) *22*, 201–17; 'Malignant Mirroring' (1989) *16*,3; 'Three Models are Better than One'(1984) *17*,2; 'The Group as Container/Contained' (1989) *22*, 227–34; 'All's Well that Ends Well'(1994) *27*, 15–24 are all reproduced here from the journal of *Group Analysis* by the kind permission of Sage Publications Ltd, London.

'The Dialogical Principle in Jungian and Group Analysis' is reproduced from *Harvest: Journal for Jungian Studies* (1994) *40* by kind permission.

The figure from *Making of Meaning* by Ogden and Richards is reproduced by the kind permission of Routledge Ltd, London.

The figure from the *Collected Papers of Peirce* edited by C.Hartshorne, P.Weiss, A.W.Burks is reproduced with the kind permission of Harvard University Press, Cambridge, M.A.

The figure from *Maps of the World* by C. Hampden-Turner is reprinted by the kind permission of Reed Consumer Books Ltd, London.

All rights reserved. No paragraph of this publication may be reproduced, copied or transmitted save with written permission or in accordance with the provisions of the Copyright Act 1956 (as amended), or under the terms of any licence permitting limited copying issued by the Copyright Licensing Agency, 33–34 Alfred Place, London WC1E 7DP. Any person who does any unauthorised act in relation to this publication may be liable to criminal prosecution and civil claims for damages.

The right of the contributors to be identified as author of this work has been asserted by them in accordance with the Copyright, Designs and Patents Act 1988.

First published in the United Kingdom in 1998 by
Jessica Kingsley Publishers Ltd
116 Pentonville Road
London N1 9JB, England
and
1900 Frost Road, Suite 101
Bristol, PA 19007, U S A

RC
510
.Z56
1998

Copyright © Jessica Kingsley Publishers 1998

Library of Congress Cataloging in Publication Data
A CIP catalogue record for this book is available from the Library of Congress
British Library Cataloguing in Publication Data
A CIP catalogue record for this book is available from the British Library

ISBN 1 85302 610 7

Printed and Bound in Great Britain by
Athenaeum Press, Gateshead, Tyne and Wear

WIDENER UNIVERSITY
WOLFGRAM
LIBRARY
CHESTER, PA

Contents

Figures

Acknowledgements

After my husband died in March 1993 I spent many hours going through all his disks on our old Amstrad and found a number of recently given papers, not yet prepared for publication, and notes for others. I tried to assemble a book from some of his published work and some of this new material, but after a few months I lost heart and simply prepared two of the most finished papers for publication, one in *Group Analysis* and one in *Harvest*. Early in 1997 I was approached by the Publications Committee of the Society of Analytical Psychology to take the project up again, with Rosemary Gordon and Jane Haynes as co-editors. I am most grateful to that Committee for their interest and persistence, which enabled me to resume work on the book. Without their encouragement the book would never have appeared.

My principal thanks are to Rosemary and Jane, who have given hours of their valuable time to reading, planning and checking for this joint effort. I am deeply indebted to them. I am very grateful also to Dennis Brown, Kate Newton, Andrew Samuels, Gerald Wooster and Cesare Sacerdoti for reading and advising on some papers, and to many other colleagues and friends for their support and encouragement.

We would like to thank James Astor and Max Fordham for their kind permission to publish the letters from the late Dr Michael Fordham which are included in chapter 7.

With posthumously published papers it is often difficult to trace the author's references and we hope readers will take an indulgent view where it has not been possible to reference a quote. Special thanks go to Renos Papadopoulos and Roderick Peters for the time and trouble they took to help us with this problem.

Finally, a big thank you to June Ansell for her efficiency, enthusiasm and patience in providing us with secretarial support.

Foreword
Malcolm Pines

Our lives intertwined. At the same age we met at the same minor day public school, The City of London. During the war we were evacuated to Marlborough where we shared buildings with Marlborough College. Ours was a melting pot school, multi-ethnic; like us many were Jews from immigrant families. Louis and I were friends amongst other friends. We had the same piano teacher though he far outstripped me as a pianist. We loved music and theatre and in wartime London went to the Promenade Concerts at the Albert Hall and to Myra Hess's concerts at the National Gallery. We queued at the New Theatre to see Laurence Olivier as Oedipus, Ralph Richardson as Peer Gynt. In blacked out London we organized poker games in each other's houses, his in the West End, mine in the East End. At 17 and 18 we had girlfriends and Louis later married Hindle. We both read medicine, he at Oxford and I at Cambridge. Amongst Louis' close friends were Ronald Senator, who became a well known composer, and Arthur Boyars, a likeable literary entrepreneur. I do not know when his interest was aroused in Jungian analytical psychology: mine began at Cambridge in my late teens and it was then that I decided to train in psychiatry and psychoanalysis. Louis wisely took his time and as a ship's doctor he travelled the oceans beginning his lifetime search for connection between cultures, for individuation and connectedness. Eventually he trained in both adult and child psychiatry and in analytical psychology which at that time was a minority interest in the psychodynamic trainings on offer in London. Years later our paths again intertwined when he came to talk to me about entering into a group analytic training, a considerable enterprise which would involve him in twice weekly therapeutic groups with Robin Skynner and over three years of clinical seminars and supervision. By then he was already a well respected analytical psychologist with a full clinical practice and hospital appointments and he was the first senior psychotherapist to complement an analytic training, Freudian or Jungian, with Foulkesian group analysis. Another interconnection: later he succeeded me as consultant to the psychotherapy department at St George's Hospital which through our efforts became a major training centre for psychodynamic psychotherapy.

Reading through his collected papers has been both an evocative and a rewarding experience. Zinkin is stimulated to work with the divergent streams of his personality and his interests, the vertical splits that he seeks to integrate. They are: (1) the Jew and the Christian, the foreigner and the Englishman; (2) as an analytical psychologist the divergence between London and Zurich; (3) Jung, Freud and Melanie Klein; (4) Jung, Freud and Foulkes; (5) Buber and Bakhtin.

Zinkin thoughtfully explores the teachings and tensions of these thinkers. He enjoys their exploration, recognizes Jung's genius but is not afraid to show the limitations of Jung's attitude to the social, his dictum that dialogue is between conscious and unconscious rather than between persons. Zinkin wears his scholarship lightly; the sequence of papers shows that he was abreast of significant developments in his field, general systems theory, child development; Bion and Winnicott are parts of his mental equipment. He writes of Jung and physics and Freud and biology, both as parts of Bohm's seamless world.

I am struck how much our interests intertwined, mirroring, dialogue, Buber and Bakhtin. We played off each other in a partly acknowledged competitiveness and it is only now through reading his writing in sequence that I can fully appreciate both his reach and his style which is gently persuasive, questioning, asking himself how to explore psyche, self, otherness. I hear his voice, his light lilt, easily broken into laughter; but he was no lightweight, for there was a strong disputatious intellect.

His life came to a sudden end after convening a workshop on endings in psychotherapy to which he had invited his much respected mentor Michael Fordham, the senior British Jungian analyst. 'All's Well that Ends Well, or is it?' Louis was in his prime, there was much ahead of him; but he left us this body of work lovingly assembled by Hindle, his wife and helpmeet over many years. I spoke at his funeral; our intertwinings continue; now his papers and mine both appear with our publisher Jessica Kingsley.

Foreword

Rosemary Gordon

So many personal and social forces went into the makeup and formation of Louis Zinkin: Jew, doctor, psychiatrist, musician, Jungian and group analyst, scientist and eager follower of the latest discoveries and thinking of physicists and cosmologists, but also bon viveur. These facets made a cloth that was almost too rich for its owner to use for everyday wear. But even if Louis had his difficulties with this splendid apparel, he wore it with distinction. His thinking was marked by its wide reach, its precision and finesse and to each of his many interests he devoted care, discrimination and critical thought and reflection.

The papers collected in this book convey, I think, the width and depth of his questioning mind. It was his paper, 'Flexibility and analytical technique', *Journal of Analytic Psychology*, Vol. 14.2, 1969, that first evoked a resonance in me to Zinkin's approach to patients and to theory, evoked some vague feeling that we operated on a similar wavelength. Such was my very private and personal reaction. This particular paper, although not included in this collection has, in fact, figured in many subsequent bibliographies and reading lists.

I now want to say a few words about some of the other papers that I found particularly stimulating. In the paper 'Psychotherapy and the Jewish Experience', Zinkin showed the willingness, courage and capacity that characterize several of his other papers: to examine, analyse, and to describe his own conflicts and doubts. He presents us with a genuine exploration of his own feelings, reactions and the relevance of these observations to theory and to analytic skill in general. I find his approach appropriate and a natural adjunct to his belief, expressed at the end of his paper, 'The Klein Connection in the London School':

> My emphasis, therefore, is on the priority of a two-person system over the model of one person plus an 'environment'. The two-person system is one in which both partners are exchanging information, about themselves, about their common culture and their common history, but doing so through the way they relate. The relationship is primary, or in Martin Buber's more biblical words: 'In the beginning is the relation'.

Indeed Zinkin considered Buber one of his most important guides and philosophers because he, like Buber, thought of relationships as being the primary and the most important event and function in our development and being. That is to say that the work of analysis is, and must be, based on flexibility, on collaboration, on co-operation and mutuality. Like Jung he considered that every valid and effective analysis of a patient also involves the self-analysis of the analyst. Zinkin's skilful and genuine self-analysis gives me special confidence in the quality of the experience of analysis and healing he offered to his patients.

Another paper in this collection that I found ground breaking and particularly meaningful was his paper 'The Hologram as a Model for Analytical Psychology'. It reveals how quickly and critically Zinkin could grasp the new developments in physics and recognize their value, their potential influence and the clarification, as well as new and holistic experiences they could bring to the science of analytical psychology. This paper, which led to the long and fascinating correspondence between Michael Fordham and Zinkin, gives us a further insight into the evolution of the thinking and theories of these two Jungian colleagues.

Zinkin demonstrated his continuing capacity to commit himself to further study when he decided, in his early fifties, to undertake a rigorous training in group analysis. Almost as soon as he qualified he wrote and published several papers which described and discussed new thoughts and speculations which reaffirmed his thesis regarding the primacy of relationship. In 'Is Jungian Group Analysis Possible?' we discover another interesting token of his character. Zinkin demonstrates his interest in bringing together and searching out whether there can be some coherence between his Jungian orientation and later studies in group analysis.

I would claim that the content of Louis Zinkin's work, in the papers assembled here, reveals that he was fascinated by the idea of bridges and bridging. It seems he was always ready to seek them out, or to build and construct them. Bridges between Jung and Freud, between work with individuals and with groups, between couples; between the analyst's work guided by empathy, feeling, intuition and the research work, for instance, of Daniel Stern. He highly respected Stern's contributions.

Zinkin also wished to push further our awareness and self-knowledge of the bridges between matter and spirit. He knew that they must both exist, not be denied, for they are equally essential to psychological survival. He also knew that we should not rail against their rejection of clarity but rather value and delight in the presence of mystery in our analytic work.

Might it be this sense of mystery and spirit that Zinkin missed in Melanie Klein's theories and metapsychology? Although he appreciated and found much usefulness in many of her observations and ideas, it seems the absence of mystery, even the mystery of relationship, led him to write 'The Klein Connection in the

London School'. He continued to wrestle with his unease. In fact his struggle with Klein was so important to him that he invited a few colleagues to form a small group in order to pursue these issues. I continue to be a regular member of this group.

I remember Louis at the end of a very successful weekend conference. He had convened it with the collaboration of the Society of Analytical Psychology and the Group Analytic Society, on the theme of 'Endings'. As I drove away I saw Louis and his wife, Hindle, hurrying across the junction of three roads. Unbeknown to me this was to be my last view of Louis Zinkin. A poignant ending to a life devoted to bridging and relating.

Introduction

Louis Zinkin worked as a Jungian analyst and a group analyst. His questioning mind was constantly stimulated by their respective points of similarity and difference. After qualifying as a doctor he trained as a Jungian analyst with the Society of Analytical Psychology. Later he found group analysis, which he came to in his fifties, compatible with his recognition of the importance of interpersonal relationships in the human drive for wholeness and identity. Zinkin had always been drawn to Jung's emphasis on the reciprocal nature of the analytical process and to Martin Buber's celebration of dialogue. He was also fascinated by the hermeneutics of individuation and the self. He read widely in other fields and disciplines and usefully connected concepts from them, such as David Bohm's ideas about the enfolded universe, and Pribram's holographic model of the brain with Jung's ideas. He explored these ideas in 'The Hologram as a Model for Analytical Psychology'.

At the time of his death Zinkin was excited and stimulated by Bakhtin's work on dialogue and on the translation of meanings across different contexts of time and space. He was beginning to relate these ideas to Jungian theory in preparation for a book. Shortly before his death, he gave a short paper at the Leo Baeck College, London, for a workshop on Judaism and Psychotherapy, and we are including it as a frontispiece as a fitting introduction to the author.

The following four papers are chosen from Zinkin's earliest work, when he was specifically beginning to wrestle with Jungian concepts and, more particularly, Jung's own, sometimes contradictory commentaries upon them. Typically, Zinkin's method was to dissect theory by questioning and linking it to his own clinical discoveries. The first of these papers, '*Death in Venice*', is unusual in that he brings together an illness, and a theory with the novel. Zinkin also explores the ethical dilemma any analyst may find himself in when a patient's 'individuation crisis' may involve anti-social behaviour.

The three papers which follow it reflect Zinkin's developing interest in the specific nature of the analytic encounter and therapeutic alliance and also reflect his desire to construct a bridge between some of the theoretical differences between Freud and Jung. In 'Paradoxes of the Self', Zinkin explores and links Kohut's ideas about the development of the self with analytical psychology. 'Person to Person: the search for the human dimension in psychotherapy', was given as his Chairman's inaugural address to the Medical Section of the British Psychological Society in 1977. It is noteworthy that this paper anticipates Daniel Stern's later research findings on the importance of early mother/baby attunement. Zinkin regarded the Medical Section as a potential bridge between adherents of Freud and Jung; this did not assuage his subsequent disappointment in his psychoanalytic colleagues' reluctance to become curious about Jungian theory and technique.

Zinkin followed Michael Fordham, and other members of the Society of Analytical Psychology, in their growing recognition of the need to incorporate Freudian metapsychology into their own developmental theories. In particular there was a growing recognition during the 1970s of Melanie Klein's contributions to the pre-oedipal phase of infancy and object relations theory. However Zinkin subsequently came to regret the increasing reliance on Klein by many London Jungians and his paper, 'The Klein Connection in the London School: the search for origins', expressed these misgivings. Drawing on Daniel Stern's work, 'The Interpersonal World of the Infant', Zinkin set out to modify his post-Jungian colleagues' reliance on Klein. This paper has subsequently become a seminal text for further academic dialogue on this controversy. His own clinical practice was characterised by its emphasis on flexibility, mutuality and the interpersonal and reflected the influence of Winnicott and convergences with the Independent Group in the British Psycho-Analytical Society.

In the early 1970s, Zinkin began a training in group analysis during which time he was a member of a twice-weekly group led by Robin Skynner, the eminent family therapist and founding member of the Institute of Group Analysis. Throughout the process of training Zinkin was constantly faced with the differences and similarities between Jungian and group-analytic metapsychology and was thereafter requested by each training body to explore possible connections. This was especially relevant as although Foulkes had posited the activation of the collective unconscious, a central Jungian concept, as the fourth group-specific factor in group analysis, he had not amplified it. Zinkin realised that Jungian and group-analytic ideas could actually be mutually enhancing and the next five papers represent his interweaving of Jung with group analysis.

The myth of the Grail quest, whose hero Perceval resolves the problems of the Waste Land by asking the right question, is one whose use analogically is familiar ground for analytical psychologists (Whitmont, Emma Jung). In 'The Grail and the Group', Zinkin uses it to demonstrate the reciprocity of need between the hero and the group, and the Jungian concept of the Wounded Healer in the conjunction of container and contained. He also explores the possibility of Jung's concept of individuation manifesting itself in the therapy group. He identified similarities between processes of individuation and Foulkes' concept of 'ego development in action'. These processes were central theoretical issues in both 'A Gnostic View of the Therapy Group' and in 'Is Jungian Group Analysis Possible?'

'The Group as Container and Contained' was given to the International Congress of Group Psychotherapy in 1988. This is a short but dense paper which elaborates on Bion's constant conjunction of container/contained, with special reference to groups. It also introduces Prigogine's theory of discontinuous changes in systems far from equilibrium as helpful in analysing group dynamics. Zinkin also invokes the value of myth and fantasy in facilitating change in the group, and the relevance of Jung's concept of the alchemical 'vas' in the myth of the Holy Grail.

'The Dialogical Principle: Jung, Foulkes and Bakhtin' was published posthumously in *Harvest* under the title 'The Dialogical Principle in Group Analysis and Analytical Psychology'. In this paper Zinkin traces the development of the principle of dialogue through Jung, Buber and Bakhtin, stressing the importance of the latter's concept of the 'inbetween', the responsivity that is integral to dialogue. He believes individuation to be facilitated by dialogue, whether experienced with the unconscious, as in Jungian analysis, or with others, as in group analysis.

In 'Three Models are Better than One', the models referred to are of the psyche as described by Freud, Jung and Buber. Zinkin suggests that each of these models contributes to a more comprehensive understanding of group processes. Whilst primarily being a group-analytic paper, it is also a statement of Zinkin's approach to psychotherapy in the group and dyadic context.

The concept of mirroring is one of the four factors Foulkes listed as specific to group analysis. In 'Malignant Mirroring', Zinkin built on Foulkes' concept as it features in the mother/baby, analyst/analysand pairings and explicates definitions of mirroring from Lacan, Winnicott, Kohut and Yalom. He then introduces his own concept of malignant mirroring and demonstrates its impact, in the group context, through clinical illustrations.

'Loss of Self in Envy and Jealousy', which refers to personal experiences of these emotions, was given as a contribution to a workshop on envy.

Zinkin felt that the question of when to terminate therapy was one of its most difficult aspects and the final paper, 'All's Well that Ends Well: or is it?' was given at a workshop for group and Jungian analysts on termination in March 1993. Within a few hours of its presentation Zinkin died of a sudden heart attack.

As editors we made a considered decision not to make stylistic alterations, except for the sake of clarity.

Psychotherapy and the Jewish Experience

Who am I? What am I? How can I be my real self? How can I be my individual self rather than some collectively defined self imposed on me by others? Is there some authentic being which I have and which I can live by and which will give some meaning to my life before I die? Do I have a choice and what do I choose?

These are questions of the utmost importance for both religion and for psychotherapy. They are questions to do with personal identity, but most religions and most forms of psychotherapy do not regard one's identity, that is to say the kind of person one is, to be given, to be fixed once and for all, but to be something one is responsible for, at least to some extent.

For the psychotherapist these questions have to be distinguished from other questions which patients ask doctors, like: What's wrong with me, doctor? What illness am I suffering from? What treatment do I need and how long will it take before I get better? It is the questions concerning our responsibility for who we are which have become the most urgent ones. We are divided selves in a divided world. It is no longer sufficient to identify with one's family, village, tribe, community, or country or race. Each of us has, in addition to all these things, to be conscious of a global identity. Each of us is responsible for the whole planet.

I would like, briefly, to look at how this problem looks to me as a Jew in the light of Jewish experience and how it looks to me as a psychotherapist in the light of psychotherapeutic experience. Psychotherapists not only have patients who are preoccupied with identity problems of this sort but themselves have to struggle with their own identity amongst all the rival schools, as well as belonging to a wider group all of whom practise something called 'psychotherapy'. I want to suggest that what we are dealing with, whether as Jews or as psychotherapists, is a vertical rather than a horizontal split, and that this vertical splitting can give us great strength if we try to heal it. Let me explain what I mean by vertical splitting through my own orientation as an Anglo-Jewish Jungian analyst.

Though I am a Jungian analyst, I owe a great deal to Freud. I have followed a particular tradition, as an English Jungian, of retaining a great deal of Freud's psychoanalysis as well as sharing to some extent Jung's criticism of Freud, which led to the split between them.

Englishman or Jew? Freudian or Jungian? Here I am faced with a double dual identity. In both cases, I have had to sort out for myself where I stood and to ask where I have to choose between them and where I could integrate or synthesize them and of course where I could say: 'A plague on both your houses!' And be myself – whatever that might mean.

Freud being a Jew and Jung a gentile, there is an obvious link between my two double identities. It surely is no accident that I have many Jewish friends at the Institute of Psycho-Analysis while, at the Society of Analytical Psychology, Jews are an ethnic minority. Why then did I, a Jew, follow Jung the gentile? I should like to be able to say that being a Jew or a gentile had nothing whatever to do with it, that I simply could see that Jung's approach was better, but I am here this evening because I know this would not be true. I was attracted to Jung at a particular stage in my development, as a medical student at Oxford, having decided to train in medicine in order to become eventually a psychoanalyst. And at this time I was struggling through an identity crisis, which included my conflict between being Jewish, which I knew there was no gainsaying, and being English, which I was not so sure about. Looking back and using a modern term which had not then been invented, I can see I was suffering from a parental double-bind. My parents saw to it that I had both a Jewish and an English education, as though these were considered to be easily compatible. But though I was told never to forget that I was a Jew, it was important to spend most of my time, at school and University, with the English. This meant learning English history, that 'we', for example, had an Empire, so all those red bits on the map belonged to us. It was important to speak and write good English, to play cricket, to dress and to behave like an English gentleman, to train in the Officers' Training Corps. In fact I was educated to be an English gentleman, though not (what was then regarded as the very apex of civilization) a Christian gentleman. I was not to attend Christian prayers and was forbidden to read the New Testament, and the name of Christ must never be spoken. Even to this day, I cannot utter it without being conscious of the taboo. I am sure that my parents, who had very little education, other than a Jewish one, could not have understood this double-bind. How could I both assimilate and not assimilate? Every Jew has a double identity. We Jews, however much we feel a solidarity with other Jews, have also to have a second national identity, based on whatever country we happen to live in, even if that country is Israel. Perhaps it is not, for everyone, a double-bind. Perhaps some choose to assimilate and others choose not to. But I, like many of my generation, at least in this liberal, tolerant and democratic country, have had no simple choice.

The double-bind, by which I mean two contradictory injunctions combined where it is not permissible to withdraw, is to be found not just in my parents' wish to see that I had a good English education but in my religious instruction. I was taught above all that there was only one God. While I understood this to mean that everybody else who worshipped other gods was mistaken, that the one God was the only one there actually was and therefore he was really the God which everybody ought to acknowledge, I found this contradicted by another idea, one which is still common in tribal societies. This is the idea that we, as Jews, have our own God and our own customs and our own Law. With this idea goes a tolerance towards other groups. They have their own gods which may suit them very well, and their own customs, but they are not ours.

I found it even more confusing (I think soon after my Barmitzvah) when I began to wonder whether God existed at all, and this seemed to me a perfectly good reason not to go to the synagogue. Indeed for me as an agnostic, it seemed to me to be rather hypocritical to do so. There were, in any case, a lot of other ways of spending a Saturday morning. To my astonishment, I was told that it really didn't matter very much. It was certainly no reason not to go on being an observant Jew. Later I was to discover that far worse than not believing and even worse than not observing was to 'marry out'. The most important thing was that the Jewish heritage should be passed on.

What has any of this to do with my being a psychotherapist or being a Jungian? Well, the main attraction for me in Jung was his conviction that whether God exists or not there is a universal religious need, just as there is a sexual one, and that if you make a comparative study of their symbolism, you find that all religions make use of the same basic patterns, the archetypes. If this is true then psychotherapists have to look for these patterns whatever the religious beliefs the patient may happen to have. For me, personally, this was such a liberating idea that I was swept up by it. Now I could relate my own need for a religious dimension not just to Judaism but to all religious practices. I could contemplate the existence of many gods as well as many forms of the same one god, not theologically but psychologically, and perhaps begin to heal the cultural split in myself by the powerful appeal to universality in the idea of the collective unconscious. Shylock's famous speech:

> Hath not a Jew eyes? Hath not a Jew hands, organs, dimension, sense, afflictions, passions … fed with the same food, hurt with the same weapons … as a Christian? If you prick us do we not bleed?

could apply to the mind as well as the body. We are still, regardless of our culture, human and, at bottom, the same.

Of course, it is not as simple as it seemed then, when I was so excited by Jung's work on mythology that it was as though I had discovered some great truth which most people did not seem to be aware of. One cannot so easily dispose of deep-seated differences between people. But I did then find a resolution of a double-bind. And I had the key which would enable me later, as an analyst, to bridge the gap between me and my patients. All therapists working in depth have to try to overcome the differences they find between themselves and their patients. By overcome, I mean cross an imaginative gap in order to identify with them and then to disidentify sufficiently to look at the differences and try to understand them. At times, but by no means always, the gap will be due to pathology in the patient, the distortions of perception which are the reasons for his or her being a patient. Now, if the therapist is conscious, as I am, of having in himself one or more vertical splits which he is trying to heal, having not only a repressed unconscious but a double identity, it can be a great help in the process of identifying with and differentiating from the patient. The two people in the room are represented by the two people in the therapist. The meeting and separating, the joining together in empathy and the moving away in differentiating, go hand in hand. This is not what is usually described as projecting and introjecting parts of the self. What I am regarding as a strength in the therapist is the containing of two identities resulting from having had to acquire two cultures. This is distinct from what is usually said to be necessary for a therapist, a firm and unambiguous notion of who you are. The double identity was important in both Freud and Jung. Freud, though a highly cultured Viennese intellectual pursuing the ideals of pure science, had a hidden Jewish mystical side; and Jung actually spoke of his Number One and Number Two personalities.

Some of my best friends are not Jewish, however, and I do not want to suggest that Jewish therapists are better than others. I do think though that Jews have a common problem which, if they are conscious of it, gives them a specific understanding of the splits in their patients. When Jews think of the history of anti-semitism they can understand why the Jews developed their fierce adherence to their differences from others. When we think of the Holocaust and identify as best we can with the victims, the split within ourselves becomes so painful we can hardly bear it. Certainly my own upbringing starts to make sense in the light of Jewish history, but the sense it makes is a realisation of deep suffering, a heightened awareness of the evils of racism which divide and split society.

One of the many differences between Freud and Jung was, paradoxically, that Freud, the Jew, was an expert in horizontal splitting and Jung in vertical splitting. Just as all analysts have to be in touch with their repressed unconscious, their horizontal splitting, to deal with their patients' neuroses, so they also have to be in touch with their vertical splitting to help their patients' personality disorders, those disorders in which people are struggling to integrate the split off parts of themselves.

The Jewish experience is not for Jews alone. Jewish psychotherapists may be in a good position to understand Jewish patients. But it is more important now for Jew to meet non-Jew. The Jewish experience, like the black experience or the female experience, needs to be experienced by those who are not Jewish, not black or not women. If this is true then we all are better off with a double identity.

Every Jew has a non-Jew within which he has to come to terms with, or rather has to enter into dialogue with, just as every man has a woman or every white woman has a black man and so on. In the same way every Jungian has a non-Jungian and every analyst a non-analyst within. In this last instance, the non-analyst within is not to be regarded as a problem, but is a necessary part of the analyst without which he or she cannot identify with the non-analyst patient and without this identification no dialogue, and therefore no analysis, can take place.

It seems to me to be incorrect to regard the double-bind as originating in the family, although it was in family therapy that the idea was first applied. Parents transmit what they are subject to and this has to be understood in some larger historical dimension, cultural, political or sociological. Getting out of the double-bind is the same as healing the vertical splits. I hope I have illustrated how my Jewish problem and my Jungian problem are the same problem, and in a way, it is everybody's problem.

CHAPTER ONE

Death in Venice

A Jungian View

In this paper I want to bring together three things: a novel, an illness and a theory.

The novel is Thomas Mann's *Death in Venice*, the illness can be labelled paedophilia, and the theory is Jung's theory of individuation. As each of these would fill a book I intend to start by limiting my aims.

I have a number of patients who brought up the story in analysis – usually through having seen the film. Two of these patients especially could be diagnosed as paedophiliacs – as perhaps could Aschenbach; but it was clear, both in the patients and in the story, that the attraction to a beautiful youth was not just an undesirable perversion, but an expression of a deep longing for an experience that would somehow give meaning to their lives. Thomas Mann seemed to be bringing out in a work of fiction something which Jung was simultaneously bringing out in his writings on psychology. The correspondence between my patients and the story, therefore, led me back to a number of Jung's ideas, and all I want to do in this paper is to try to show what light this threw, for me, on what one is trying to do as a Jungian analyst.

The story

Let us start with the story. It is quite short – only a novella – but quite extraordinary in its evocation of atmosphere, its power to grip the reader and lead him to a conclusion which seems inevitable. What is it about? Like all great works of art its meaning is ambiguous and cannot easily be translated into terms other than itself. Each re-reading seems to yield new aspects of meaning, and on close scrutiny every sentence seems to be significant, although this is not always immediately apparent. Thomas Mann brought to it a deep interest in mythology, in classical antiquity, and was deeply impressed, as was Jung, by the works of Goethe, Schiller, Nietzsche and Freud. He had certain conscious intentions in writing the story, particularly in bringing out the Apollonian–Dionysian opposites. His symbolism is partly conscious and he particularly intended to depict in Tadzio, as well as in other characters, the symbolic motif of Hermes Psychopompos, the guide who led souls to death. He brings in a great deal of mythologizing towards the end of the story; but despite all this, Mann has described how he was carried along by the story which at first he intended as a 'hymnic' evocation, but which became a kind of moral fable. It is ironic that in spite of all the acclaim it received the author, secretly, viewed the story as a failure. For me, however, the story, with its blend of highly sophisticated conscious working and unconscious driving, is a masterpiece. Its symbolism is ultimately non-allegorical, its intellectualism irrelevant. It is a mythic story. Although it can be discussed in terms of the intellectual and artistic problems of its day, or as an allegory of sick Europe (it was written in 1911), I want to treat it as a story of an individual, Aschenbach; and as a story of what can happen to an individual regardless of time or place.

A Jungian view

I should now like to formulate this happening in Jung's terminology. It is a story of an individuation crisis with splitting of the self, dissolution of the persona and ending in death of the self. Whether this death is final or a kind of rebirth is highly problematical. In the course of the process there is intense archetypal activity. The persona becomes a kind of empty shell, the self appears as a number of archetypal images, the principal and central one being that of the *puer aeternus*.

In all discussions among analytical psychologists there is a tendency either for woolliness, when we think we are agreed, or dispute about the meaning of our terms. These terms include 'archetypes', 'self' and 'persona'. The disputes need not be divisive. As psychological knowledge advances, our concepts may need revision both in expanding and in limiting their scope. There is a very real problem also in that workers in psychology who are not Jungians develop similar concepts – even sometimes using the same names – and we have to decide to what extent their thinking and their insights can be assimilated into our own. A recent example, in The Society of Analytical Psychology, was a sharp disagreement as to whether the persona could be equated with Winnicott's 'false self'. Such a discussion in my view is very necessary. If following Jung in his break from Freud means ignoring the work of psychoanalysts ever afterwards, the loss will be immeasurable. However, there is also the opposite danger, that in the process of studying other ideas the essence of Jung's contribution may be lost; but surely the important thing is to be aware of that danger rather than to cut ourselves off. I am seeking not to define or re-define Jung's terms but to apply them in a particular context in my own way.

Individuation

The first point to be made is that in my two patients the compulsive homosexual longings have not been cured – in spite of many years of work. These two analyses would do very well in a statistical research study purporting to prove the uselessness of analysis. Nevertheless, neither I nor my patients would regard their analyses as having failed. It is still desirable to relieve the patient of the compulsion, and one cannot deny one's failure or try to make a virtue of it. At the same time it is possible to see that the converse could have occurred: the symptoms could be cured and the analysis have failed. To understand this one needs to understand the idea of individuation. In *Death in Venice* Aschenbach, too, cannot free himself – he cannot leave Venice even though he knows of the danger, but that is because to return home would be another kind of death. His work, for which he has lived, no longer has meaning: he can still write as well as ever; no doubt he would be as successful as ever in the eyes of the world; but to himself he would be dead.

I have, therefore, called the central problem an 'individuation crisis'. One of the difficulties in Jung's idea of individuation is to know whether it is a process that goes on in everybody from birth to death, or whether it involves only a very few people at certain periods of life. Michael Fordham reviewed this controversy in a paper given to the International Congress of Analytical Psychology in 1965, in which he contrasted what he calls the extended thesis (individuation as a process from birth to death as expounded by Baynes, Harding, Perry and Jacoby) with the classical concept in which individuation is seen as a specific feature of the second half of life (Jacoby 1958, Fordham 1968).

My own position falls midway between those two. If, as Fordham suggests, the essential part of Jung's definition lies in it being the development of the individual from the collective psychology, then it seems to me that this may be a lifetime task of the individual from birth to death, as it is in the schizoid personality, but characteristically it occurs in moments of crisis when the integrity of the individual is threatened. Such a crisis may occur at any time, but there are three main periods in life when it usually becomes crucial:

1. The establishment of the individual in *early childhood*. This is the area in which Fordham and others are mainly working (Fordham 1944).

2. *Adolescence*, in which an identity crisis may occur. This term elaborated by Erikson is very clearly related to the problem of individuation (Erikson 1968).

3. *The mid-life crisis*, in which Jung was especially interested.

In *Death in Venice* the mid-life depression seems to precipitate a crisis in which Aschenbach loses the meaning and purpose of his life. As in the classical view of Jung, this produces the invasion of archetypal images, the first being the Stranger at the cemetery gates. At the same time, his persona becomes split off. None of the characters he meets responds to him as a great writer except the hotel manager who only treats him with fawning flattery.

For my two patients, however, there is no question of a mid-life crisis, although I think their problem is the same as that of Aschenbach. They have lived in a secret state of crisis all their lives, and for such patients the task of individuation has immediate meaning. My view of individuation really derives from my regarding it as a *task* or *goal*. I do not believe that it involves all people throughout life. Many people even pass through adolescence and mid-life without it being activated in them. Recently a perplexed father of an adolescent girl said to me, 'She keeps saying, "I don't know who I am." I can't understand it; I always knew who *I* was.' Of course, the crisis of not knowing who you are is the crisis of establishing the individual out of the collective. It is dangerous and frightening because it may succeed and it may fail. Even to talk of it is dangerous – it sounds like madness, particularly if you are not an adolescent. Both my patients found it easier to talk of their homosexuality than of this. But once admitted, then the task, the task of self-realization, begins.

The persona

This is a troublesome concept of Jung's. It did not appear to have had much difficulty for him, nor did he expect it to have for his readers. He states: 'The problem of the persona should not present any great difficulties.' He wrote about it mainly in 'Two essays on analytical psychology' (Jung 1943) and although he referred to it in his later writings he continued to regard it as a simple idea, as compared with the 'dark inner world', an idea which was 'accessible to everyone'. In a recent paper on the persona, Blomeyer noted the dearth of literature on the subject, which he regards as a scotoma among Jungians, compared with papers, say, on the self. He points out that Jung falls prey to a fallacy that accessible 'in the sense of being approached', is equated with accessible 'in the sense of capable of being understood' (Blomeyer 1974). I would add to this that there is an analytical bias which regards 'deep' structures as more important than superficial ones, which sees analysis always as an 'uncovering' process. The words 'superficial' and 'profound' carry these connotations – that of 'trivial' and 'important' – whereas it is obvious if we are relating to another human being that the face is infinitely more expressive than the heart. The face, which can be looked at, expresses what is within; the heart, which is hidden, expresses nothing – except blood. Jung found also, as he dug deeper and deeper into the psyche, that the profound truths he was seeking turned out to be collective and impersonal facts. On the other hand, the face *can* be a mask and the mask can be used as either a social signal – what sociologists would call a role-sign – or it can be used to hide and disguise a person's real attitude to others. The point is that the persona *becomes* a mask at the onset of the individuation process, because it is split off from the self. It is at this point that individuation becomes a necessary task, and, as Jung says, 'the aim of individuation is nothing less than to divest the self of the false wrappings of the persona on the one hand and the suggestive power of primordial images on the other' (Jung 1943). On the same page he also writes: 'Individuation means becoming a single homogeneous being, and in so far as individuating embraces our innermost last and incomparable uniqueness, it also implies becoming one's own self.'

I would like to draw attention to the word 'innermost' in that formulation. Jung discovered that as he delved deeper into the psyche he ultimately reached not individual uniqueness, but impersonal collectivity. This is the problem for the introvert. For Jung it had seemed obvious that collective values were external and that uniqueness lay within. But it was not as obvious as all that and Jung's important contribution became, therefore, the discovery that deep inside the psyche of everyone lay the same collective forces threatening to destroy the unique individual. Therefore he saw the persona, which represents the external attitude, as quite obviously not the same as the individual. The core within, which he was seeking, does exist, but though deep inside it can be established only with the help of another person – originally the mother in the very beginning of infancy. Later it may need a relationship with *another person* to maintain it.

In *Death in Venice* it is only in the crisis, i.e. at the beginning of the story, that it would be correct to regard the persona as a false self. Aschenbach is a great writer and there is absolutely no suggestion that in the past there has been any kind of false front. It is true that he is a 'solitary', that his wife has died and his child grown up and gone away (these statements also have a symbolic meaning); but, nevertheless, he has been alive through his work. Aschenbach has no doubt that his work, which expresses his innermost being, is understood by his readers. The hero he has developed is 'the concept of an intellectual and virginal manliness, which clenches its teeth and stands in modest defiance of the swords and spear that pierce its side'. It is this *self*-representation which is enshrined in a beautiful idea which eventually fails. The split occurs eventually because through the discipline of his work, his courageous 'rejecting of the rejected', his relentless search for the ideal, he neglects the child in himself who then appears as an archetypal image. It is then that his work and, therefore, his position, become meaningless and empty. Both my patients have difficulties in their work, which is in constant danger of breaking down. This does not mean that their work and all the social achievement attached to it is unreal and meaningless, but in both cases it can become so.

Aschenbach sees in the young boy, Tadzio, all the perfection he has been struggling to achieve. The boy has it already: it has nothing to do with his work – in fact he is forever playing while Aschenbach himself has not used his youth in play but has always devoted himself to serious work. This is a viable way of life until it breaks down in late middle life. There is then a dissolution of the persona. It is interesting that the Stranger at the cemetery, who starts off his urge to travel, is at first observed by Aschenbach when he realizes that he is himself being observed in a most hostile way. This is really one of the themes of the book; he tries to retain his solitary position observing others, but others keep observing *him*. Sometimes they seem to know more about him than he knows himself. They relate to something in himself which he cannot recognize. They seem to understand his fate. What he has achieved as a writer is no longer a reflection of what is real in him. The persona no longer functions either to express himself to others, or to conceal himself from them.

The archetypes

Many archetypal images occur in the story. The mother-archetype is in the background and is impersonal; it is depicted as the sea, as Venice, and above all as death. All the characters who matter in the story are male and nearly all have archetypal qualities.

Apart from Tadzio the most significant figures are:

1. The Stranger at the cemetery.

2. The old man on the boat trying to be young, who treats Aschenbach with undue familiarity.

3. The Boatman who knows where Aschenbach's destination is, who knows that 'the signore will pay', but asks for no payment.

4. The Street Musician, the mountebank, who also conveys great hostility.

It is difficult to know whether to regard those figures as real people or to take them as symbols. They can certainly all be seen as self-representations in that they seem to stand for split-off and rejected parts of himself, and if we are to read the story as containing several people, then Aschenbach is projectively identifying himself with them. They have a great deal of luminosity, and Mann certainly uses them as powerful images in spite of the almost matter-of-fact prose style with which he describes them (quite different from the language he uses to describe Aschenbach's dreams). This gives them a subtly invasive quality (quite lost in Benjamin Britten's opera, in which they appear as eerie and ethereal).

I would like to discuss the significance of these four figures and then separately discuss Tadzio as a *puer aeternus* figure.

My patients, who could be labelled as paedophiliacs, arouse both in themselves and in others hatred and disgust at their compulsive activities. This is based on the idea of innocence, a precious quality they seek to contact but which, in contacting, they fear will be destroyed. Thus they see themselves, as they approach a boy, as being evil. Both my patients at times regard themselves in this way. The boy they approach appears to have everything that is desirable, but it is all contained in innocence. If they try to enter into a relationship with a boy all they have to offer is their knowledge and experience of the world and this gift if accepted will destroy the thing they love (to use Oscar Wilde's telling phrase; Wilde brought about his own self-destruction in a similar way to Aschenbach). Even if the boy willingly accepts this instruction into sexual pleasure, he is thought to be corrupted in the process. The word 'assault' contains the legally reinforced social assumption of the aggressive nature of these compulsive activities. In both my cases also the aim of sexual contact itself is to give pleasure to the other and both patients regard their own sexual satisfaction in these encounters as an irrelevance.

Three of the four important male figures in *Death in Venice*, the Stranger at the cemetery, the Boatman and the Mountebank, all personify a kind of evil knowingness. In each case Mann throws in the detail that they are of foreign extraction. They do not belong where they are found. Thus they are shadow figures. They act as split-off bits of the self, alien and dangerous yet demanding a special and unsought relationship with Aschenbach and he is stripped of all persona and is himself innocent when facing them. It is because these aspects of himself are split-off that he cannot find any satisfactory way of making friends with Tadzio.

This problem of making friends is due to the lack of a model of satisfactory father–son relationship. In my two patients there was the familiar family pattern of the over-possessive infantilizing and seductive mother, and a father who could not be reached. Both revealed in their analysis, despite strong resistance, a desperate longing for a friendly affectionate relationship with the father, and were trying in their approach to boys to bring this about. That involves role-reversal, but the essential pattern is the wish to bring about a meeting of father and son. In both my patients there had been a desperate bid for acceptance by the father during adolescence. In one case this had partially succeeded. In the other the boy had attempted a jump into a false kind of adultness. This had involved harsh internal attacks on the child in himself. What he had lacked was the normal initiation into the male world in which the adult's apparently sadistic attacks on a youth are a necessary component of acceptance of the youth, a re-creation of growth. If the aggressive aspect of the father is split off from his love for the son, a shadow aspect of the father emerges. He then becomes alien, devoid of innocence or beauty and expresses rejection and contempt. The Stranger at the cemetery, the Boatman, and the Mountebank, all have this attitude of contempt, unmodified by tenderness. The fop who is old and trying to be young represents a false solution, a false basis of relationship, and he arouses Aschenbach's contempt. Later

Aschenbach himself is drawn into attempting the same false solution when he submits to the barber's cosmetic skills.

Henderson in his very rich study of initiation regards initiation itself as an archetype, and when he is considering initiation in the process of individuation makes the following comment:

> In analysis the archetype of initiation appears especially in the material of those who in their youth were older and wiser than their years or who during the second half of life are striving to regain some of the youth which they originally lost. (Henderson 1967)

Both those conditions apply to Aschenbach, and although I think it misleading to speak of initiation itself as an archetype, I would very much agree with Henderson's treatment of it as a process of psychic development with a characteristic grouping of archetypal images. It is thus delineated as a developmental crisis with a definable beginning and an end, and it is for this reason that I have introduced the term 'individuation crisis'. In *Death in Venice* these figures represent the father, seen as evil shadow figures but also containing knowledge of the world and the ability to survive – which, if they can be assimilated, could enable the boy to be initiated into manhood. Whitmont, in discussing male psychology, draws attention to the link between the *puer aeternus* and the father archetypes. Having delineated father as the voice of collective authority, as well as protector, he says: 'The opposite orientation of the father is that of *puer aeternus*, companion and brother. This is an entirely different form of maleness from the experience of the man as father and is in this sense opposed to it' (Whitmont 1969, p.182). Those three figures in the story then are the father as shadow, seen as inferior and malevolent, but they are in control of Aschenbach and lead him to his fate. Their opposition to the *puer aeternus* is absolute, an indication of the deep split in the self of Aschenbach.

Puer aeternus

We come now to Tadzio. I think that *puer aeternus* is the best description of him. Jung introduced this term into analytical psychology in his *Symbols of Transformation*, but he gives it more meaning in his later paper, 'The psychology of the child archetype' (Jung 1951). It now has an established place in the literature of analytical psychology, where there is a tendency to regard it as an archetype in its own right. However, I think it better to use it as Jung did, as one particular manifestation of the archetype of the child.

The correspondence between Mann's delineation of Tadzio and Jung's description of the child archetype is so close that the essay could easily be taken for a commentary on the story rather than as a companion to Kerenyi's essay (Kerenyi 1940). Tadzio is beauty itself, he is perfection, 'beautiful as a gender young god emerging from the depths of the sea and sky'. He is also described as delicate, slim, graceful, a pampered darling, as indeed in his first appearance he is contrasted with his sisters and the governess whose appearance is severe; his golden ringlets and pretty clothes indicate 'feminine softness' and tenderness in keeping with Jung's idea of the hermaphroditism of the child. He has incredible charm but is also vulnerable, destined to die young (a fact which gives Aschenbach unaccountable pleasure) and yet is immortal. In the end he survives and it is Aschenbach who dies. He symbolises life and joy but, finally, he is the summoner (really the psychogogue). He is a radiant light in the greyness of a diseased Venice, but is he really innocent? He plays all the time in a most childish way for a fourteen-year-old; he appears to be living a 'provisional life', to use Baynes' well-put phrase, and yet he knows, he undoubtedly knows! When he gazes back at Aschenbach it is with the utmost seriousness. When the Street Musician sings and everybody laughs, it is he alone who does not laugh. Another strange detail, which belies his innocence, is the look he gives the Russian family:

> ... the sight of the Russian family leading their lives there in joyous simplicity, distorted his features in a spasm of angry disgust. His brow darkened, his lips curled, one corner of the mouth was drawn down in a harsh line that marred the curve of the cheek, his frown was so heavy that the eyes seemed to sink in as they uttered the black and vicious language of hate. (Mann 1979, p.30)

Here is a glimpse of the shadow aspect contained in this beautiful child, whose smile can melt Aschenbach's heart. It appears more clearly in the terrible dream of the Dionysiac orgy where he is the 'Stranger-god', the stranger who was 'sworn enemy to dignity and control'.

The stranger god is the Thracian Dionysus and he is the enemy to Aschenbach's Apollonian ideals. Dionysus is one of a series of dying and resurgent gods and the sacrifice to the god is also the sacrifice *of* the god in the initiation rite. The rite is symbolic and in it the loss of reason is only temporary and the initiate is the recipient of priceless knowledge.

Application of these ideas in clinical practice

Interesting though it may be to speculate on this story, teasing out the symbolism and relating it to our knowledge of individuation and the archetypes, we, as practising analysts, devoting nearly all our time to working with patients, have now to apply what we have learnt to that work. It is in this area, applying our knowledge therapeutically, that there is the greatest amount of controversy in analytical psychology. Whether or not to use reductive methods is only one aspect of this controversy. The problem arises for the followers of Jung because Jung's own way of working was suitable, by his own admission, to very few patients – to those who were also capable of active imagination. It seems to me that with those patients Jung could make a protracted therapeutic alliance; with others, the vast majority, he seems to have made only brief contact. Very often he dismissed them or firmly rejected their way of life. This seems to be because they lacked what he regarded as the moral courage and will to embark on an individuation process.

Before considering the case of the paedophiliac it is worth looking briefly at the *puer aeternus* type, the well-known problem of the patient who is identified with the archetype, who lives out the eternal youth. Marie-Louise von Franz, in her seminars on this subject, follows Jung and gives a beautiful description of this type of patient, amplifying her understanding with a wealth of mythological material. She approves of Jung's idea that hard work is the cure for the *puer aeternus* type and says 'it is not much good just preaching to people that they should work, for they simply get angry and walk off'. Nevertheless she does seem to fall into this very trap herself. She gives an example from her own work where she warns a young man to give up promiscuity and drinking, otherwise it will ruin his life. He rejects her advice and then gets polio (von Franz 1970). If we wish to avoid such tragedies with patients who break off treatment we must indeed avoid preaching. We should examine why these patients make us want to preach and this involves an awareness of the transference, and, especially, the countertransference. Here it is clear that the analyst is liable to feel rejecting towards the *puer aeternus* type. Indeed nothing can be imagined more likely to annoy an analyst than the apparently stubborn refusal to grow up. The analyst is more likely to keep his patient and develop a therapeutic alliance if he recognizes that split-off rejecting – indeed, even murderous attitude to the child – may be projected into him.

If we now turn to the paedophiliac, it can be seen that his rejecting attitude to the child is directed towards the child in himself. He is therefore the opposite of the *puer aeternus* type and it is made explicit in *Death in Venice* that Aschenbach has rejected the child in himself. By 'reject' I mean a more serious problem than is usually implied by repression and reaction-formation. It is a split in which a whole aspect of the self, the loved and hated child, is actually split off and disowned. When it reappears in archetypal form, embodied in an actual boy, it is hardly possible to call it a projection. It no more truly belongs to the object than to the subject. At the same time, just as von Franz has perceptively described, in the *puer aeternus* type there is always also a shadow figure around. He is full of 'cold rage and contempt'. He is the rejecting part of the self equally split off in hatred of the child's values and it is he who is personified in the shadow figures in *Death in Venice*. These figures, as I have suggested, are also father-figures – and father in the negative relationship with the child as constellated in the unresolved Oedipal situation.

How has Aschenbach lived until the beginning of the story when his decline begins? In Freudian terms, clearly by sublimation in creative work – but this sublimation is achieved by a number of mechanisms. The boy is identified with the mother, which leads to a homosexual relation with the father (introverted Oedipus complex). This is then denied and the author constructs a manly hero who rejects weakness and sentimentality (along with playfulness and charm). But the libidinal object is not really lost. There is an identification and desexualization of it in the attempt to arrive at a kind of intellectualized beauty, and the child is turned into a work of artistic creation. Although artistically successful, the author's personality structure finally breaks down, with disruption of his internal world of objects. He is emptied of this internal world (mid-life depression).

In recent years psychoanalytic theory has come nearer to analytical psychology in its development of Hartmann's concept of self-representations and in the idea that self and object representations become merged in regressive states (Hartmann 1950). So that these 'objects' which invade Aschenbach's awareness of the outside world are really both self and object representations.

Roy Schafer, the psychoanalyst, in his work on internalization, discusses 'the fates of immortal objects' (Schafer 1968). By 'immortal' he means that in primary-process thinking, death of the object, in the sense of ceasing to exist, cannot occur; the object is transformed into, say, a vengeful spirit. So Aschenbach's objects return in both evil and beautiful form and finally become sexualized once again in a dream of a Dionysiac orgy. But this regression was for Jung the prerequisite of initiation and the death is really a rebirth in the individuation process.

The 'internal object' of psychoanalysis is not, of course, an actually perceivable object, not a 'thing'. It is an abstract concept, just as is the concept of the archetype. The existence of the child archetype had to be postulated by Jung because of the universal appearance of its images.

Thus in paedophilia the analytical psychologist can recognize the archetype; it produces images which occur in phantasy and are then projected on to a suitable actual child. The images exert a compulsive demand on the patient to act out. However, the archetype does more than produce images. The child archetype (just like other archetypes, such as the shadow, the anima or the old wise man) produces self-representations in the form of sub-personalities. The integration of these sub-personalities form part of the task or goal of individuation.

Individuation, therefore, needs to be the shared goal of the analyst and patient – not symptom-removal as such. We have then to reject the crude medical model and try to establish a true therapeutic alliance which grows stronger as the meaning of individuation becomes real to the patient. How to set about this with a patient such as a paedophiliac needs a great deal more attention from analytical psychologists than it has received up to now. We have long recognized that knowledge of theory and technique is not sufficient and that we need to relate to our patient as a real person, but we have tended to believe that this is an art which cannot be taught as can theory and technique. I believe that we can learn a great deal about it by using an interactional model and studying its setting. In a previous paper I have considered how a mother and baby can interact as whole persons from the beginning, long before 'whole objects' are said to be perceived in psychoanalytic theory (Zinkin 1978).The formation of split-off 'sub-personalities' obviously makes this whole person relationship difficult, and a work like *Death in Venice* can be used to illuminate the problem.

Perhaps Aschenbach could have been saved if he could have found a way of relating to Tadzio as a real person. In this case it would have had to be based on a father–son model. His problem would be very much the same as we might see the problem of a father trying to relate to his own adolescent son. The father has to maintain an affectionate friendship, helping to initiate him into manhood and acting as a model for identification, but at times opposing the son as an authority. He has to try to allow for the boy's needs to regress to a more infantile level at one moment and to recognize his emerging adulthood the next: all this depends on his being in touch with, and in control of, his own sexual and aggressive impulses – the wish for union on the one hand, and his competitive hostility on the other. It all sounds very complex, but it depends ultimately on the father's having kept alive an adolescent boy in his inner world. Aschenbach has not succeeded in this. This desirable father–son relationship can also be a model for the true alliance between analyst and patient.

It is difficult to make a true therapeutic alliance with the *puer aeternus* type, but it is even more difficult with the paedophiliac which is the *puer aeternus* in reverse. It is easy to make a false alliance based on a crude medical model in which the paedophilia is a symptom – something bad which must be cured – but this attitude allies the analyst with the patient's persona and endeavours to sustain it. A true alliance does recognize the undesirable anti-social symptom, but it also recognizes in the patient:

1. The responsible adult (father) who cares about children and wants to protect their innocence.

2. The evil (shadow father) adult who wishes to destroy childhood.

3. The beautiful, innocent, vulnerable, child who wishes to remain a child for ever.

4. The child who really knows about evil and wishes to lure the adult to destruction.

Those four sub-personalities all exist in the paedophiliac patient just as they all exist in *Death in Venice*. In the analysis of the paedophiliac death may strike at any time. The great fear in both analyst and patient is that the patient will be caught, his illness defined as a 'crime' and he will be finally disgraced and humiliated by society – society, of course, acting quite properly and correctly within its own terms, but destroying the individual.

It will be observed that each of those four sub-personalities has a wish. For individuation to take place all four of them have to have their wishes granted in some measure, but each has to make allowances for the other three. Each acts as a guide towards the final goal – whether seen as positive or negative – just as all the characters in *Death in Venice* have a Hermes aspect.

As I have indicated, the analyst has to identify sub-personalities through their appearance in the transference and countertransference. He has to do more, though, than interpret these. He has actively to try to find a true centre in his patient to which he can relate, just as one imagines Aschenbach relating to Tadzio as a person, were he not the victim in the power of the archetype. The story, as I have said, became for Thomas Mann a 'moral fable' – rather against his will. But the enigma remains. What is the moral? It all depends on whether we read the death as Aschenbach's ultimate disintegration, or as a symbolic return to the mother to be reborn. Is Aschenbach's attempt to rejuvenate himself to be taken as a symbolic rebirth, or is it a bitter ironic comment that it is too late? Discussion with other readers has revealed a wide divergence of opinion on this point. As in many works of art, the meaning is ambiguous and the question is left in the reader's mind, though, not even stated clearly as a question by the writer.

I have chosen to take paedophilia and *Death in Venice* as my theme, but I could have taken any other symptom because any symptom can lead to individuation becoming the mutually acknowledged task of the analysis. It is only when this happens that curing the symptom becomes a secondary goal and we, as analysts, can defend ourselves against the statisticians.

References

Blomeyer, R. (1974) 'Aspekte de Persona.' *Z. Analyt Psychol 5*, 1.

Erikson, E.H. (1968) *Identity – Youth and Crisis.* London: Faber.

Fordham, M. (1944) *The Life of Childhood.* London: Routledge & Kegan Paul.

Fordham, M. (1968) 'Individuation in childhood.' In J.B. Wheelwright (ed) *The Reality of the Psyche.* New York: Putnam's Sons.

Hartmann, H. (1950) 'Comments on the psychoanalytic theory of the ego.' In *The Psychoanalytic Study of the Child.* New York: International Universities Press.

Henderson, J.L. (1967) *Thresholds of Initiation.* Middletown, Conn: Wesleyan University Press.

Jacoby, J. (1958) 'The process of individuation.' *Journal of Analytical Psychology 3*, 2.

Jung, C.G. (1943) 'Two essays on analytical psychology.' *Collected Works 7.*

Jung, C.G. (1951) 'The psychology of the child archetype.' *Collected Works 9*, 1.

Kerenyi, K. (1940) 'The primordial child in primordial times.' In *Essays on a Science of Mythology.* Bollingen Series XXII: Princeton University Press.

Mann, T. (1979) *Death in Venice.* London: Secker and Warburg.

Schafer, R. (1968) *Aspects of internalization.* New York: International Universities Press.

Von Franz, M-L (1970) *The Problem of the Puer Aeternus.* Zurich: Spring Publications.

Whitmont, E.C. (1969) *The Symbolic Quest.* New York: Putnam's Sons.

Zinkin, L. (1978) 'Person to Person: the search for the human dimension in psychotherapy.' (Chapter 2 of this volume; originally published in *British Journal of Medical Psychology, 51*, pp.25–34).

CHAPTER TWO

Person to Person

The Search for the Human Dimension in Psychotherapy

The Medical Section is a meeting place for those concerned with psychotherapy. We come from different schools, each of which has its own ways of thinking and its own ways of approaching patients, but over the years we have learnt to communicate extraordinarily well with each other, and looking back I can remember very few occasions when I have felt there to be a serious gulf between us. I do not mean that there has been lack of disagreement, but there has been a growing understanding of each other's point of view. I am not sure that this is a reflection of what is happening to psychology in general. Here I find that I am constantly going through a cyclical process, where I see rival schools coming together and I have rising hopes of unity, only to have these hopes dashed as new schools, new approaches, new conceptual models come into existence.

As a Jungian, of course, I have been taught to view these developments in much the same way as early Christian sects; that is not simply to ask the question, 'Who is right?', but also to ask, 'What psychological need is expressed by the new point of view?'

It used to be easier than it is now to use agreed criteria based on the natural sciences. Now we have rapidly changing ideas of the nature of scientific enquiry itself, and now it is possible to have quite different conceptual models which can simultaneously be fruitfully used. This is at the same time both exciting and bewildering. It liberates us from constraints in our thinking which we used to take for granted, but this very freedom threatens us, because we may lose our bearings altogether. In this respect psychology is only reflecting a rapidly changing world, where all values can be questioned.

In this paper, I shall try to focus on one area in which, in spite of all the confusion, common ground is being established, and this is a growing clarification of what it means to be human. This is the problem which faces every psychotherapist when he tries to present a case. Can his experience of his patient as a unique, living person be translated into a common, psychological language, which has evolved to deal with an abstraction, like the mind, or the human psyche, or people in general, or even particular categories of people? This is the challenge made by the existentialists to the psychoanalysts. How *can* you, they ask, talk of people in terms of mechanisms? And surprisingly, psychoanalysts find this difficult to answer, even though their insights come from hours spent with people seen on their own, totally absorbed with them and what they have to say. Does the difficulty arise from the analytic process itself, which consists of a kind of dissection into bits?

The Gestalt principle, whereby the whole is greater than the sum of its parts, can be applied here. We may conclude that analysts are doing what Solomon proposed to do to the baby that the two women were quarrelling over, but I think this would be quite the wrong conclusion to make. This is because, although I am attracted, even impressed, by the existentialist standpoint, I regard analysis as having produced infinitely richer results, in terms of understanding people. We *need* mechanistic explanations. The mechanism of projection is the most obvious and most simple example, known about, of course, long before psychoanalysis. Here it is obvious we have understood something about a person when we realize he is seeing in another person a quality in himself, which he does not recognize but which we can see. Unquestionably, psychoanalysis has revealed the enormous subtlety and complexity in the continuous interplay of such mechanisms. Nevertheless it remains true that this kind of insight, however elaborated, still misses the uniqueness of the person.

Analytical psychology, although it makes much less use of mechanisms than psychoanalysis, is open to the same charge. Archetypes are impersonal and the deepest levels of the human psyche are collective, so where is the individual, the person who can be loved?

Uniqueness is a very troublesome concept. It is much emphasized in existentialist philosophy, but it is difficult to incorporate into the traditional scientific approach which prefers to deal with the demonstrable, the repeatable and the general. Therefore, individuality, so prized and respected in psychotherapy, may appear to be outside the realm of scientific enquiry.

Jung was always very conscious of this problem and said in 1916:

> From matters of individual psychology science ought, in fact, to withdraw. For, to speak of a science of individual psychology is already a contradiction in terms. It is only the collective element in the psychology of an individual that constitutes an object for science; for the individual is by definition a unique re- ality that cannot be compared with anything else. A psychologist who professes a 'scientific' individual psychology is simply denying individual psychology.

He exposes his individual psychology to the legitimate suspicion of being merely his own psychology. The psychology of every individual would need its own manual, for the general manual can only deal with collective psychology.

Nevertheless, Jung did not withdraw from 'matters of individual psychology', nor give up his claim to be scientific. The whole of his work can be seen as an attempt at resolution of this conflict and individuation seems to me to have as its central task the bringing together of the individual and collective aspects of the person. However, I do also think that Jung and analytical psychology have not paid sufficient attention to the need for the other person in a loving relationship, who will recognize, enhance and treasure the uniqueness of the person.

When we look at what happens in analysis the emphasis has been on the analyst's function in enhancing the relationship between the patient and his 'unconscious'. But as well as this we can see that the common understanding of the unconscious fantasies (a negotiated agreement to look at them in the same way) enhances the relationship between analyst and patient; and my thesis is that it is this second process which may be by far the most important because it facilitates development of the patient as a person. It is, as I have pointed out in a previous paper, dependent on circular, interactional processes rather than the linear ones used in the medical model when we talk of the patient 'making progress' or getting better.

Now the difficulty about uniqueness is that it cannot be observed outside this interaction. To give an example, recently a patient I had in analysis went to a funeral. Her grandmother, of whom she was quite fond, had died in her nineties. My patient had felt almost nothing at her death and went to the funeral hoping that this experience would bring her more into reality with it. She was impressed and moved by the ritual, but it seemed to have nothing to do with her grandmother. When the minister, who had never met the grandmother, was giving his address, her mind began to wander. When she started listening again, she found that he seemed to be drawing a comparison between the grandmother's death and the death of Christ, a comparison which seemed quite inappropriate to my patient. While this was going on she suddenly found herself recalling that the grandmother's death had been on a bed-pan. 'She would!', she thought, not unaffectionately. 'How typical!' All her life Grandma had seemed to be preoccupied with bowels and lavatories. As she told me this, she began to laugh. In fact we both laughed. This thought had of course been private and quite unsuitable for a funeral, but it *had* been about her grandmother, the actual very human person who had died. To my patient the bringing together of the private joke with the awe-inspiring collective fact of death, through laughter in the analytic situation, was I believe therapeutic. The joke consists in the apparent incompatibility of the personal idiosyncrasy with the transcendental nature of death. The priest knew so much about the nature of death, but he didn't know the grandmother.

This illustrates a major dilemma in psychology. It presents itself as soon as we try to demonstrate theory through giving clinical examples. It is most acutely present in the supervision of trainee therapists. The trainee tries to describe his patient to the supervisor. Every word and gesture can be recorded and reported – even videotapes can be used nowadays. The supervisor then observes all this material, but he cannot himself interrelate with the patient. In practice, he imagines himself doing this, but this is full of pitfalls, because if he were himself the therapist the patient would act and talk differently – unless he were very ill indeed. Therefore both supervisors and trainees have to concentrate on what *can* be discussed – mechanisms once again. The problem is not simply the well-known one of selectivity by the trainee, but the fact that only he has personal knowledge of the patient. In other words, the priest at the funeral could not refer to the bed-pan, even if the grandmother had described it to him, because it could not be an affectionate joke. So it is in supervision: ultimately the experience of the patient as a person cannot be shared. The danger is that this fact leads to the neglect of a human dimension in both psychological theory and analytic technique.

Another patient was fascinated by the Ingmar Bergman film *Wild Strawberries*, where the old distinguished doctor had a dream of being a medical student again and taking an examination, and failed because, with all his knowledge of heart disease, he could not diagnose a broken heart. I could of course take up this material in a transference interpretation – that the patient was attacking me as the impersonal doctor. I could then consider if the attack was justified. What cannot be doubted is that her memory of the film provided her with a means of stating something which *might* have been correct. As an analyst I can diagnose depression, for example, through direct observation, or I can infer its existence even though it is disguised by defences. So, too, might you, if I reported the case fully to you. We have in common a body of knowledge which would enable us to do this. It could therefore be argued that the analyst can be impersonal, that it does not matter, or even that it is an advantage, because he is not biased through being 'emotionally involved'. However, we know this to be a false position, that this kind of knowledge is very limited, that the 'depression' we have diagnosed is not the 'broken heart'. We know that empathy between therapist and patient is essential. Therefore, analysts have devised a more sophisticated model to include empathy. This is based on the somewhat mechanistic, theoretical concepts such as Klein's projective and introjective identification and clinical concepts such as Michael Fordham's syntonic counter transference. Few would doubt the enormous value of these concepts. I would suggest, however, that we need to know a great deal more about how these processes come about and more specifically what are the optimal conditions in which they occur. I would also suggest that analysts, or analytically oriented therapists, have been inhibited in acquiring this knowledge through certain assumptions which they make.

As a starting point, let us consider the situation when the therapist *fails* to empathise with the patient. One can immediately imagine a number of reasons why this may be which would include defensive reactions on the part of the patient, but more fundamental are the cases where there is something which is simply lacking in the patient – there is nothing to empathise with. A severely autistic child would be an example.

As psychotherapists, we are constantly confronted nowadays by patients who are not alive, not real, not themselves. Sometimes they are aware of this and complain about it; sometimes it is the therapist alone who is aware of it. Sometimes both miss it. These patients may, or may not, also have diagnosable states such as phobias, obsessions, addictions, etc. Although these qualities, like being real, being alive, being a person, are so hard to define, so difficult to measure (even to use such words sounds quite unscientific), they retain their central place when we consider the ultimate goals of any therapeutic endeavour. Both analytic theory and academic psychology are beginning to find a place for them. Once the quality which, for want of a better name, may be called 'humanness', is acknowledged, we can all contribute in studying it. We can describe its manifestations and we can define the conditions which enhance it and those which diminish it. This does not mean abandoning the idea of an impersonal, underlying structure. On the contrary, it is essential that we hold on to it. Behind the human face is the inhuman skull.

In the severely autistic child it could be said that the quality I have called humanness is what is absent. Very often it is present at birth and later disappears. By this I mean that the mother reports that the baby relates to her normally at first and perhaps like previous babies have. It is this capacity of the baby to relate to the mother from the beginning which seems to constitute a kind of innate humanness which it is so difficult to account for in analytic theories of development. It is significant that it is the mother on whom we rely to tell us that it is there or not there.

One proposition then, that we can all consider from our different standpoints is this: *the mother who regards her baby as a person from the very beginning is not deluded.* By this I mean that she is not always simply attributing qualities to the baby he does not possess. Let me give you an example of what I mean. A young woman in analysis had a baby which from time to time she brought with her to the sessions. I do not know how often this happens with other analysts, but certainly it worked well in the case of this patient. This was a sensitive mother and there were no serious problems with the baby. On the occasion which I am recalling, the baby, which was I think about ten weeks old, was placed in a carry-cot next to the couch the patient was using and had been fed about one hour previously. It was awake, but was lying quietly while my patient was talking and more or less free-associating, but after a while it began crying, not very loudly, and my patient, after some conflict as to whether to do anything about it, got up, picked him up, and then sat on the couch with him. She began to talk to him and to smile at him, and became quite absorbed in this. His crying gradually stopped and he made little noises back to her, as well as smiling back. This exchange went on for a few minutes, after which the patient resumed her talk to me, continuing to hold and pat the baby, but no longer looking at him. She said that the baby had 'needed to have a little chat'. Now, how can we understand this claim of the mother that she had been having a little chat with a ten-week-old baby? Is she joking? Is she using a metaphor? Is she simply projecting something onto the baby which doesn't belong? Or is it possible that having a little chat is exactly what she had been doing? Certainly it seemed to describe very well what I had been observing. And what of her idea that this was what her baby had needed? Could this be a basic need of babies? If the answer is 'yes', then it must be given central importance in any theory of child development and we cannot do this without seriously questioning the conventional wisdom of existing theories.

My own belief is that the interchange does take place and is basic. It is one of a number of important reciprocal interchanges that must take place *from the beginning* to establish the humanity of the individual. However, the arguments against this come from many sides. Academic psychologists would point to the absence of object constancy at this age, physiologists to the undeveloped neurological apparatus, and even the ethologists might say that the baby perceives the mother's face only as a sign stimulus. However, all these objections, based as they are on sound observations, are not sufficient to demolish the mother's claim. Ethological studies, for example, may mislead us here. Spitz, whom we may now regard as a psychoanalytic pioneer in this field, argues, on the basis of experimental findings, that the infant of three months who smiles at the mother's face is responding to a sign Gestalt, consisting of a forehead, eyes, nose, mouth configuration, preferably in motion. This acts as an innate key stimulus, triggering off an innate response. Although the evidence he presents for this mechanism is strong, it can easily be misinterpreted. The fact that a baby will smile indiscriminately at any face, even at a mask, should not lead us to conclude that this is all he is perceiving in the mother. The mother herself may be smiling and this smile may come and go in a reciprocal relation with the baby's smile, and it is only one of the many modalities of the relationship. These include the talking, her way of holding the baby, her smell – all of which are also expressing her emotional state. There is thus a rich interplay of expressive acts directed at the baby which are at the same time responses to the baby's expressions.

We now have some evidence that the baby does combine these sense modalities in his early perception. Just to take one example, Carpenter's (1974) work with babies of two to seven weeks, in which the baby turns away from the mother if her face is matched with another person's voice. Spitz does acknowledge, even stresses, the importance of the emotional climate and the reciprocal relationships in development, but does not always avoid drawing false conclusions from artificially isolating one aspect of the situation for experimental purposes. For example, after describing how a baby stops smiling if the experimenter turns his face sideways, he says:

> This experiment shows that the three month old is still unable to recognize the human face in profile. In other words, the infant has not recognized the human partner at all. He has only perceived a sign Gestalt of a forehead, eyes and nose. (Spitz 1965)

But this conclusion is quite unjustified. We can only say that his *smile* does not show that he has recognized the human partner and we are indeed beginning to get some evidence that babies do respond differentially between mother and a stranger in the first weeks of life. Moreover, Spitz later mentions that it is difficult, after the profile has been presented, to elicit the smile again on presenting the face. So even in this experiment it is clear that more is going on than first appears. Spitz, as I have said, was a pioneer. As he says in the Foreword to *The First Year of Life*, he was a lonely figure when he started in 1935 to use systematic infant observations. He also refers to the avalanche of publications which have since appeared and which are increasing exponentially.

Most of this avalanche consists of work being done, not by psychoanalysts, but by experimental psychologists. This is as it should be. They can conduct systematic, detailed research, far beyond the scope of any practising therapist. There has in recent years been an impressive shift in the direction of infant observation largely as a result of the influence on psychology of other disciplines. The swing is away from the study of infants as experimental animals and towards studying them in the more natural environment, taking into account the sociological setting and implicitly putting into practice Winnicott's famous adage that there is no such thing as an infant. Ethology has had a considerable influence and Bowlby's work on attachment has established a vital link between ethology, psychoanalysis and experimental psychology. I can do little more in this paper than draw attention to this recent work. I can recommend an excellent short summary by Mary Boston (1975), although I think that the implications of this work require a much greater modification of psychoanalytic theory than she suggests in her paper. The work which is most relevant to my theme is the study of the socialization of the infant. We cannot meaningfully speak of 'deprivation' unless we have detailed knowledge of the way socialization *normally* develops in the infant, through mutual interaction with the sensitive mother. Sophisticated electronic devices, such as videotapes, are revealing the complexity of these interchanges. Prominent among workers in this field are Richards and Bernal in Cambridge, Schaffer in Glasgow, and Ainsworth and her co-workers at Johns Hopkins. The richness and complexity of the observed social interchanges are confirmed and supported by other closely related fields of study such as the early development of language, the acquisition of motor skills – in the work of Bruner for example – and the perceptual apparatus and perceptual capacities of infants, such as the work by Fantz on visual perception. These studies of early socialization have led to emphasis on mutuality, reciprocity and what is called 'inter-subjectivity', which seems to me a term closely related to Winnicott's 'subjective object'. It will be observed that these notions apply only to two people, not to one person studied individually. They are regarded as essential in establishing 'lasting emotional bonds', as Schaffer (1971) would say, or autonomy, which Shotter calls the 'development of personal powers'. Autonomy in human relationships has to be distinguished from autonomy over inanimate objects. The power a baby has to make his mother smile is quite different from his power to manipulate a rattle. In fact, what is called socialization is really so much more than that. Perhaps 'humanization' is a better word, the kind of concept which workers with autistic children, such as Mahler and Bettleheim, have found necessary.

It is of interest here that there is evidence that babies react differently from the beginning to people and to things. Martin Richards, for example, describes some experimental work with Trevarthen, of which he says:

> These first observations indicate that when infants are given an interesting thing to look at they concentrate attention on it. The eyes narrow and scan over the object, the body posture seems tense, the arms, hands and fingers are orientated towards the object in incipient pointing gestures. With social situations, the infant seems to sit back, the body is loose and the hands and arms drop, the eyes widen and the attention appears less focused. The face is more mobile, with many mouth movements, and of course smiling is common. (Richards 1974)

This very early human interchange needs a place in psychoanalytic theory. It also needs a place in analytical psychology, where there is a tendency to regard the deepest layers of the human psyche as impersonal and relatively undifferentiated.

Perhaps we have all been regarding the human baby as primitive in the same way that anthropologists used to regard primitive societies as primitive. John and Elizabeth Newson in the November 1975 *Bulletin of the British Psychological Society* speak of the 'primacy of social responsiveness in human infants', and the Newsons refer to the host of recent observations which have begun to suggest that the human infant is a much more complicated organism than previous generations of developmental psychologists have led us to believe. Perhaps we can say the same in analytic circles of previous generations of analysts. In this country, and indeed in this Section, it is Winnicott's voice which has been the most persuasive and has profoundly influenced both those Freudians and those Jungians who have listened to it, and Winnicott can be seen in his later papers to be developing a theory of early reciprocal mother/infant relationships, very much in line with so-called academic psychology. It was, however, derived from his own experience with patients and made use of a highly personal metaphorical language. A key paper is Winnicott's 'The mirror role of mother and family' (Winnicott 1971). In this paper, characteristically short and concise, he acknowledges the influence of Lacan's 'La stade du miroir'. It is an extraordinarily rich paper which shows Winnicott's gift of using metaphor to convey meaning to his readers. The idea is the very simple one that the baby looks at the mother's face as in a mirror, while the mother through her face reflects to the baby himself. The case illustrations he gives are all about patients who had difficulty in feeling themselves to be real.

Of course, such a metaphor loses its meaning if taken too literally or concretely. A mirror reflects in a mechanical way and the mother is really doing much more than this. She is looking at her baby and responding emotionally and radiates back to him what she sees and feels, through the constantly changing expression in her face. The baby is doing the same thing. Also, over a period of time the expression of each is influencing the expression of the other, probably in an alternating sequence. If we grant that all this might have been taking place in my patient's chat with her baby, we still have to add a great deal: the holding and handling of the baby, which Winnicott says must be taken for granted, and the noises. It is the interchange of the mother's special way of talking to her baby and the baby's little noises which seem to constitute something like a conversation. It is therefore important if we single out a single sense modality, like vision, that we do not forget that in the natural state all these sense modalities are working simultaneously. It is in this highly complex sense that we can understand something of the way the mother's face can act as a mirror.

In this paper Winnicott does not commit himself by making a clear statement as to whether the baby is perceiving a whole object. As he includes a reference to Gough's work on the baby looking at the mother while feeding at the breast, he must mean before the depressive position is reached, particularly as he dates the depressive position rather late. He does, however, bring in his idea of the subjective object – the object which is presented in such a way that the baby's sense of omnipotence is not violated. The result can be that the baby is able to use the object and to feel as if the object is a subjective object and created by the baby.

Now it has always seemed to me that this idea which Winnicott came to stress so much, of the importance of illusion, is only half-true. The baby may not be omnipotent in reality, but at least his powers are real. By this I mean that, given the right conditions which Winnicott says have to be taken for granted – and I think these conditions were met in the example of my patient – the baby can experience autonomy. He can *really* elicit a smile on his mother's face for example, or he can cause the smile to disappear. In this sense he does create and it is not an illusion. However, this only happens when the mother attaches meaning to the baby's expressions. Once again, in the mother's case she is responding to something that is really there. She is endowing with meaning that which has meaning already, and not simply projecting her fantasies, as in a Rorschach test, on an arbitrarily produced pattern. Mothers do, of course, frequently have illusions, even delusions, about their babies' expressions, but cannot then act as a true mirror.

A second reason why I am not happy with the use of the word 'omnipotence' is that it implies, and is usually used in psychoanalysis to imply, a denial of outside powers and I am sure that the baby in this special situation is also experiencing the mother's autonomy – her spontaneous smile for example. If the illusion of omnipotence simply means, however, that the whole experience is like a miracle, then I am in complete concordance with it.

Winnicott, of course, developed his ideas while remaining a psychoanalyst and without systematically modifying psychoanalytic theory as he went along, or trying to fit the ideas into a theory as it then existed. There are, of course, obvious reasons why psychoanalysis has not dealt adequately with early human interaction and this has been well discussed by Guntrip (1961). Libidinal drives have been given primacy in emotional development, and the original Freudian homeostatic closed-system model, with the idea of drive reduction being a basic aim, has led to a great concentration on highly charged emotional states which can be observed at the height of instinctual experiences, such as feeding, or not feeding, a very hungry baby. There has therefore been little emphasis placed on quiet states, such as in the conversation I witnessed. There has thus been a tendency to regard the infant as either in a state of rest or under the spell of powerful drives, seeking satisfaction in order to achieve homeostasis. These states do of course occur, and it is likely that splitting into part objects and the defence mechanisms of projective and introjective identification do occur in highly excited states associated with powerful instinctual drives. It is also likely that there are periods of quiescence, in which the children's world is undifferentiated. These two states would correspond to Michael Fordham's description of states of integration and de-integration. However, there are many intermediate states and the sensitive mother, as in my example, uses an in-between time to make a social or human relationship. If the baby is awake, but has been fed, it is quietly alert. These periods have not been the main concern of psychoanalytic theory, yet it is in such periods that the baby is best able to enter into a mutual reciprocal social relationship with the mother, as well as to explore its powers over inanimate objects.

The concept of circular interchanges between mother and infant is only slowly finding a place in analytical thinking. The infant's world was originally described with little reference to the part played by the mother. Then gradually notions of good and bad mothering have been brought in, principally the mother's need-fulfilling role, that of satisfying the libidinal drives, then the importance of what Winnicott calls handling and holding. Only recently has stress been placed on the specific maternal function in establishing personal identity through reciprocal human relationship.

In analytical psychology there has been a similar problem. There has been a tendency to see the analyst solely in terms of helping the patient to be in touch with, and have some understanding of, the inner world. (I say 'the inner world' rather than 'his inner world' because of the importance we place on the collective nature of the unconscious, but of course we do regard the personal unconscious as important as well.) Individuation is very often seen as having this goal. But this way of thinking leaves out the other person and his direct relationship with the patient. Jung did value this in practice, as those who knew his way of working with a patient will testify. The fact that he valued it gave rise to a different technical approach to analysis from Freud's, sitting face to face with the patient, with more spontaneity of expression from the analyst and so on. But it remains difficult to derive this approach from the theoretical basis of Jung's work, based as it was on the elucidation and amplification of archetypal images. Again, the emphasis has been on highly charged rather than quiet, emotional states. For Jung it is the numinosity of experience which gives it value. Numinous experiences, when they occur, can be of enormous positive importance in such varied states as profound religious or aesthetic experience or falling in love, or can be destructive, as in Nazi Germany, or in schizophrenia. But again, these states can be overemphasized. For most ordinary people, these experiences are comparatively rare, and I would imagine that this is true both in modern and in primitive society. Reading *Memories, Dreams, Reflections* (Jung 1983) can easily lead one to the mistaken impression that Jung's life consisted only of such experiences. Most of us are engaged in living lives which can be full and rewarding at a much lower emotional temperature and anyone who has had experience of analysis, Jungian or Freudian, knows that it does not consist of blinding revelations all the time, and that as well as powerful affects, a good deal of more natural, more ordinary interchange takes place, which can even be called 'conversation'.

Sometimes this conversation can have the same miraculous significance as in the baby's conversation with the mother, when patient and analyst are understanding each other and enhancing each other's existence, though again it can easily be undervalued or ridiculed by outsiders – as, I think, conversations with very young babies have been.

Now, what can we do to correct this bias? First I think it must be recognized that the findings of analytical dynamic psychology are in no way negated by these recent discoveries. It remains true that the developing infant has the task of mastering instinctual drives and that in the process he will tend to live in the either/or world which consists of either fusion or highly affectively charged part-objects. Archetypal images at their most primitive and impersonal form can be seen to express the same states of mind, whether or not we agree that they are actually derived from infancy. Nevertheless, we do not have to develop all our theory from these facts. For example, the theory that at first the infant has only part-objects and that whole objects can be arrived at only through the achievement of ambivalence, where good and bad part-objects are brought together, needs another dimension. Melanie Klein, of course, held that the depressive position can be achieved only if good experiences outweigh the bad. What are these good experiences? Not simply the satisfaction of instinctual drives. Any account of good maternal care cannot leave out the conversation, the mirror role of the mother. Surely she is at that moment showing herself as a whole person?

A highly important factor, also, is that of distance. It is the distance receptors – vision and hearing – which are in use, and regulation of distance very largely defines the nature of human relationships, although the two variables emotional distance and physical distance have both to be considered. I did not mention when I spoke of the mother and child having a chat, that the mother held the baby sitting facing her on her lap, about 18 inches away. It is known now that at birth a baby's eyes can function perfectly, except for accommodation, and that, at birth, 18 inches is about the distance at which it can see clearly. This is a very good distance in which two people can address each other. They are sufficiently close to see each other's face, to the exclusion of other visual stimuli, and yet there is an important space separating them from each other. If they are closer, fusion or confusion with each other may take place. If a long way away, they may not see each other's expressions. If a very long way away they cannot recognize each other.

Second, the way of looking at the other person is important. We may speak of seeing without looking, looking at, looking into another's eyes, or looking right through another person. It seems to me that the mother, looking for meaning in her baby's expression, is not simply looking at the surface of the baby nor through him. She is looking at a hypothetical centre in the baby, and in this way she is helping him to find a centre in himself. It is in this sense that mother and baby are seeing each other as a whole, and perhaps in this context it is better if we avoid using the word 'object'. I would suggest that this early experience of wholeness in the form of a friendly human mother quietly relating to her baby, through her voice and face rather than through her breast, giving him the whole of her attention, is a normal and a very early experience. It considerably precedes in time such achievements as object-constancy, unit status, or the depressive position when good and bad are brought together. Extremes of good and bad do not occur at these times and the baby does have some awareness of another person. In fact it seems to me likely that such experience is a precondition for the much later bringing-together of split-off good and bad and the achievement of symbol-formation. (By 'much later', I mean a few months.) It also seems to me that we must look for the lack of, or distortion in, this early experience to understand the genesis of psychotic and schizoid states. For instance, some patients create exciting emotional states because they cannot tolerate quiet states and not because of lack of libidinal satisfaction as such. It may be that in these patients it is the quiet being-together which is what has been lacking in early infancy.

At the same time we should not forget that, vital though it is, the establishment of the capacity to form friendly or loving relationships with others is not the only goal of development. We need to flee from, or attack, enemies. (The differentiation between friends and enemies need not involve splitting as it does in paranoid states where everybody is seen as either an enemy or as an ally. Friends and enemies are not really simple opposites. Friendship requires a negotiated reciprocal interchange but having enemies does not.) Also we need to know how not to relate to the many strangers who surround us, those who are neither friends nor enemies. Sometimes, although it is unpopular to say so, we must even manipulate other people. We also have to negotiate with others in changing these relationships from enemy to friend, for example, or stranger to enemy. As well as this, we must develop and learn to recognize the limits of our powers over the non-human world, both living and inanimate. In addition, we have to learn to live with ourselves.

In reminding you of what is really very obvious I am trying to establish a separate status for what I call the human dimension. It is important, but its importance can only be understood in a context where non-human functions are also really human, though I hope that I have made it clear that I am using the idea of humanness in a special way.

In psychotic states, friends, enemies and strangers are, of course, often confused. For example, recently a borderline young man told me that a man at work had been watching him. Probably this was delusional, but the delusion derives from misinterpreting 'looking at' for 'watching'. Probably the man was just looking at him, perhaps idly, perhaps with interest, but probably not with the intensity implied by the word 'watching'. My point is that, to make this discrimination, 'friendly looking at', as opposed to watching or observing, has to have been experienced from early infancy. If not, the task of the analyst is to supply and enhance this missing experience, or at least provide the opportunity for the experience to take place within the analytic setting. This is not primarily a paper on technique, but you can see that it has numerous technical implications.

I have avoided until now the use of the terms 'ego' and 'self'. This is to avoid confusion. Both of these terms are abstractions which have not been derived from the kind of reciprocal interactions I have been describing. We can say, for example, that the ego has the function of regulating distance and emotional expression which are the moment-to-moment responsibility of the mature individual. That the mother, in her conversation with her baby, provides an opportunity for ego-development, in recognizing and establishing the autonomy of the baby. We can also say that the mother is establishing the baby's sense of self, because it is his unique self that she is recognizing and responding to. These statements are both correct up to a point, but they carry a suggestion that these entities, 'ego' and 'self', can exist in themselves without the continual need for other people, and this misses the essence of reciprocity. The mother cannot look into the baby's eyes if the baby looks away. The adult may have an ego which enables him to regulate distance to some extent. He can be friendly or hostile, warm or cold to another person, but the other person can do the same and the resultant interaction and distance has to depend on both partners and on the degree of mutuality which can be established.

I can illustrate this with a final and very brief clinical example. A patient had a long series of dreams about a boy. He was a homosexual with a compulsive need to seek out pubescent boys. In the dreams, he kept seeing the boy from different angles and distances, in different positions, in different states of dress and undress, in different moods (for example, the boy looked sad or preoccupied), but in all the dreams the patient was an unseen observer and always the boy acted as though regarding himself as alone. The crucial need which emerged was that the boy should look back at him. In fact the whole case hinged on the need for a man and boy to see each other and recognize each other. Of course I made frequent interpretations that the boy was himself and that the man was himself, but this is not sufficient. His 'acting out' indicated that it had to be another person and in the analysis the mutual recognition had somehow to be realized in the patient's relationship with me, by which I mean much more than transference and counter-transference.

I mean that I really had to recognize and reflect back to him, himself. When I try to express to you what took place between us, I cannot do so except through the symbol of the man and the boy who look at each other. Perhaps this is father and son (and this particular man had never been seen as he was by his father) but its prototype lies in the very earliest mother–baby interaction.

You will recall that in Thomas Mann's *Death in Venice* this mutual recognition between the old man and the young boy becomes the only really important thing. The whole of the hero's previous life is as nothing compared with this, and afterwards he dies. This meeting with the boy, which for the man is so momentous, is not even noticed by anyone else. Perhaps his death is an indication that he has encountered the Divine Child and it is said that no man can look into the face of God and live, or perhaps it simply indicates that he has now at last truly lived: his life is complete and he can die. Many interpretations are possible, but one that I would not accept is that it is simply a homosexual infatuation, a projection of an unconscious fantasy, because this leaves out the mutuality which is essential to it.

I have tried to indicate some of the ways in which we can extend our conceptual framework to do justice to the kind of mutuality that my patient was seeking in his dream, and that Thomas Mann was expressing in his short story, but we have a long way to go. We can, however, support this endeavour with systematic observation, which we can agree to call scientific and gradually we can be conscious in our therapeutic work that we are more than analysing observers and interpreters.

References

Boston, M. (1975) 'Recent research in developmental psychology.' *Journal of Child Psychology, 4*, 1 pp.15–34.

Carpenter, G. (1974) 'Mother's face and the newborn.' *New Scientist 61*, p.742.

Guntrip, H. (1961) *Personality, Structure and Human Interaction*. New York: International Universities Press.

Jung, C.G. (1983) *Memories, Dreams, Reflections*. London: Flamingo.

Richards, M. (ed) (1974) *The Integration of a Child into a Social World*. London: Cambridge University Press.

Schaffer, H.R. (1971) *The Growth of Sociability*. Harmondsworth: Penguin.

Spitz, R. (1965) *The First Year of Life*. New York: International Universities Press.

Winnicott, D.W. (1971) *Playing and Reality*. London: Tavistock Publications.

CHAPTER THREE

The Collective and the Personal

Introduction

Running through Jung's work is the contrast between 'personal' and 'collective'. It seems a simple enough contrast and we are inclined to take it rather for granted. However, these are not simple opposites. Surely the opposite of 'personal' should be 'impersonal' and the opposite of 'collective' might well be 'individual'? Jung clearly wished to say something more than these straightforward oppositions imply. Many difficulties arise from his particular usage. One instance is his idea that the persona is a segment of the collective psyche (Jung 1926). Here the persona is individual but not personal, i.e. both individual *and* collective. Another instance is to be found in the introduction to *Psychology and Alchemy*. Jung discussing Christ as a symbol of the self together with other religious figures, states:

> Not only is the self indefinite, but – paradoxically enough – it also includes the quality of definiteness and even that of uniqueness. This is probably one of the reasons why precisely those religions founded by historical personages have become world religions, such as Christianity, Buddhism and Islam. The inclusion in a religion of a unique human personality – especially when conjoined to an indefinable divine nature – is consistent with the absolute individuality of the self, which combines uniqueness with eternity and the individual with the universal. The self is a union of opposites *par excellence*, and this is where it differs essentially from the Christian. (Jung 1944, p.19)

Here Jung is taking Christ as a collective symbol which he regards as a symbol of the self. He is therefore seeing the archetype combining, as opposites, *both* collectivity and individuality. This leads to difficulty, in practice, of identifying 'personal' material. Mary Williams has pointed out that Jung acknowledged the problem of drawing a boundary-line between the personal and collective unconscious (Williams 1963), and Rosemary Gordon has shown how symbols may act as a bridge *between* the collective and the personal (Gordon 1977). In general, analytical psychologists on the look-out for archetypes tend to regard the rest of the material produced by patients as 'personal' by a process of exclusion. This does not do justice to the nature of the personal, which has certain positive characteristics lacking in the collective. Numinosity, which is usually regarded as accompanying the experience of an archetype, may perhaps be more likely to result from a simultaneous presentation of collective and personal features. The presence of a personal element may be denied in religious experience, but is more difficult to deny in other experiences of the numinous. In the realm of aesthetics, a Mozart quartet, for example, can be seen to exhibit a highly formal and predictable structure (which may have archetypal characteristics) but at the same time a certain tension exists between this collective aspect and a highly personal quality emanating from Mozart the person. Without these personal qualities the formal structure would seem bare and empty. Again, in the realm of interpersonal relationships, falling in love is a phenomenon which is not adequately expressed by the formula of projection of the anima or animus. It also includes the prizing of highly personal, perhaps even idiosyncratic, features of the other person as a unique individual.

I believe the mother–infant dyad to be a very special case in point and I shall be giving it particular attention in this paper as constituting the infant's first experience of a combination of collective and personal.

The collective–personal dichotomy has a bearing, also, on the analytic relationship. The analytical psychologist, in his daily work, is likewise *combining* his impersonal, collective knowledge with an activity best described in such terms as 'getting to know the person'. This second activity can be adequately described only in a special language concerned with the reciprocal nature of relationship. In a previous paper I tried to schematise this dual activity as combining a linear model – a one-way observational process going in one direction – with a circular model which involves the two-way process of entering into a living relationship with another person (Zinkin 1978).

I believe this double activity of the analyst can be easily recognized by the analyst as constituting his work. Unfortunately there is a tendency to regard only the first of these activities as a scientific one and the analytical approach has, for this reason, been subject to much criticism from existentialist and phenomenological psychologists as being impersonal and mechanistic.

Jung's work places all the emphasis on collective aspects of the psyche. I would like in this paper to suggest that the balance should be redressed to give much greater weight than Jung did to the personal, while accepting his distinction between personal and collective, despite its difficulties. I shall consider in relation to Jung the philosopher Martin Buber with his well-known 'Ich–du', even though in him perhaps the bias lies the other way.

Jung's theory of the psyche

This paper, then, is a theoretical one of a very fundamental kind. I have up to now used 'collective' and 'personal' as though they were nouns, but it is legitimate to object to this and to ask *what* is thus described. If they are applied to the conscious or the unconscious these words, too, are really adjectives. To conceive them as entities (which need not imply reification) means seeing them as parts of a system called by Jung the psyche. The concept 'psyche', however, is fraught with difficulties and when Jung tried to define it he could do so only in the most tautological terms: 'By the psyche I understand the totality of all the psychic processes both conscious and unconscious' (Jung 1921, p.463).

Jung is here distinguishing psyche from soul and he is only drawing attention to its totality, rather than giving a full description of what it is. It is perhaps inevitable that the most fundamental terms of any theory should be undefined. For Jung it was axiomatic that what he was studying as a psychologist was 'the psyche'. He shared with other psychologists, including Freud, the idea that there was such an entity, that it had a reality as valid as 'material reality' and that it had a structure.

Jung's individual contribution lay in his special idea of its structure, rather than the idea of the psyche as such, which he took for granted. If we take the archetypes as Jung's most important theoretical concept, we can see that they required the idea of the collective unconscious. Jung regarded the archetype as the 'indispensable correlate of the idea of the collective unconscious' (Jung 1936). The collective unconscious in turn can only make sense if distinguished from the personal unconscious and the unconscious needs likewise to be distinguished from the conscious.

Jung's diagrams

It is after some hesitation that I reproduce three of Jung's diagrams of the psyche in this paper, as used by Jacobi in her introductory work *The Psychology of Jung* (Jacobi 1942). When I presented them to an audience of analytical psychologists they aroused little interest (in spite of being in Jung's suggested colours) and were thought not to do justice to Jung. It is true that Jung regarded them as only a rudimentary kind of sketch map and that he used them only when giving extempore lectures or seminars and not in his serious published work. Nevertheless they do show the structure of the psyche in the sense that they show how Jung thought of the parts of the psyche as being related to each other. If we try to understand this from the written work, we find that Jung still had recourse to spatial metaphors; the persona is the most *superficial* layer of the psyche. The ego is the *centre* of consciousness. Consciousness is like an island rising out of the sea of the unconscious. The reader can only conceive these relationships in visual terms. He will form a mental picture approximating to Jung's. We might as well then use Jung's own pictures. Although they merit extended discussion, I wish to make only four points here which are related to my theme.

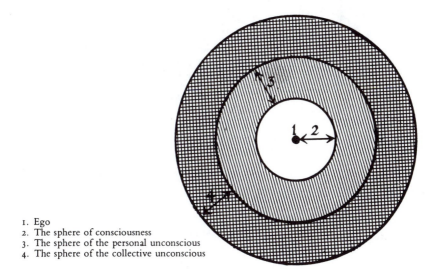

1. Ego
2. The sphere of consciousness
3. The sphere of the personal unconscious
4. The sphere of the collective unconscious

Figure 3.1 Jung's model of the psyche 1

A. That part of the collective unconscious that can never be raised into consciousness
B. The sphere of the collective unconscious
C. The sphere of the personal unconscious

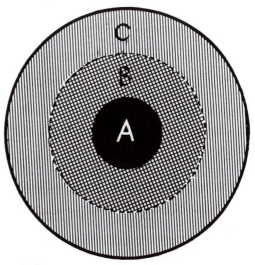

Figure 3.2 Jung's model of the psyche 2

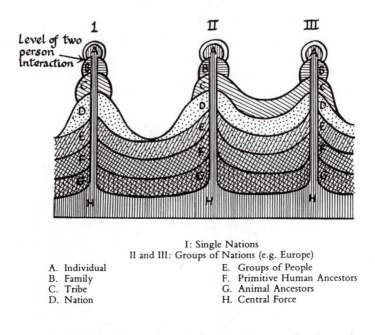

I: Single Nations
II and III: Groups of Nations (e.g. Europe)

A. Individual   E. Groups of People
B. Family   F. Primitive Human Ancestors
C. Tribe   G. Animal Ancestors
D. Nation   H. Central Force

Figure 3.3 Jung's model of the psyche: relationship between collective and personal elements

1. First is the problem of *the* psyche. This usage does not necessarily imply there is only one psyche. The psyche could, like the liver, be identical in structure for each individual. The structure can be studied in spite of the fact that no two livers are exactly alike. On the other hand, the appearance on the diagram of the collective unconscious does suggest that there is really only one collective unconscious. The word 'collective' can mean, as Murray Jackson has suggested, 'shared' (Jackson 1960). In this sense, Jung also sometimes spoke of a collective consciousness. Figure 3.3 is most interesting in this respect because it does indicate that only the peaks correspond with anything we call individual.We are all, in that sense, only superficially separate; we are all connected at some level with everybody else and there is a central force like a subterranean sea which unites us all as it reaches into every individual.

2. A further difficulty in conceiving of the psyche in the singular is perhaps less obvious, but very important to my theme. It cannot deal with two persons communicating with each other. It leads to what Rickman called a one-body rather than a two-body psychology (Rickman 1950). The collective–individual dichotomy contrasts the

large group with the single person. It does not account for the special case of one individual in relation to another. This special case of the one-to-one seems to be of crucial importance when considering the personal. The intimate dialogue of the analytic relationship cannot be understood on the basis of a single 'psyche' and I shall be using the writings of Buber to illustrate this.

3. A curious feature of Jung's diagrams is that he is quite ready to turn them inside out! The centre in Figure 3.1 is the ego surrounded by consciousness, the personal unconscious and the collective unconscious. In Figure 3.2 the collective unconscious is in the centre and the most conscious parts of the psyche are on the periphery. Jung is indicating by this that it is simply a matter of viewpoint which way we put them. I can accept this on the grounds that at times we need to consider the central position of the ego and at other times the superficiality of consciousness compared with the 'depth' of the unconscious. It should be noted, however, that the boundary of the psyche in each case indicates what lies *outside* it. In the first case, it is the 'outside world' or external reality; in the second, the collective unconscious itself seems to be all there on the outside. In neither case is it another person. To call another person part of the outside world, or 'environment', is correct, but it leaves out the special nature of the personal encounter (Buber 1970).

4. Such a model cannot depict the 'I' of the I–you. The ego as the centre of consciousness, despite its great organising powers, is simply not the I that addresses, or recognizes itself when addressed by, another person. It is true, of course, that Jung did not regard the ego as the centre of the psyche. At times the self is given this place – although the self also represents the entirety of the psyche. The self acts as that which unifies the psyche and Jung gives no special consideration, as far as I know, to it having a function in relating to other people. Again, I think his model did not allow of this possibility.

Martin Buber

Although Buber was primarily a philosopher and Jung a psychologist, they were not as far apart as these titles might suggest. Both were steeped in the German philosophical tradition, both had great knowledge of comparative religion and both were particularly interested in man's relationship to God. Above all, both developed a view of man which was based on personal experience of a highly numinous kind. Jung's early numinous experiences, as recounted in *Memories, Dreams, Reflections* (Jung 1963), can be paralleled by intense and powerful experiences which Buber had had and both developed a highly individual view in which these experiences played a vital part. Buber, who lectured at an Eranos conference, was a great admirer of Jung (despite certain criticisms). He regarded Jung as 'the world's leading psychologist'. Both, moreover, wrote in a rather high-flown style, Buber even more than Jung. His writings abound in metaphor and paradoxical utterances, often apparently contradictory statements written in the heat of inspiration. For this reason, some readers are put off, while others are fascinated and profoundly influenced by Buber, as they are by Jung.

Buber's perhaps over-simple division between I–Thou and I–it is also a very powerful one. I shall follow Kaufmann's translation where in the text 'Ich–du' is translated as 'I–you'. As Kaufmann explains, two-thirds of 'I and Thou' does not refer to God and in English we do not refer to each other as 'thou' (Kaufmann 1970).

It can be very easily grasped that one feels most of all an 'I' when addressed by another as 'you', or when addressing another as 'you'. It is also intuitively apparent that there is a quite different sort of experience when thinking *about* something or someone, when there is an object of our thoughts, the I–it. Buber regards the 'I' of I–you as different from the 'I' of I–it. For Buber, God is the 'Eternal Thou', but the 'you' need not be God – it can be another person, an animal (as in Buber's childhood experience of a horse), or even a stone. The important thing is that a dialogue is taking place. Even with a stone one can address it and allow oneself to be, in a sense, addressed by it.

For the purposes of this paper it is not necessary to follow Buber in all of this. We need not accept dialogues with God or with stones (though Jung surely did not regard either as an 'it'), but we cannot easily deny the reality of dialogues between persons. My own view is that the experience of dialogue with another person from the beginning of life, primarily with the personal mother (or mother-substitute), is at the root of all other forms of dialogue – whether it be with God, with stones, with the outside world, or with 'contents of the unconscious'.

Most of what Buber has to say about dialogue is specifically applicable to intra-human dialogue. This is most clearly brought out in *Between Man and Man* (Buber 1947). In this book, which is an extension and clarification of the ideas presented in *I and Thou*, Buber distinguishes three ways of perceiving a man who is 'living before our eyes' (Buber 1947, p.8). These he calls observing, looking on and becoming aware. Observing corresponds roughly with the medical model. The observer is intent, he is looking for traits, he probes the other so that he may write him up and he makes notes. The onlooker is more like a classical psychoanalyst. 'He takes up the position which lets him see the object freely and undisturbed awaits what will be presented to him' (Buber 1947, p.9). He lets himself go and he is 'not in the least afraid of forgetting something'. But it is 'becoming aware' which is for Buber the true dialogue. At this point, Buber says, the man 'says something' to me if I am receptive – something which cannot be grasped objectively, he speaks to *me*. He addresses me and this sense of a saying or speaking while not meant literally is, according to Buber, emphatically not a mere metaphor. At this moment, something happens which is completely different from observing or looking on – and which cannot be put into words.

These three states or ways of perceiving can easily be recognized by the analyst. All three seem to me to be essential, but it is only the third which does justice to the state of affairs when the analyst is really in touch with his patient and which, because it is so difficult to describe, gets left out of most descriptions of technique. It is at this point that the analyst ceases to be an observer or an onlooker, but becomes a participant in a dialogue.

The personal in Jung's psychology

Jung regarded the personal unconscious as equivalent to Freud's concept of the unconscious; that is, it consists of contents which were once conscious but later repressed and which might just as well be conscious. (This is somewhat of a distortion of Freud. It is true that his great contribution placed greatest emphasis on repression, but he made numerous references to the unrepressed unconscious, as Matte-Blanco has shown (Matte-Blanco 1975) and certainly his followers, particularly Melanie Klein, have developed the idea of unconscious phantasy as that which was never conscious. Jung's use of the term 'personal unconscious', therefore, simply means that part of what is personally experienced which is later repressed.)

'What is personally experienced' would thus constitute 'personal consciousness'. Jung sometimes referred also to collective consciousness, but this seems to mean simply contents of consciousness which are common to many people and therefore unlike collective unconscious contents required no special demonstration.

When Jung refers to the personal mother or father, he uses the word 'personal' to distinguish them from collective representations. This direct common-sense appeal, this assumption that we all know what is meant by the personal, seems to me to bypass a whole area of psychological enquiry. How do we come to perceive other persons as such and how do we experience ourselves as persons? Jung was not alone in neglecting this area. It is only comparatively recently that psychoanalysts have concerned themselves with such questions. It is not that Jung was unaware of the importance of 'experiencing one's self as a person'. His concept of individuation, the achievement of 'wholeness', cannot be understood without this dimension. Analytical psychology, as well as psychoanalysis, seems to assume that, if only the patient will withdraw projections, other persons (including the analyst) can be experienced easily enough. This idea has led some analysts to over-emphasize the analysis of the transference with the idea that it is only the transference that stands in the way of the patient seeing the analyst as real. In this context, it matters little if the distortions of perception are thought of as coming from the repressed unconscious or are archetypal, i.e. derived from the collective unconscious.

The same error is made by those analysts who do not see the analysis of the transference as of prime importance, but who nevertheless see their work entirely in terms of helping the patient to integrate his unconscious 'bits'. Here again it may be assumed that the capacity to relate to other persons will somehow emerge once distortions are corrected. These assumptions all derive from a one-person psychology.

The conflict between Buber and Jung

In his *Eclipse of God*, Martin Buber makes a number of criticisms of Jung (Buber 1953) and Jung's reply to these criticisms appears in Vol. 18 of the *Collected Works* (Jung 1952). Buber replies to this in an appendix to *Eclipse of God*. Buber, like other theologians sympathetic to Jung's psychology, such as Victor White, cannot accept that God can be considered entirely in terms of 'psychic reality', nor does he believe that Jung is consistent in remaining within the realm of the empirical psychologist. Buber attacks particularly Jung's attachment to Gnostic concepts of God (he is in general very hostile to the idea of *gnosis* as opposed to *devotio*) and above all to the identification of the self with the Self and the Self with God, as in Hindu writings. Jung's rather testy reply reveals some sensitivity to this kind of attack. Whether God exists other than as part of Man's psyche can rightly be regarded as a question outside the subject matter of psychology. (Buber and Jung are agreed about that.) The existence of other persons, however, is not in question, and it seems to me that if what Buber has to say about dialogue can be understood in intra-human terms, without reference to God, then his I–you, I–it dichotomy can readily be accepted as within the realm of psychology.

The personal mother, if conceived of as 'you', then assumes enormous importance, particularly if she is regarded as the first 'you' for the baby.

The *a priori* of relation

Buber says, 'In the beginning is the relation' and he speaks of the '*a priori* of relation' and the innate You:

> In the relationships through which we live, the innate You is realized in the You we encounter: that this, comprehended as a being we confront and accepted as exclusive, can finally be addressed with the basic word, has its ground in the *a priori* of relation. (Buber 1970, pp.78–79)

For Buber, the *a priori* of relationship means that I–you *precedes* I–it.

While acknowledging the force of Buber's prose style, I can only justify introducing him into a paper on psychology by translating him so that his statements look less like *ex cathedra* pronouncements and rather more like testable hypotheses. The biblical phrase 'In the beginning' has then to be thought of as 'in the first few weeks of life' and we are speaking the language of the psychology of infantile development. This area of psychology can never become an exact science, in so far as we are attempting to imagine what it feels like for the infant. It is a science only in so far as these imaginings are limited and informed by objective observations. In this, infant observation is a great deal more reliable than analytic reconstruction. Even here, however, there is an important difference between observing an infant in the manner pioneered by Spitz, which is a one-body psychology, and watching mothers and babies together. I would regard this as an essential exercise for all analysts, though much more precise and refined observations are to be made by experimental psychologists watching in relatively controlled conditions. A great deal of work has established that in the very first weeks of life an early form of 'conversation' takes place between mother and infant – sometimes called 'proto-conversation'. What is more, there is a good deal of evidence that this takes a very special form for the individual mother and baby. It is now established, for example, that the infant recognizes his mother in the sense that he differentiates her from other adults; also babies can be observed to be differentiating people from things. I have referred more fully to the importance of this work in another paper (Zinkin 1978).

Buber, as I have said, does not limit I–you to interpersonal communication. He refers to very early I–you relationships with the moon or the pattern of the wallpaper. Buber also states that a man can be in an I–you relationship with another man, even though the other man is unaware of his presence. There is a need for caution here. It is probably true that the infant, like the 'primitive', experiences all the world as in relation to himself. The idea would correspond to the idea of object-relations, although there is some controversy as to whether object-relationships begin at birth. Nevertheless, it is important to distinguish this general phenomenon from the special case of the dialogue, or early conversation with the mother. It is clear to the observer (or onlooker) that in this case there are two active and aware partners involved in the dialogue and it can also be seen that the baby is behaving quite differently at these times from the way he behaves at others. This means that, although at other times the baby may be said to hallucinate, such hallucinations are not the same as are found in psychosis. In other words, the baby seems to know whether there is a real person there or not. Buber's I–you, then, is the very general mode of relating which precedes I–it. The 'innate You' seems to refer to a genetically laid-down potentiality, a reaching out or groping towards a You. The personal mother becomes the 'you' for the baby at the times when the baby is a 'you' for her. It seems to me that it is only at these times that I–you can be called personal.

I–it comes later. This is also in agreement with our knowledge of infant development if we take the 'it' to mean a relatively high level of abstraction – the stage when the mother can be conceptualized when not being related to. This is very different, however, from placing the perception of the personal mother late.

Buber goes to great lengths in separating I–you from I–it. He even says that I–you is not an experience. In his world: 'Feelings one "has"; love occurs. Feelings dwell in man but man dwells in his love' (Buber 1970, p.66). The poetic strength of this statement should not deter us from trying to translate it into psychological language. I think two points are being made which can be seen if we think of babies and mothers. The first is that what is taking place cannot be understood by looking into the baby. The relationship between the two is the love which the baby is part of: it is not described in terms of his emotion.

The second point *can* be related to the infant as a single individual. It is that loving the mother represents a higher degree of abstraction than participating in a relationship. As soon as the baby is able to say 'I feel love for mother', this is a high level of abstraction, an observation of his experience, therefore I–it. This suggests an either–or quality about abstracting, whereas there are actually many levels. Let us look more clearly at this problem.

Levels of abstraction

It seems to be a basic necessity of the human mind to divide things into two – to see things in terms of opposites. Very early in his career, at the time of his break with Freud, Jung proposed *two* ways of thinking, directed and undirected (fantasy) (Jung 1916). More generally accepted is the equally dualistic distribution between concrete and abstract thought as proposed by Goldstein. It has proved useful, for example, in understanding schizophrenic thinking, to oppose concrete to abstract.

Korzybski in his *Science and Sanity*, a work on semantics, demonstrates that there are an infinite number of levels or orders of abstraction. Korzybski has shown that the language we use constantly brings about confusion of levels. He attributes this to the persistence for two thousand years of Aristotle's logic, with its laws of identity, contradiction and excluded middle. A word, as Korzybski never tires of reminding us, is not what the word signifies; the map is not the territory. A word may be defined by extension, i.e. by pointing – as we teach children – 'look: this is a dog' – or by intention, when certain qualities are abstracted from the direct experience, giving rise to a dictionary type definition, where a dog would be defined as a *class* of animal with certain characteristics (Korzybski 1953). Whitehead and Russell in their 'Law of Logical Types' have clarified this problem, that a class and the members of a class belong to different orders and must not be identified (Russell and Whitehead 1910). Korzybski shows that there are many words which are multi-ordinal, i.e. they may be used at many different levels of abstraction, and, to be clear, the level has to be pointed at. The earliest use of words uses very low levels of abstraction. The lowest level exists before words are used. This he calls the 'unspeakable level'.

This provides a way of conceptualizing the early 'I–you', the 'conversation' between mother and infant. It occurs at the unspeakable level – at an extremely low level of abstraction. The baby does somehow abstract certain characteristics of the mother which enables him to recognize her. He does not *know* that he abstracts: this would be a higher order and one which would enable him to use words, leading to higher and higher levels of abstraction.

The archetypes

Korzybski suggests that the hierarchic arrangements of levels implied in orders of abstraction is mirrored in the hierarchic structure of the nervous system. He distinguishes man very fundamentally from the animals by the enormous development of the cerebral cortex making possible very high levels of abstraction (also making possible a high degree of confusion of levels leading to insanity – particularly if animals are copied by man).

Jung has also paid attention to the hierarchic structure of the nervous system and the importance in individuation of achieving harmony between levels. The diagrams of the psyche very clearly show a hierarchic arrangement of layers. Although they can proceed in either direction – conscious to unconscious or unconscious to conscious – the *order* remains the same.

When Jung speaks of the baby being 'unconscious' and of consciousness as 'arising from the unconscious' it leads to the idea that the baby first perceives a kind of impersonal, collective mother, expressed in archetypal images like the great mother or the terrible mother, and only later as an actual person. (In psychoanalytic theory a similar view is held in the form of part-objects preceding whole objects.) It is not certain that Jung was committed to this view: he was not much concerned with a detailed account of the development of consciousness. It is undoubtedly true that archetypal imagery is easy to demonstrate in young children and also in primitive people, whom Jung also saw as being 'unconscious'.

But does the child first experience 'motherness' and gradually discriminate his own personal mother out of it, or does he, on the contrary, first experience *his* mother, albeit in a very simple way, and generalize this into an idea of motherness?

This question seems to depend on a very careful distinction between archetype and archetypal image, a distinction which Jung often made, but found it difficult to stick to. An archetype can be operative in the absence of an archetypal image. We can suppose that this must be a genetically laid down, innate pattern of expectation in the infant, with certain universal characteristics which enable the mother to be perceived at all. We can also suppose the archetypal image is not itself perceived when the personal mother is there, smiling and talking to the baby. If she is either absent when the baby needs her, or present but not relating personally to the baby, the baby may *then* be having an experience, i.e. an image of the archetypal mother – blissful or terrible according to the infant's affective state at the time. Neither of these states depends on 'consciousness' in the sense of the ability to use high levels of abstraction.

What I am proposing is an intimate interplay between personal and collective from the beginning rather than the development of one from the other.

As to the development of language, it is by no means certain that this occurs by the kind of abstracting process that Korzybski supposes, i.e. that the child first sees *a* dog and then generalizes the abstract class of 'dog'. Another possibility is that we have an innate sense of 'dogginess' and we recognize a 'dog' when it fits into this. Chomsky's theories support this latter view. It is quite possible that both processes occur and supplement each other – in which case it might be useful to see Jung's model in the two ways he draws it, i.e. personal > collective and collective > personal.

The idea of a double process can also be supported on neurophysiological grounds on the basis of recent discoveries of the importance of bilaterality of the central nervous system, particularly experiments in dividing the connections between the cerebral hemispheres. There is some evidence to suggest that one hemisphere is primarily responsible for discriminating and the other for 'seeing things as a whole'. These two functions acting in a co-ordinated way may explain how, from the beginning, both ways of perceiving are necessary and that it is not sufficient to think simply in the vertical dimension of levels, where lower levels operate earlier than higher ones, as the central nervous system works as a whole from the beginning. Translated into psychological terms, such evidence would support the idea that collective (archetypal) and personal (individual) forms of perception occur from the beginning. (An interesting study of the implications of these discoveries for analytical psychology has been made by Rossi (1977).)

Michael Fordham

In Fordham's work is to be found an extensive study of the development of the psyche within the framework of analytical psychology. His work is based on a great deal of experience of child analysis as well as studies of infantile development, and he lays great stress on the importance of direct observation of infants.

Although he has always acknowledged the influence of the personal mother, there can be discerned in his work a gradual shift from considering the psyche in the impersonal language of the 'ego', the 'self' and 'the environment' (a one-body psychology), towards considering the baby as a person from the beginning or in relation to the mother as a person (an interactional two-body psychology). Perhaps the turning point occurred with his publication of *Children as Individuals* (Fordham 1969).

Fordham now very much stresses that the baby is an individual from the start. He attributes this individuality to the self – called the primary self – and suggests that this implies a primary separation from the mother. There is a kind of circle round the baby (corresponding to Jung's idea of a 'magic circle' or *temenos*) which, from birth, acts as a defence separating him from the mother – a defence operating unconsciously. He also makes an important distinction between defences of the self and ego defences (Fordham 1977).

The picture that Fordham gives of the baby as an individual from the start is often difficult to reconcile with other statements he makes, e.g. that the baby treats the mother as part of himself (Fordham 1969). This latter state of affairs would exist only if there were no boundary or circle around the baby, separating him from the mother. Also Fordham follows Klein in the idea that, at first, the infant perceives part-objects and only later perceives the mother as a whole.

Perhaps Fordham, in drawing attention to the boundary around the baby, has over-emphasized the defensive factors of such a boundary (although this is particularly helpful in understanding schizoid pathology).

It seems to me that the boundary, while it has a constitutional basis, needs to be recognized and affirmed by the mother and that the baby is given a sense of his own individuality by the mother communicating it to him, as part of a two-way process. A territory need not be defended when it is not being attacked or felt to be in danger of being attacked.

Dialogue precedes self-awareness

Martin Buber's *a priori* of relationship in the 'I–you' implies, for me, that dialogue with another person precedes any possibility of self-awareness or 'dialogue' with one's self. In a sense, dialogue with one's self is imaginary dialogue – so is dialogue with the outside world, and only with another person is real dialogue possible. Buber would deny this, of course, but in regarding his kind of dialogue as secondarily derived from interpersonal dialogue, I do not wish to imply any diminution in its significance in individuation, whether thought of as religious or not.

The primary self, which can be postulated as an abstraction, does not exist as such for the baby. The experience of the self comes gradually out of the mother's experience of him – which she communicates to him – and we need a communication model to understand this. At all times, our abstract concepts have to be kept clear of what we imagine a baby experiences.

If I–you precedes I–it the 'I' which relates exists from the beginning. It is not, however, the same as the 'ego' of Jung – the centre of consciousness, because consciousness always implies self-awareness. Awareness of the other in a dialogue does not imply more than a very low level of abstraction – the unspeakable level of Korzybski, the basic word You of Buber.

A communication model

It may seem an abrupt switch to turn from Buber's language to that of communication theory, but I believe it to be necessary. The personal dimension can be intuitively grasped. How mothers and babies actually communicate with each other can be studied empirically. This is a different field of study from the study of babies as such and it requires a different model – not of 'the psyche', but one which conveys how two individuals communicate with each other. This kind of model has often been shown diagrammatically, but here I should like to draw my own diagram to bring out certain points in the simplest way.

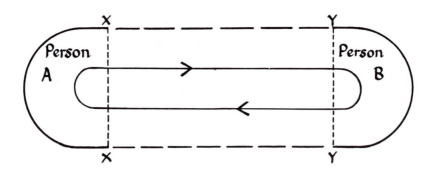

Figure 3.4 A communication model

This is the simplest representation I can make of two persons communicating with each other. It shows:

1. Reciprocity (the circular nature of the interchange).

2. A relatively open boundary, dotted lines x–x and y–y between persons A and B; otherwise no communication could get through.

3. A *distance*, x-y between the two persons.

4   A relatively closed boundary limiting the input of each person to the output of the other.

The diagram is very over-simplified. It does not show how information is stored or how signals are transformed.

If we apply this model to the case of the mother-and-baby interaction, we can see that they are preoccupied with each other, open to each other, and speaking to each other. Buber would say You 'fills the firmament'.

This scheme does not indicate *what* is communicated. We can imagine a technically good feed given quite mechanically, but the all-important personal element can best be understood by Bateson's concept of meta-communication (Bateson 1972). Bateson is here adapting Carnap's concept of metalanguage.

Meta-communication is a secondary kind of communication. It is assumed that information is transmitted which is regarded as primary, but there is some additional information which makes a commentary, so to speak, on this information. The commentary is an explanation of the nature of the communication which is being made. In practice, when dealing with persons, it is often difficult to say exactly what is communication and what is meta-communication. Usually when words are used it is taken that the words constitute the communication and non-verbal expression the meta-communication. If this concept is applied to the earliest interchanges between mother and baby, which of course is non-verbal, the impersonal elements (whether collective or individual) can be separated from the personal. The impersonal communication is accompanied by a personal meta-communication which gives it a special kind of meaning.

Let us take the mother feeding the baby as an illustration. We can identify the same two components:

1. *Communication* of sense impressions – the warm, sweet taste of the milk, the feeling of being held, the mother's smell, the sight of the mother's face, the sound of her voice, and so on. We would have to suppose that some genetically laid-down expectation of the baby has to be met for the baby to organise these impressions in some way, e.g. certain basic features of the mother's face (as Spitz has shown). All this is impersonal.

2. *Meta-communication*. This is the mother's personal way of addressing the baby. This includes her way of holding the baby, e.g. holding him at a comfortable angle. But, however the mechanics of it are analysed, she is the mother who, in Erikson's phrase, 'lives through and loves with her breasts' (Erikson 1950). She is expressing something like, 'You are my special baby. Feeding you gives me pleasure.' She may be communicating this by speaking or smiling, but somehow she communicates these things.

The first component is impersonal. The second is the personal. The genetically laid-down expectation would correspond to the archetypal mother: the mother's unique way of handling the baby and addressing him as 'You' would be a personal mother.

Of course, the second component can be missing: the mother can be preoccupied with something else, or feeding the baby mechanically. There is then no personal mother. This is perhaps an extreme case. It is difficult to imagine no personal mother whatever in practice. Even the autistic child seems to be defending *against* a personal mother. The fact is that it is very difficult not to communicate something interpersonally. Even the most schizoid individual who tries silently to express nothing always communicates *something* of his feeling about the other person. One cannot *not* communicate.

Levels of interaction

Look at Figure 3.3 as a three-dimensional model and imagine looking down on it from above. You will then see concentric rings with the individual in the centre somewhat resembling Figure 3.1. Now imagine a series of transverse sections. The top one will consist of the solitary individual. Successive ones will show wider and wider circles, with the family, the group, the nation, etc. Now each of these levels can be seen as a field of enquiry. At each level, the meaning of the individual changes. My two-person model, as exemplified by mother and infant, would be seen in a section close to, but not quite at, the top. Below this would be a family group.

These fields of enquiry can be seen as 'systems', each with its own special characteristics. The strength of Jung's model lies in its ability to contain, and relate to each other, these different models. (Freud's model was much more limited in this respect.) Its weakness lies in the ease with which the levels can be confused. Specifying or pointing to the level is essential if confusion is to be avoided. Unfortunately, Jung does not always point clearly to the level he is discussing. His variable usage of the word 'self', for example, has given rise to much confusion as to whether it refers to the totality or to a centre. A diagram such as Figure 3.3 helps to show the *total* area of study embraced by psychology. Now that analytic interest has spread to marital pairs, families and to stranger-groups, we need both to differentiate and to integrate the findings appropriate to the particular areas of study which are all subsumed under 'psychology'. That the archetypes are collective, i.e. transcending the individual, is easily seen in Figure 3.3, by the presence of the 'central' force which penetrates all levels of interaction. I have indicated on Jung's diagram where I think the level of personal dialogue could be placed.

Systems theory

Modern systems theory has clarified the hierarchic ordering of levels which can be seen in the nervous system as well as in the 'psyche'. The whole universe can be seen as a hierarchy of systems. If we take the organism as a living system (following Miller 1965) we can see sub-systems – organs and cells, the supra-systems – groups, organisations, societies and supra-national systems. Living systems are a special case of concrete systems and Miller carefully distinguishes concrete or real systems which exist in physical space–time, from abstracted and conceptual systems. Abstracted and conceptual systems are also distinguished. A conceptual system uses symbols like words or numbers, in relationships, and the system may or may not be isomorphic with a concrete or with an abstracted system. An abstracted system is one in which the observer selects relationships from his theoretical standpoint, which are observed to inhere and interact or coact in concrete systems. Note that some of the relationships in an abstracted system have to be empirically determined, but this is not true of a conceptual system.

This terminology is helpful when looking at Jung's diagrams. They clearly represent a conceptual system. The problem is to know if there is a concrete or an abstracted system which is isomorphic with it.

One of the advantages of Jung's model is that it does not stop short at the boundary of 'the organism' – it can embrace two individuals (as in the analytic relationship), the family, the group (as in a therapeutic group), the nation, etc., until we reach some such concept as 'Man in his totality', or collective man.

Each level shows different phenomena and the level – or 'system' – or field of enquiry has to be specified, or 'pointed to', as Korzybski would say, so that the meaning of words which are multi-ordinal terms should be clear, and so that levels of abstraction are not confused.

The 'personal' which Jung tries to include in his model, as distinct from the 'collective', seems to me to have no meaning (1) when considering the individual in isolation or (2) in the very large group. (Jung was well aware of this second point.) It comes into its own when considering small groups – or in the family – and has a very special meaning in the dyad, with the roots in the mother and infant pair.

Jung's model is therefore more like a globe of the universe than a map of a small village. The map of a small village has its place on the globe, but to find one's way round the village it is more useful to limit oneself to the map.

In discussing the controversy between Jung and Buber we saw how difficulties arose between them because Buber wanted to establish that God was *other* than man and Jung wanted to restrict himself to psychological representations of God. This stance, which Jung often took, was part of an attempt to remain scientific. In the course of his argument with Buber, he makes the following remarkable statement:

> The 'reality of the psyche' is my working hypothesis and my principal activity consists in collecting factual material to describe and explain it. I have set up neither a system, nor a general theory, but have merely formulated auxiliary concepts to serve me as tools, as is customary in every branch of science. (Jung 1952, p.666)

This disclaimer of Jung's cannot be accepted. Of course Jung has set up a system, a general theory. His working hypothesis of the 'reality of the psyche' *is* his system. No scientist can collect facts without a system. Facts in science are really relationships and the relationships are components of a system, as general systems theory has made clear; for example, when Jung triumphantly showed his patient the 'scarab' he was *relating* it to his patient's dream (Jung 1963). The psychotic patient's statement about the sun was *related* to the undiscovered papyrus. His whole theory of archetypes and the collective unconscious was painstakingly built up of the observing and collecting of such relationships. This was his factual material.

It is unfortunate that Jung, when dealing with adversaries, even sympathetic ones, found it necessary to retreat to the position of a humble 'fact-collector'. This always drove him back to regarding all his material as intra-psychic.

The term 'intra-psychic' implies a boundary to the psyche. If we regard the psyche as a multi-ordinal term, however, the boundary and what is regarded as inside or outside will depend on the level or system being studied. Before considering the clinical implications of all this it is worth here pointing out that the analyst is dealing principally with two separate systems: what is going on *in* the patient and what is going on between himself and the patient. In the latter case he is *in* it, not outside it. He cannot abstract from it without turning I–you into I–it, and this is what makes the personal so hard to describe.

A note on symbols

In discussing the collective unconscious Jung repeatedly says that it gives rise to symbols, that the archetypal images 'arise' from it and symbols are products of the psyche. This way of thinking seems to exclude, for him, the 'fact' that symbols develop so that people can communicate with each other. In this sense, the baby's smile is just as much a symbol as is a mythological motif. Myths are stories which people tell one another. Surely this is an interesting psychological fact? It belongs, however, to a different order from that of the 'fact' that they arise from the collective psyche.

Jung's insistence that a symbol, as distinct from a sign, represents something unknown has obscured the consideration that symbols are forms of communication between people. They may of course be communication at a very low level of abstraction. Nevertheless, when communicated, these are at a certain level known by both the person transmitting the symbol and the person receiving it. The analyst interpreting a patient's symbols is not simply regarding them as products of the unconscious. He is regarding them also as communications *to* him. Interpretation, often thought of as 'making the unconscious conscious', is perhaps better regarded as relating the material to higher levels of abstraction.

Some clinical implications

In a mainly theoretical paper I can only touch on clinical implications.

Patients after experiencing psychotherapy are inclined to attribute improvement not to insight, not to the knowledge they have acquired about themselves, but to the relationship which they have had with the therapist. The analyst knows that they are engaged in a dialogue, that it is vital to get into a special kind of relationship with the patient (Hobson has rightly called analysis a special kind of conversation; Hobson n.d.), but lacks a theoretical basis for doing this. Trainee analysts having supervision are particularly prone to agonizing conflicts between being friends with the patient and being properly analytical.

Many attempts have been made to express what is required in the analyst's attitude. Lambert calls it 'agape', but I find this still too detached and elevated an attitude (Lambert 1973). It seems to me that the problem (which exists for the patient as well as for the analyst) can be solved only by a recognition of what Buber calls the two-fold nature of man – the words 'I–you' and the words 'I–it' must *both* be spoken. I still adhere to the notion that interpretation is the principal therapeutic tool the analyst has.

Interpretations are very largely I–it statements. They presuppose a very high level of abstraction and represent the analyst's efforts to make detached, objective – even scientific – observations about what he sees when he looks *at* the patient. All communications, however, including interpretations, need to be addressed *to* the patient and for this a reciprocal, dialogical mode has to be established. This is the 'I–you' and the task is not really very different from the mother trying to get in touch with her baby. It is based on a knowledge of highly personal, individual characteristics of the other person.

The task of establishing the I–you arises at the beginning of the analysis – as it does, for the mother, at the beginning of the child's life – in the very first session. There is, I think, a mistaken idea that only at the end of analysis can the patient be expected to view the analyst as a real person. We need to see the *a priori* of relation.

To conclude, I shall give you a very tiny fragment of a long analysis to show how the I–you can be lost and then regained.

The patient was a highly intelligent woman and this session occurred after many years of analysis, which on the whole had gone very well. She always had difficulty in starting, however, and this particular session started badly.

She lay down on the couch and was silent for perhaps three or four minutes, but it seemed an age. She was obviously very tense – anguished would perhaps describe it better. She then suddenly said, 'I'm wasting *time*. That bloody clock's ticking away – *why* do you have such a noisy clock?' I made no comment. She then said, 'I can't talk – it's no good. I've got lots of things to tell you but you'll think it's all so *stupid!*'

I tried to interpret this. I said, 'There seems to be a bit of you that's pleased to be here and wants to tell me things, but there's another bit that's very angry. First you attack yourself – then me and this bit of you is very –'

I don't know how long I might have gone on in this vein, but she interrupted me with a great shout, '– Oh *bugger* the bits of me!' and then began to cry.

After a while I said a very unanalytic thing. I said, 'I'm sorry. We weren't in tune.' Being in tune was the patient's own phrase, but by this time we both understood it. She often said, 'The trouble is I just can't get in tune with you.' My saying it then was an appeal to this personal common language. When I said it she immediately relaxed, stopped crying and told me 'lots of things'.

If reduction of anxiety is the criterion, this worked better than an interpretation. Perhaps it *was* an interpretation? I do not think that, unless the term be stretched out of all recognition, it can be called that. I should prefer to call it, at least in this paper, getting back to the personal 'I–you'.

Summary

In this paper I have tried to reassess the meanings of the words 'collective' and 'personal' as used in analytical psychology. Jung's main work was to concentrate on collective aspects of the psyche, particularly to develop a theory of archetypes and the collective unconscious. In doing so, he contrasted 'collective' with 'personal', but tended to take the personal for granted.

In this reassessment, I have used Jung's own diagrammatic illustrations of what I believe to have been his working model of the psyche. As well as acknowledging the enormous scope of this model, I have pointed to its limitations in that it is basically designed to present a one-person kind of psychology. I have suggested that 'personal' can only be understood on the basis of (at least) a two-person model.

In illustrating this, I have drawn on the philosophy of Martin Buber and have tried to show its scientific applicability by relating his notion of dialogue, the I–you, to very early interaction between mother and infant which gives added meaning to Jung's concept of the personal mother.

I have suggested ways in which communication theory and systems theory can be used to clarify the field of psychological enquiry which would enable dialogue to be studied as well as intrapsychic events.

Finally, I have given a very brief clinical example of the importance of the personal 'I–you' in analysis.

References

Bateson, G. (1972) *Steps to an Ecology of Mind: Collected Essays in Anthropology, Psychiatry, Evolution and Epistemology*. London: International Textbooks.

Buber, M. (1947) *Between Man and Man*. London: Kegan Paul, Trench, Trubner & Co.

Buber, M. (1953) *Eclipse of God: Studies in the Relation between Religion and Philosophy*. London: Gollancz.

Buber, M. (1970) *I and Thou*. Translated by W. Kaufmann. Edinburgh: T & T Clark.

Erikson, E. (1950) *Childhood and Society*. New York: Norton.

Fordham, M. (1969) *Children as Individuals*. London: Hodder & Stoughton.

Fordham, M. (1977) 'Maturation of a child within the family.' *Journal of Analytical Psychology 22*, 2, pp. 91–105.

Gordon, R. (1977) 'The symbolic experience as bridge between the personal and the collective.' *Journal of Analytical Psychology 22*, 4, pp.331–342.

Hobson, R. (n.d.) 'Notes on the technique of interpretation' (unpublished).

Jackson, M. (1960) 'Jung's archetype: clarity or confusion?' *British Journal of Medical Psychology 33*, 2.

Jacobi, J. (1942) *The Psychology of C. G. Jung*. London: Routledge & Kegan Paul.

Jung, C.G. (1916) 'Symbols of transformation.' *Collected Works 5*, pp.7–33.

Jung, C.G. (1921) 'Psychological types.' *Collected Works 6*.

Jung, C.G. (1926) 'Two essays in analytical psychology.' *Collected Works 7*.

Jung, C.G. (1936) 'The concept of the collective unconscious.' *Collected Works 9*, 1.

Jung, C.G. (1944) 'Psychology and alchemy.' *Collected Works 12*.

Jung, C.G. (1952) 'Psychology and religion: a reply to Martin Buber.' *Collected Works 18*, p.666.

Jung, C.G. (1963) *Memories, Dreams, Reflections*. London: Collins and Routledge & Kegan Paul.

Kaufmann, W. (Trans) (1970) Introduction to *I and Thou* (M. Buber). Edinburgh: T & T Clark.

Korzybski, A. (1953) *Science and Sanity*. Lakeville: International Non-Aristotelian Library.

Lambert, K. (1973) 'Agape as a therapeutic factor in analysis.' *Journal of Analytic Psychology 18*, 1, pp.25–46.

Matte-Blanco, I. (1975) *The Unconscious as Infinite Sets*. London: Duckworth, pp.72–79.

Miller, J.G. (1965) 'Living systems: basic concepts.' *Behavioural Science* (July).

Rickman, J. (1950) 'Methodology and research in psychiatry.' Contribution to a symposium, British Psychological Society, 26th April.

Rossi, E. (1977) 'The cerebral hemispheres in analytical psychology.' *Journal of Analytical Psychology 22*, 1, pp.32–51.

Russell, B. and Whitehead, A. (1910) *Principia Mathematica.* Cambridge University Press.

Williams, M. (1963) 'The indivisibility of the personal and collective unconscious.' *Journal of Analytical Psychology* 8,1, pp.45–49.

Zinkin, L. (1978) 'Person to person: the search for the human dimension in psychotherapy.' *British Journal of Medical Psychology* 51, pp.25–34.

CHAPTER FOUR

Paradoxes of the Self

Introduction

This chapter is not an attempt to encompass the whole of the topic referred to in its title. It is a response to a stimulus. In April 1983, in the issue of the *Journal of Analytical Psychology* (Vol. 28, No. 2) there appeared an article by Redfearn entitled 'Ego and self: terminology' (Redfearn 1983). Its author hoped to stimulate discussion particularly among those who teach and write in the field of analytical psychology. I was duly stimulated. Nevertheless, my wish to respond in writing was hampered by such difficulties that I several times nearly gave up the attempt. The questions of the nature and the relationships of the ego and the self to each other are big questions indeed, and it is not clear to what extent Redfearn attempted to deal with them in fifteen pages of text. He does attempt to circumscribe questions by regarding them as terminological ones. One difficulty for me was that, not being content with this circumscription, I could take up the issues he raises only by widening their scope still further. As will be seen, I was mostly taken up by the first seven lines of the paper which refer to maps of the mind, the 'real thing' in the case of the mind, the mind consisting of more maps and 'much else'. I could see that much depended on these few lines. Perhaps they were meant as a simple introduction to be taken for granted, but I could not easily do this, having long been engrossed in knotty questions of maps and models and what they refer to.

I was caught up too in the comments by Jacoby (Jacoby 1983) and Schwartz-Salant (Schwartz-Salant 1983) and in Redfearn's reply to these comments. It became apparent that the issues he raises are not only of the utmost intellectual difficulty but carry also a high charge of affect. I found that I was the victim of a number of double-binds of which I could identify two. One concerns the audience. Is this really 'those who teach and write', or is it second-year analytical trainees who need the simple guide? At a recent conference on supervision, attended mostly by very senior analysts, the most pertinent question was raised by a trainee. He asked, 'Who supervises the supervisors?' The infinite regress helped me to understand the nature of my confusion. Are we teachers getting together to agree on our use of words so that we can better teach what we all know about, or are we students trying to understand something which we can only half grasp?

The second double-bind concerns the use of the term 'terminology'. This suggests it is not the concepts 'ego' and 'self' that are being discussed, only the words being used. But as one reads the paper it rapidly becomes apparent that it is indeed the concepts which are under scrutiny, as well as the words. The whole paper places the reader in the very map and territory problem of models of the mind, so lightly raised in the first few lines.

Before giving up in confusion, I managed to resolve the first problem by deciding I would join in the discussion only at the higher level, that of a senior student. The second-year students would have to wait a while before we, the teachers, could resolve our difficulties and provide them with a simple guide. In coming to this decision I took some comfort in the thought that the students might be quite interested in our discussion and even join in, and also reflected that one can learn to drive a car without knowing the history of the internal combustion engine. The second problem of words and concepts, I realized, requires a third term such as 'things'. One cannot have meaning with a dyadic structure, one needs a triad like that shown in Figure 4.1.

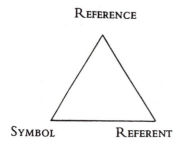
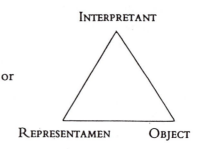

Figure 4.1 Triangles of meaning
Source: Richards and Ogden (1923)   *Pierce (n.d.)*

This semiological formation of a triangle (Eco 1976) fits in with our analytical notions about infantile development and the onset of the ability to symbolise, which I understand not as being the stage when things mean something (they seem to do that from the start), but when a second order is reached: the meaning of the meaning. I could then see that we required not only 'unconscious' and 'conscious' but also 'consciousness of consciousness' or 'self-consciousness'. I could then see that a number of problems arise from:

- confusion between the two levels, not often distinguished by analysts, the distinction between consciousness and self-consciousness, and

- what happens when this little word 'self' is introduced into depth psychology, whether Jungian or Freudian.

As soon as we see *ourselves*, which animals and babies cannot easily do, we are in the world of paradox. The task then becomes one of finding the limits to paradox.

My own position

No paper can be written without bias and I have a strong one, in favour of psychoanalysis, which I believe is shared with most of my colleagues in London. I see the break between Jung and Freud as a tragic though very productive historical episode and see the two schools as being involved in the same enterprise, with great potential for coming together as each struggles with the problems it meets from its own perspective. I know that not all analytical psychologists share this view. My energies and interests are mainly clinical, but not restricted to individual analysis, being deeply involved in group and marital work too. By this I do not mean jumbling together ideas from different theories, but I do enjoy trying to work with different models and endeavouring to combine their better features into new models, in a way which I believe does no 'violation to the spirit of Jung'. I am, therefore, highly in favour of what Redfearn is trying to do in his paper, and my criticisms stem from an appreciation of the inherent difficulties of such an endeavour.

Maps and models

Although both Freud and Jung built up vast theoretical systems or, as I would prefer to put it, models of the psyche, the comparison with maps raises certain difficulties. Redfearn states that Jungians and Freudians need different maps because they have different methods. He is thinking therefore of the practical use of a map for getting about, but his statement leaves out the question as to how it has come about that we have different methods. Surely we have different methods *because* we have different maps, and we have different maps because we have two different models of the psyche. The word 'psyche' may also raise questions of terminology and it may be said that Freudians and Jungians use the same word to mean quite different things. At this point the nature of the psyche is the very object of psychological enquiry, the very thing that psychologists are trying to find out about. It cannot be defined in advance by any school of psychology. Ultimately it may be possible for all schools to disappear, as they have done with other sciences, as we reach agreement as to the ways the psyche can be talked about. Despite the difficulties, there is much to be gained by comparing models with maps, and I have made a similar analogy myself. There is a sense in which a model, like a map, should faithfully represent something else, something which needs to *be* mapped, something which has an independent existence from the map. This is the territory. The problem which Redfearn seems to bypass when he speaks of methods is that it is very difficult, in the field of psychology, to go and inspect the territory which the maps are purported to depict.

Schwartz-Salant, in his Comment, goes to the opposite extreme. He sees the problem I have outlined above only too well but he seems to propose that we abandon altogether the kind of comparison that Redfearn attempts and study each writer only in his context, according to 'his own purposes'. This would suggest that each writer can have his own separate map, that each individual can have 'his own purposes' and that there is no common enterprise, no actual territory which we are all trying to explore. Perhaps he only means that this has to be done *before* careful comparison can be made but, if so, if we ever did begin to compare, a great deal would be lost, because each writer would be almost incomprehensible if one tried to read him without reference to others. This is why there is always a list of references. In other words, a writer's own context always includes his reading of others.

The place of the 'self' in models of the psyche

The break between Jung and Freud is one which needs constant reviewing as new developments take place in the two schools. When the break happened, there was no place for the self in Freud's model. Perhaps this was one of the reasons why it did happen. Freud seems to have sensed the difficulty of bringing it in, and stuck to the use of the ego concept. He did this long after he had described narcissism. Jung, on the other hand, apparently unworried, quickly moved towards it and it became the centre of his whole system. The possible differences between the two men are:

1. The type of patient each was interested in, Jung being more interested in patients with identity problems than was Freud.

2. Their own personalities: Jung himself had a greater identity problem than Freud did.

3. The greater scope of enquiry in Jungian psychology: although it is hard to generalize here, I think that there is no question that Jung wanted to look at man as a whole and not just as patients and their illnesses.

4. Freud took the self for granted because he took the individual for granted, which Jung did not.

5. The greater wish of Freud, both in his writings and in his practice, to remain 'biological', 'objective', and 'scientific' as he conceived of these terms.

6. Freud's wish to avoid paradox which Jung was ready to embrace.

I shall touch further on these factors, which are all relevant to our theme, but, whatever the reasons for these differences between the two great men, the same questions beset their followers. Both schools have changed in time and diversified into sub-schools, and great changes are occurring in psychoanalysis with the advent of 'self-psychology'. Kohut, far more than any other psychoanalyst, seeks a major place for the self in a model of the psyche when he sees the development of a cohesive self as a separate line from the development of the drives and their vicissitudes. It is in making this vital separation that he has broken the ranks of psychoanalysts and we, who have believed ourselves to have had a 'self-psychology' from the beginning, need to take stock again. Kohut's considerable following seems to reflect an ousting of the Oedipus myth by the Narcissus myth in the collective psyche. As a result, analytical psychologists have become more interested in the meaning of the Narcissus myth as evidenced, for example, by Schwartz-Salant's book (Schwartz-Salant 1982), and we have even adopted the term 'narcissistic personality disorder' which has appeared like a quite new diagnostic category to describe the sort of patient in whom we Jungians have always been interested. One very stimulating suggestion is that made by Murray Stein that Jung was talking about narcissism all the time in his idea of introversion (Stein 1976). I am sure there is a great deal in this.

The self, narcissism and paradox

In listing the possible reasons for the great interest in the self by Jung, following his break from Freud, I have considered the personalities of the two men as well as their divergent interests, and in this respect have been influenced by Peter Homans in his book *Jung in Context* (Homans 1979). Jung was deeply concerned with the cohesiveness, as well as with the identity, of his own self during his 'creative illness' following the narcissistic injury which Freud inflicted on him. Thus his involvement was on three levels: his own self, that of his patients, and the self as a psychological concept. Freud, despite his own injured narcissism, was able to take the self largely for granted, both his own self and that of his relatively unconfused patients, and did not have the same need to introduce it as a psychological concept. Although he altered his theories, he never deviated from a model of conflicting instinctual drives which bore such fruit in his study of the neuroses and even in the more organised forms of psychosis. Freud was able to develop a detailed psychopathology of these conditions as he developed his own theory and his model was strong, consistent and illuminating, though restricted in its application. Jung's theory, by contrast, was weak and inconsistent, and it led to paradox though it was much wider in its application. Although at times he expressed great contempt for Freud he never rejected the value of Freud's theories within their own restricted field and always retained them as part of his own model.

Certain differences as well as striking similarities appear in a comparative study of Kohut and Jung, as both Schwartz-Salant and Jacoby have pointed out in their comments on Redfearn's paper. But, for my part, I am satisfied that the differences result from the complexity and enormity of the topic which they both encounter. It is true that Kohut tries to confine the term more than Jung does. He is less ready than Jung to accept the 'I am the universe' statement as being true, seeing it as an illusory expression of a grandiose self. But Jung also recognized grandiosity which he called inflation, attributing this to the ego rather than to the self. Moreover, Kohut speaks of the self in its restricted and wider sense. In one paper Kohut developed the idea not of one line of development but of several lines, the existence of *multiple* selves (Kohut 1978), and this is very similar to Jung's thinking. Jung not only had two personalities but was very interested in multiple personalities. I think also that Jacoby's discussion of Kohut's essay on the bipolarity of the self, and particularly his quotation from Kohut which resonates so much with Jung, does make it clear that we are not 'poles apart'. There are many such passages in Kohut's writings; he concentrates more than Jung on the need for self-esteem and on the function of the parents, and later of therapists in providing this, but this supplements in an important way rather than contradicts Jung's work. My own view, therefore, is that it is quite wrong to think that there is a 'Kohutian self' which is different and distinct from a 'Jungian self'.

Puzzles and paradoxes

Having noted with approval a convergence of thought between analytical psychology and psychoanalysis, and having also observed that Jung's model is both weaker than Freud's and richer in seeking to explain a wider range of phenomena, I should like now to draw attention to a point where I think this weakness is a positive advantage. Psychoanalytic explanations have always been linked to a developmental model in a way which Jung's were not. By this I mean that psychoanalytic theory is very largely a theory of what goes wrong in infantile development. To understand what goes wrong it has to posit a theory of normal development and if this theory is shown to be incorrect, then a great deal of psychoanalytic theory has to be re-thought. Although a number of Jungians, notably Fordham and Neumann, have used Jungian ideas – with Jung's approval – developmentally, Jung's own model did not *depend* on a historical approach and, if challenged, Jung could always retreat to an historical non-linear one. Although a great deal has been achieved by the linear, one-way study of development, it is also a source of error.

There has been a natural assumption among orthodox Freudians that babies start off in a state of boundary-confusion, and only gradually get things clear. A simple linear progression is assumed with a straightforward correlation between the degree of consciousness acquired and the 'correct' perception of reality, so that the baby cannot at first distinguish itself from others but can only gradually do so; the more consciousness develops, the more clearly they can discern their selves. This idea, so taken for granted, is now being shown to be incorrect and in my view is the exact opposite of the truth, which is that the more consciousness develops the *more* problematic, mysterious, uncanny and paradoxical does such discernment become. There is a great deal of evidence from the study of infants in interaction with their mothers which flies in the face of this psychoanalytic error. Mothers could not have conversations with their babies in the first few days of life (and they do) unless the baby could distinguish itself from its mother. Animals, even fairly lowly ones, do know their own boundaries. They make it quite clear that they can distinguish between themselves and others, so we are obliged to say that they are conscious of this difference. I would have no objection even to robots being described as conscious. Artificial intelligence seems to differ from human intelligence only in the degree of self-awareness which humans have. My statement that babies, knowing their own boundaries, must be conscious is often met with an objection such as, 'No, we don't know that because they can't tell us. We can only say they behave *as if* they did.' This seems to me to confuse two levels of knowledge, to confuse consciousness with *self*-consciousness. Jung did recognize these two levels but he used a somewhat strange phraseology. Animals and babies, according to him, were 'unconscious' (see, for example, Jung 1928). Of course they are not literally so. What he must have meant is that they are not self-conscious, which is another way of saying that they are not self-aware, have no knowledge of self.

Colloquially, 'self-conscious' often implies a state of embarrassment. Such embarrassment can be seen to be due to confusion brought about by a confrontation of one's own self-image with the image other people have (or are thought to have) of one's self. As I have discussed elsewhere (Zinkin 1983), looking in a mirror can have dire consequences because of epistemological problems, and this is why Lacan sees mirroring as the primary source of alienation. Psychologists, once they include the self in their model of the psyche, face the same dilemma. They become aware that their study is of themselves. They then have to try to do something seemingly impossible. They have to separate themselves from themselves in order to see themselves. This impossibility is the main reason why the study (or contemplation) of the self gives rise to paradox and Jung was ready to embrace this paradox while Freud was most reluctant to do so. The kind of paradox generated by self-contemplation is well typified by Angelus Silesius which Schwartz-Salant quotes from Jung's quotation. For convenience I here quote it yet again:

> I am God's child and son, and he is mine.
> How comes it that we both can combine?
> God is my centre when I close him in;
> And my circumference when I melt in him.
> The hen contains the egg, the egg the hen,
> The twain in one, and yet the one in twain.
> God becomes 'I' and takes my manhood on:
> Because I was before him was that done!

(Jung 1954, p.110, n.71)

What do we do with such offences to our logic? Schwartz-Salant tries to do two things at once. First, he says we must not violate the mystery. Then he explains it all away with a simple Venn diagram. In fact this does not explain very much. It might explain such phenomena as to how I can both be a doctor and an analyst, while someone else is both a social worker and an analyst, but it does not explain how anyone can be the son and the father of the same man or, for that matter, to use Redfearn's example, both the branch of a tree and the tree of a branch. Redfearn also, of course, knows the value of paradox and the need to stay with it, despite his wish to make things simple for students, as can be easily seen in his many other writings. The question is, though, should we even try to explain these puzzles? It is generally accepted that poets and mystics are better psychologists than we are (Hobson 1974) so should we just leave it to them? To this my reply is a decisive, 'No'. If we are scientists at all it is our business to explain, as best we can, what poets and mystics amaze us with, to find ways out of the amazing maze, to make maps for this purpose. There are limits to this possibility of explanation, but we must find those limits.

Some possible ways out

First there must be a distinction between mystics and madmen. Angelus Silesius obviously knew that in a sense he was breaking the law of logic, whereas a schizophrenic might not. Redfearn suggests we must accept the branch's joyous assertion: 'I am the whole tree' or 'I am the universe'. True, but supposing the branch were to claim it was the branch of another tree? In other words we must distinguish between statements which are just wrong or nonsensical and those which in some sense are profoundly true.

Our task, as scientists, is a heavy one. We have to try to produce theories like Einstein did before the truths of nuclear physics could approximate to the truths of the mystics. Jung's marked relativism has given us a start. When he says, as he often did, about his contradictions: it is a question of the point of view, he did *not* mean by point of view that any opinion would do but that some things look different when seen from different directions, ourselves especially.

The 'I' and the 'we'

In this paper I sometimes say 'I' and sometimes 'we'. Writers of scientific papers usually avoid the use of both these terms in their wish to be objective. The statement, 'I would like a cup of tea,' while it might be true, is not like saying, 'the earth revolves on its own axis'. Why is this considered more objective, more scientific? One reason is that it is a 'we' statement or a 'collective truth' an appeal to a general rather than a particular experience of the world. As analysts we frequently do not accept the 'I' statements of our patients. If, for example, the patient says, 'I have nothing but admiration for my father', we instinctively look for unconscious contempt. But in doing this, we too are, perhaps unconsciously, making not an 'I' statement but a 'we' statement, like 'we analysts, from our study of many other patients, have a theory which would lead us to doubt the truth of your statement'. We try to understand our patients, not only by our own unique response to them, but by reference to pooled knowledge of *other* people. All 'interpretations' involve doing that. Jung was always highly aware and troubled by the fact that psychology generalizes about the individual and that the more deeply into the unconscious we go, in our efforts to find the unique individual, the more collective the unconscious becomes, the more shared with humanity at large. It is never clear in Jung, never finally resolved, whether he prizes more the attainment of unique individuality, or the awareness of our timeless generality. He never really argues this question, but both are somehow subsumed under the goal of individuation.

Nevertheless, it seems to me that we do all understand it in part. We know that as we help people to become more aware and more objective about themselves, they simultaneously become both larger and smaller. They increase in the sense of more things becoming part of them and they diminish in that they become more part of the world. We often have to imagine the outer world growing as the inner world grows, rather than one growing at the expense of the other. Nor can either be taken as a fixed point of reference by which the other can be measured. It is all relative, and in any case there is no indisputably real outer world and inner world. It is a distinction we make purely for convenience; it is all a matter of point of view.

If I am right in suggesting that both processes are taking place simultaneously in everyday analytic work, then this has implications too for our ego–self distinction. Both the ego and the self are being expanded in one sense and diminished in another. They are not reciprocally related, i.e. the self expanding while the ego diminishes, or the ego expanding at the expense of the self. The distinction between ego and self like the distinction between inner and outer, or the distinction between collective and personal, does not depend on relative size. The 'size' may depend on the point of view (the cup of tea may be 'bigger' to me than the earth's revolutions).

Inner and outer: parts and wholes

Although both Freudians and Jungians agree in distinguishing an inner and outer world, and in seeing the outer world as being represented in the inner, there are important differences between the two groups. Jungians are less ready to regard the outer world as being outside the *person*, and the inner world as being inside him. Introversion and extroversion are two equally valid orientations, and this has profound implications in our understanding of what psychoanalysts would call 'external reality'. I may say, for example, 'I am in London' or 'London is in me' and both are true, but a schizophrenic patient recently said to his analyst, 'I can't make out whether I am in analysis or in London.' Of course, both were true, but the confusion was not simply between inner and outer. In the outer world I am part of something larger. In the inner world that same something is a small part of me. My thinking in the second way, e.g. that 'London is part of me', implies no inflation of the ego nor grandiosity of the self, provided:

1. I recognize that I am not the only one of whom London is a part.

2. I am not speaking literally.

Putting these two considerations together we arrive at a common metaphor.
It is worth noting here that the division between inner and outer is one which we make only when we become *self*-conscious. Consciousness is not sufficient, but also the distinction is never a literal one. We do not, by inner and outer, mean inside and outside the body.

Literalness

The ego and the self are not things, so statements about them should never be taken literally. This is easily said, but how then should we take them? To what extent can scientific statements become poetic or mystical statements? This is at the root of the controversy which arises between Redfearn and Schwartz-Salant. To what extent is clarity and to what extent is a sense of mystery to be valued?

Although they seem to be poles apart on this, they are both trying to recognize the need for both.

Literalness is equated by Barfield with idolatry (Barfield 1957). He attacks Freud for a kind of idolatry of the body. He considers that Freud saw dream images as representing parts of the body, but did not recognize that the material body and its parts are also representations. Jung comes under attack too, for trying to build his concept of the collective unconscious on the foundations of idolatry. Jung is reproached for 'insulating the archetypes from the world of nature, with which, from their own account, they were mingled or united'. These criticisms of Jung and of Freud have some validity and it is helpful to see them as map and territory problems, following Korzybski (Korzybski 1935). If one is trying to speak not literally but symbolically, then to what do the symbols refer – to other symbols? When Jung says that the self is an archetype, he means we do not and can never know what its symbols ultimately refer to. Symbols are not signs. The idea of the totality of the psyche never has a simple literal meaning. This is only a pointer to something unknowable. At this point the triangles in Figure 4.1 can again be useful, the introduction of the third term. We need Figure 4.2.

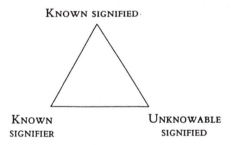

KNOWN SIGNIFIED

KNOWN
SIGNIFIER

UNKNOWABLE
SIGNIFIED

Figure 4.2 Triangle of known and unknowable signified

The unknowable signified does not *need* to be known, but it does need to be there. Korzybski also objected to the one-to-one correspondence between concepts and things conceptualized. In doing so he stressed the importance of levels of abstraction (Korzybski 1935).

It may appear, when speaking of levels of abstraction, that all this applies only to intellectual theorising, but it should be remembered that if intellectual formulations of the theory provide a good model of the psyche, the most unthinking sorts of everyday experience of the self (and the self as a datum of experience might mean just this low intellectual level) can be 'mapped' on it. Thus a man may feel, and indeed be, whole if he has lost his legs, his sight, his hearing, even his reason. He is not using his bodily boundaries as his territory. On the other hand, one may feel and be incomplete without one's car, one's wife, one's house, or one's membership to a professional body. When I say 'feel and be' I refer to the fact that in common parlance we often do not need to distinguish phantasy and reality, what is felt to be so and what *is*, because the level of abstraction is understood. The self referred to is not the human body. Its boundaries may be greater or smaller than that of the body. If we try to make a model of this 'self' it would have to allow for all its different 'sizes'. Jung attempts just such a model and draws map-like diagrams (see Figures 3.1 and 3.2, p.57) which can be turned inside out to reflect the point of view adopted, and also they show a hierarchical arrangement of levels corresponding to levels of abstraction. The self may thus be larger or smaller than the individual.

Although the body is not meant literally in statements about the self it may be used analogically and 'as if' is understood; for example, when we say a person is 'equated' with a phallus, say to a patient, 'you want to scoop out my breast', 'you want to show me your penis', or 'don't lose your head', or not to be heartless. Again, most people can understand these statements without a lengthy intellectual analysis but such an analysis could theoretically be made, or at least up to a point through differentiating levels of abstraction. Perhaps even Angelus Silesius's statement could be analysed in this way. Again I would have to add 'up to a point' and I never suggest, as perhaps Korzybski does, that this need be a very precise point.

Although greatly helped by Korzybski's formulations, I do feel there is something to be said for merging map and territory, not only for poetry, but also for science. I am sure of this, at least for psychology, but I expect it applies to all the sciences. The merging needed is only partial and does not mean confusing, or identifying the map with the territory. When Barfield speaks of saving the appearances, he means that we are always dealing ultimately with collective representations. We cannot know what is unrepresented. To understand metaphors like 'I am the universe' we have to allow *some* confusion between levels. Some participation must take place; not 'participation mystique' but a little bit of meaningful ambiguity. This is perhaps what Schwartz-Salant means by 'the spirit of Jung', which is not to be violated. And it may be that I am speaking here of the very overlap which he is trying to show in his Venn diagram. It is difficult for analytical psychologists to agree about how much of this blurring or ambiguity can be tolerated. To some extent tolerance of ambiguity seems to be an individual matter.

The limits of Jung's model

Although our toleration threshold may vary it is never infinite. Like the alchemists, we accept confusion but not forever. Jung's model of the psyche developed out of a need to widen his world, to break through restrictive boundaries. Just as he had to break out of the restrictions of his early village life and his father's restricted view, so he later had to break out of the restricted vision of Freud. His own model of the psyche tends always to extend to infinity. It appears cosmic, includes everything, can embrace any other model – including Freud's, including Christianity and eastern mysticism and pre-history.

Jung, however, to remain (personally) sane and to become (impersonally) a cogent scientist, had to build in restrictions on his model. He had to draw *some* kind of map and the very act of drawing a map, even drawing a line, is an act of division which creates a boundary and a boundary imposes a limit. It was not to be the limited map of Freud, the literal body, developing from beginning to end in an orderly, predictable sequence of stages within a sexual orientation. It is arguable, of course, whether Freud's model is really quite as restricted as this, but at least this was how Jung saw it. Whether Freud really took the body as literally as I am suggesting he did, by introducing the self, Jung broke through the idea of limitation by the body; for example, it did not depend on having legs but might depend on having a house. Also, it could be understood as surviving the death of the body. I have said that Freud's model, though restricted, was strong and that the introduction of the self into the psychoanalytic system has led it into error, because it cannot easily accommodate itself to the idea that the self is not limited in space or in time to the limits of the body. The self may be given a small or a very large 'S', but the body is always spelt with a small 'b' (I may be discounting here some interpretation of Freud's theory, especially Norman O. Brown's way of relating the body of psychoanalysis to the mystical body (Brown 1966), and to the Body Politic as in Hobbes's *Leviathan*).

Jung sometimes sees his system as a supra-system that includes others, but sometimes he sees it as a sub-system, along with other sub-systems such as Freud's and Adler's, of some greater supra-system. This is entirely consistent with his view of the self and of parts and wholes as relative. I have tried to show elsewhere how the individuation model can be seen as a sub- or supra-system to the medical model and also how Jung's model can be combined with other models in group psychology (Zinkin 1984). The limits of the model, the lines which make differences, can be seen both in Jung's diagrams of the psyche and also in his textual descriptions of it (see Figures 3.1–3.3, pp.57–58). Two particular limiting features stand out:

1. Its circularity. Although the circle shows an unlimited continuous movement as one follows its outline, it also shows discontinuity. It gives the model an inside and an outside and a centre, i.e. a point which can only be in one place.

2. Its hierarchical structure. There is an ordered sequence. Though the model can be turned upside down or inside out, it remains an ordered

sequence. So if, for example, ego and self are to be mapped on this system of concentric circles, the ego can be in the self, the self can be in the ego, both or either can be infinitely large or small, but they are always being seen in relation to each other and they cannot be in entirely separate, unrelated locations. Perhaps this is why Redfearn chose a tree and its branches in his reply to Schwartz-Salant. The branch of the tree *can* be the tree of the branch, but it cannot belong to another tree.

In Jung's model the archetypes have their ordered arrangement. Although Redfearn can use Jung's model analogically to apply to the 'personality' and then speak of 'sub-personalities', it is not actually a model of the personality any more than it is a model of a tree or of the human body or of the universe. It is a model of the psyche which may be mirrored by these three things among many others. It is like a map on which tree, body or universe can be located if one wishes to use it in this way, but of course the tree, the body and the universe must be understood, not literally, but psychologically. It may be that the word 'soul' will convey better what I mean by understanding things psychologically rather than literally, although I am somewhat hesitant about the use of this word. James Hillman has re-visioned psychology and has plumbed the depths of meaning of the word 'soul' (Hillman 1975), though I am afraid that for the average reader who has not studied the background of this word it does not have quite the right connotation. This is a good example of the difficulties of simply referring to 'terminology'.

The symmetry of circularity

Jung's circles represent circular rather than linear thinking, a distinction I made previously following Harley Shands (Shands 1960) in considering the baffling problem of finding a basis for being flexible in analytic technique (Zinkin 1969). Following a circle means ending at the beginning and this raises the paradox of the identity of beginning and ending and threatens the Aristotelian, left-brained law of contradiction, broken so happily by Angelus Silesius and the like. The symmetry of the circle is the symmetry of the logic used in dreams. If we wish to understand dreams we have to use dream-logic. Dreams are neither without logic, nor are they illogical, but they have a logic which has its own separate rules and its own inner consistency, and Matte-Blanco has shown that this logic is symmetrical as opposed to the asymmetry of high level conscious discursive thinking (Matte-Blanco 1975). He uses set theory and the notion of the infinite set in order to elucidate his exposition of this logic. In the dream world parts and wholes are not mutually exclusive but can be identified. Now it seems to me to follow from Jung's valuation of the unconscious as compensatory to consciousness that the logic of the unconscious has to be accepted alongside that of consciousness. This giving equal weight to the two is quite different from the traditional Freudian attempt to translate unconsciousness into consciousness. Jung's model of the psyche can be understood only as an attempt to incorporate both kinds of logic. It follows naturally from placing the self rather than the ego in the centre, the place where symmetry and asymmetry meet.

Although many present-day Jungians have taken many steps back in Freud's direction, this is the step which the Freudians need to take in our direction, the placing of the self rather than the ego in the centre of the psyche. Some, like Kohut and Winnicott and (I would add) Searles, Lacan, Masud Khan and Foulkes, have begun this process by introducing the self into their system. The reflective nature of self-awareness creates paradox and as the more orthodox psychoanalysts try to grapple with the new ideas the two become confused and muddled. I think we should welcome them and join in with them because their muddle is similar to ours.

I hope I have shown that it is possible to throw a little light on the muddle which, if not making everything crystal clear for teaching students, at least may help us to move in the direction of collectively meaningful ambiguity.

Like Schwartz-Salant I have much else to say in response to Redfearn's fifteen pages but perhaps, for the time being, I have said enough and perhaps, too, there are many others who will join in.

Summary

In this paper I have addressed myself to the question of the validity of various paradoxes generated by the concept of the self, particularly in relation to the concept of the ego. These paradoxes may be seen as profoundly true or hopelessly muddled formulations. The problem gave rise to a heated exchange between Redfearn and Schwartz-Salant in the April 1983 issue of the *Journal of Analytical Psychology*. I have tried to do justice to both these opposing views and to suggest ways of distinguishing between meaningful paradox, which I regard as inevitable, and meaningless confusion resulting from loose thinking. The paper is not intended to be an exhaustive treatment of this topic but a contribution to discussion.

References

Barfield, O. (1957) *Saving the Appearances*. London: Faber & Faber.

Brown, N.O. (1966) *Love's Body*. New York: Random House.

Eco, U. (1976) *A Theory of Semiotics*. Indiana University Press.

Hillman, J. (1975) *Revisioning Psychology*. New York: Harper & Row.

Hobson, R.F. (1974) 'Loneliness.' *Journal of Analytical Psychology 19*, 1, pp.71–89.

Homans, P. (1979) *Jung in Context*. Chicago University Press.

Jacoby, M. (1983) 'Comment on "Ego and self: terminology".' *Journal of Analytical Psychology 28*, 2, pp.107–109.

Jung, C.G. (1928) 'Child development and education.' *Collected Works 17.*

Jung, C.G. (1954) 'Mysterium Coniunctionis.' *Collected Works 14.*

Kohut, H. (1978) 'Remarks on the formation of the self.' In *The Search for the Self.* New York: International Universities Press, II, 737–770.

Korzybski, A. (1935) *Science and Sanity.* Lakeville: International Non-Aristotelian Library.

Matte-Blanco, I. (1975) *The Unconscious as Infinite Sets.* London: Duckworth.

Peirce, C.S. (n.d.) *Collected Papers.* (Ed. C. Hartshorne, P. Weiss and A. W. Burks). Cambridge, Mass: Harvard University Press.

Redfearn, J. (1983) 'Ego and self: terminology.' *Journal of Analytical Psychology 28*, 2, pp.91–106.

Richards, J.A. and Ogden, C.K. (1923) *The Meaning of Meaning.* London: Routledge and Kegan Paul.

Schwartz-Salant, N. (1982) *Narcissism and Character Transformation.* Toronto: Inner City Books.

Schwartz-Salant, N. (1983) 'Comment on "Ego and self: terminology".' *Journal of Analytical Psychology 28*, 2, pp.111–114.

Shands, H. (1960) *Thinking and Psychotherapy.* Cambridge, Mass: Harvard University Press.

Stein, M. (1976) 'Narcissus.' *Spring.*

Zinkin, L. (1969) 'Flexibility in analytic technique.' *Journal of Analytical Psychology 14*, 2, pp.119–132.

Zinkin, L. (1983) 'Malignant mirroring.' *Group Analysis XVI*, 2.

Zinkin, L. (1984) 'Is there still a place for the medical model?' *Spring.*

CHAPTER FIVE

The Klein Connection
in the London School
The Search for Origins

What is the origin of the archetypes? Though they would have to be thought of as having an existence before they exist in any individual, even though this pre-existence is hard to conceptualize, the question of origins can also be asked in the form: 'How do the archetypes come to exist within the individual?' Jung's answer to this question was in terms of inheritance, though not in terms of the generally accepted notions of genetics. His view that there must be a collective unconscious from which individual consciousness arises, creates many problems, and if we concentrate on the life of the individual it is not easy to determine how the archetypes actually play their part in infantile life from the beginning. As with all inheritance, we know that there is a continuous interaction between the genes and the environment throughout the whole course of life, but at any stage it is difficult to determine what is cultural and what is laid down by the genes, and is therefore acultural, without invoking a Lamarckian theory of the inheritance of acquired characteristics. In the infant we need to be on the lookout for recognizable and repeated patterns. Even if these are clearly seen in the infant's behaviour they may or may not be in the infant's awareness.

In this chapter, I shall re-address this question of origins in a way that is, I think, novel for analytical psychology because, at least in London, we have looked for answers by making links with psychoanalytic theories of infant development. These, until recently, have tended to disregard the findings of infant research. This is particularly true of Kleinian theories of unconscious fantasy, which have always been regarded as themselves somewhat fantastical by the majority of Freudians throughout the world. It seems to me that now is the time to review the Klein–Jung links in the light of infant research in the process of furthering our understanding of the earliest manifestations of the archetypes in the psychological life of the individual. This approach will try to avoid one source of error in the traditional psychoanalytic approach: the supposition that the fantasies of the adult or even those of young children are evidence for the existence of similar fantasies in the first few months of life.

To clarify my orientation: my principal focus is not to compare the baby with the adult, but rather to compare two *relationships*, that between the mother and her baby and that between the analyst and the analysand. I do not want to suggest that the analytic relationship can be exhaustively described in these terms, but I am sure that it can add greatly to our understanding of what is going on between us and our patients to consider how the first important relationship of our lives is made. As we learn more about this first relationship, so we can understand more about later relationships. This reverses the usual psychoanalytic method, which works backwards, from transference to infancy and uses patients' fantasies to 'reconstruct' the infant.

My emphasis on the importance of infantile development will, doubtless, mark me out in Jungian circles as a member of the so-called London School and a few remarks on how I see the development of this school may help the reader to locate my position within it.

This school has arisen largely through the influence of Michael Fordham. It is he who has repeatedly drawn attention to the processes of individuation described by Jung as occurring from the beginnings of life, and who first described the early appearance of archetypal forms in the young child, challenging Jung's emphasis on individuation as belonging specifically to the second half of life (Fordham 1968). In my view, Fordham's account of de-integration and reintegration has been his most original and valuable contribution to this question (Zinkin 1986).

Another characteristic feature of Fordham's work has been the maintaining of contact with developments in psychoanalysis, particularly those of the British School of object-relations theory. This school has developed its ideas from the seminal work of Melanie Klein and her followers, though these should not all be called Kleinians. Though accepting certain parts of Kleinian theory, they have to various extents introduced modifications of it. Prominent among these post-Kleinians are Wilfred Bion, D.W. Winnicott and, more recently, Donald Meltzer, all of whom were closely in contact with Klein herself. These three writers receive frequent mention in papers from members of the London Society of Analytical Psychology, particularly from those members trained in child analysis.

In a recent historical survey, Fordham (Fordham 1988) gives special prominence to Klein as the third great figure to be placed alongside Freud and Jung. It is clear from his essay that Fordham, in contrast to most analytical psychologists outside London, continues to see Jung as complementary rather than as implacably opposed to Freud and his followers. This has led to a most fruitful attempt at synthesis, a continuation of a tendency to be found in Jung himself, when placing his own psychology in a complementary relationship to that of Freud and Adler, as he so often did.

Because the developmental approach characterising the London School is so influenced by Kleinian meta-psychology, much of this paper can be read as my attempt to modify this influence. This is not my primary aim, however. My view is that it is still valuable to forge links with Kleinian theory as well as with other psychoanalytical schools, but that we can only perform this act of unification if *all* theoretical positions are modified by new findings, whatever the source of these findings may be.

Meta-communication

In the words of a popular song:

> It ain't what you say, it's the way that you say it.
>
> It ain't what you do, it's the way that you do it.
>
> That's what gets results.

In the song it's not very clear what sort of results are being sought, but it seems clear that the advice is of a technical nature. It is well known that patients after a long analysis do not actually remember many of the interpretations they have been given. Perhaps they remember the general gist but not the specifics. Though it can be argued that this does not matter in the least provided the interpretations were effective at the time, this is very much an analyst's argument. What the patient does remember is the relationship with the analyst, whether good or bad, and even though it may be, with some analysts (and certainly with Kleinian ones), that the content of the interpretations is *about* the relationship, it may nevertheless be the manner in which they are conveyed that is important. This may consist of the tone of voice, the timing, the pacing, and many other non-verbalised messages which are sent all at the same time and received during the analytic encounter. This may well be more important than the content of what the analyst says, though, in a good analysis, it seems more likely that the manner and content go together. Certainly the manner and even the mannerisms of the analyst are often picked up by the patient, and it is part of the folk-wisdom of analytical circles that you can tell who analysed whom by the way people talk.

In terms of communication theory, the term 'meta-communication' is used to refer to what is conveyed together with whatever message is primarily meant to be conveyed. In human communication, whatever the content of the verbal message, there is always also at least one other message that forms the meta-communication. This second message, which may be non-verbal, is one that gives information to the other as to the nature of the relationship between the two. One may speak deferentially, for example, to convey one's social inferiority, and this message is picked up whatever is said in this manner (or one can say exactly the same thing conveying a refusal to be deferential). It is because there is always meta-communication that Bateson has pointed out that it is impossible not to communicate, and this concept was essential in his theory of the 'double-bind' (Bateson 1956, pp.251–264). Very often one of the conflicting messages in the double-bind is verbal and the other non-verbal. However, these simultaneous messages do not normally conflict in the sense of a violent contradiction, defying the laws of logic and thus confusing the recipient. There seems to me, though, to be an enormous range in the extent to which simultaneous messages are harmonious or discordant.

It is not very clear in practice as to which is the communication or main message and which is the meta-communication or secondary message. The analyst, for example, is trying to listen not only to what the patient is trying to say but what is being said, at the same time, about the relationship. Sometimes this is contained in the content of the patient's talk, but more often the analyst relies on non-verbal clues, the tone of voice, the hesitations, the body-language and so on. This constitutes the *manner* in which one is being told whatever it is one is hearing. Hence the relevance of the popular song. The distinction between messages resembles Freud's division into 'manifest' and 'latent' content, but it does not necessarily rest on one message being repressed, though this may be the case. Sometimes the manner is more carefully attended to than the content, though more usually it is relatively unconscious. What is true for the analysand's communications is true also for the analyst's. The analyst may or may not be aware of the way he or she is speaking when making an interpretation or other contribution. This may be far more important to the patient than what is being said. The patient is often listening to what the statement is stating about how the analyst is feeling towards or understanding the patient at the time, that is, how the analyst is conceiving of the relationship between the two. These meta-communications go on all the time, each one affecting the meta-communication of the other in a continuous reciprocal exchange.

In trying to understand how analyst and analysand communicate, it is most instructive to consider how mothers and babies communicate with each other, particularly because there are levels of regression at which, as in the young infant, words are not available. Whatever the mother does with her baby has more than one function. Feeding and changing the baby do not satisfy simply its nutritional and excretory needs but enable the mother to express her love (or, unfortunately, her lack of love) for her baby. Though we loosely talk here of 'love', it is better to think of what is being conveyed as the way in which the relationship is being conceived.

Infant research and infant observation

Infant research in a general sense should be distinguished from the infant observation which, having been pioneered by Esther Bick, is now increasingly becoming part of the training programme for analysts. Let me say at once that I am very much in favour of analytic students learning about babies from direct observation. Whether or not they are or have been parents themselves, analysts need a good deal of experience with actual babies if they are to understand the baby in the adults they work with. However, it is important to recognize the limitations of sitting with a mother and baby once a week compared to the systematic and detailed research which is available to the specialists. There are also limitations stemming from the fact that they are being taught by analysts who in the seminars are naturally inclined to interpret the observations according to analytic theories. They watch babies and supervise students with the eyes and ears of the analyst. Kleinian analysts assume that babies have unconscious fantasy. They therefore interpret what they see as the expression of unconscious fantasies and then they may use their observations as evidence to prove the existence of unconscious fantasies, thus perpetuating their own ideas. Because they think there is an initial oral phase and the breast is the first object of any importance to the baby and they believe the baby is driven by libidinal and destructive impulses, they concentrate their observations not only on feeding but on *frustrating* feeding experiences, on states of very high arousal, on the more dramatic and exciting events, on what goes wrong rather than on what goes right. They may overlook the possibility that it is precisely when the baby is not frustrated and angry but quiet and contented that the most rapid development takes place, and that it is at these quiet times that the baby has its richly varied experience. The Kleinian tends also to argue from pathology to normality, that what is pathological for the adult is normal for the baby or young child. Though this certainly may be the case, it overlooks the possibility that what is normal in adults may be a continuation or development of what is normal in infancy and that most of the patients we see did not have very satisfactory early experience, even if not heavily traumatized. Psychotic manifestations in adults who confuse fantasy with reality are taken to be regressing to very early infancy, and therefore 'bad' persecutory fantasies are thought to be the order of the day in the first months of life. It is further assumed that the first organisation of the baby's experience is into two extremes, the good and bad breasts, the so-called part-objects, elicited for the baby by the two extremes of utter bliss and ungovernable rage. Kleinian observers often seem to detect a baby in a rage with assumed sadistic oral fantasies of biting, tearing or scooping out a breast by every means at its disposal, or else a blissful baby united to its fantasied good breast (Klein 1932; 1946). These contrasting fantasies suggest a baby with a sort of dual personality, which is then called 'splitting of the ego'. Only when the actual breast survives, they consider, do these fantasies become modified. Only then can a baby gradually get the idea that the breast is not simply all good or all bad.

There is much to be said, therefore, for analysts paying attention to those who explore the beginning of psychological life without these analytic assumptions. What emerges from current infant researchers is a totally different baby. Their study of the infant throughout the twenty-four hours of the day has shown that they go through different levels of consciousness or awareness, have different needs at different times from stimulation to soothing, and these states are inseparable from the mother who regulates them. This regulation will depend on the mother's sensitivity and the extent of her level of attunement to the baby. The baby displays sociability from the start, and the mother is vitally important in fostering the baby's readiness to relate. She is not just attending to the baby's basic bodily needs, and in fact the most important interactions take place when the baby is neither hungry nor wanting to sleep but quietly and contentedly awake. It is at this time that she and the baby may play games and talk to each other, and perhaps most enjoy being together. These interchanges constitute an early form of dialogue. The emphasis is on a harmonious rather than disturbed or discordant relationship. As a result, the researchers see a different baby from the one the Kleinian analysts see. This baby is a basically friendly and contented one, with a great interest in the world, with a built-in preference for the human face, with the ability to recognize the mother's smell in the first days of life and the mother's voice soon after and even her face by about two months.

Infant research has revealed a much more capable baby than anyone thought possible, one that can discriminate split-second differences, for example; and this has resulted not only from having more sophisticated techniques for observing the infants than analysts customarily employ but from devising ingenious experiments for testing hypotheses. They have ways of 'asking' babies questions about what they are perceiving which are not available to the analysts who watch babies for perhaps one hour a week.

But it is not only the behaviour and the cognitive powers of babies which are studied. There has been a great deal of research on the affects which infants display at different ages and in various situations. Interestingly, although researchers recognize distress as an affect they do not especially note anger, which (together with sexual desire) Kleinians pay so much attention to. They do note fear, joy, disgust and interest, for example, and these are not usually seen in extremes but are finely graded. There is a continuous gradation, for example, from interest to pleasure to excited joy. In a typical game, the mother gently leads or in reciprocal interaction follows the baby through these fine gradations of feeling.

The work which I think should be of the greatest importance to Jungians is that of Daniel Stern. Not only is he a psychoanalyst as well as an infant researcher, but he has concentrated on the development of the subjective sense of self and has concluded that this emerges during the first two months (Stern 1985). The *sense* of self has always seemed to me to be of more interest than discussions as to whether there is an objective self which exists or not at any particular age. Stern has shown that it is reasonable to conclude that the sense of self in the baby as being distinct from the mother begins to emerge from birth and that by three months the baby has a sense of having a core self. By then she or he has a sense of agency, continuity, coherence and distinctive patterns of self-feeling. All these go together and contribute to the baby seeming more of a person at this age. There is no suggestion that he has the ability for self-reflection, and above all there is no suggestion that the baby has images of himself or has a representational world. What we call an 'inner world' would be possible only after fantasy and reality are distinguished, and this would depend on the baby being able to conjure up images outside the action-sequence that gives rise to them. For example, the baby, on gazing at the mother's face, has, of course, an image, but does not have this image in her absence. He quickly learns to recognize the face when it is re-presented because the laying down of the memory pattern which makes this possible does not require an image. Lichtenberg reaches a similar conclusion and refers to an imaging capacity which does not begin to develop until the end of the first year (Lichtenberg 1983).

A study of the supporting evidence as found in the books by Stern and Lichtenberg provides a convincing refutation of the Kleinian idea of fantasy in the first, all-important year when the baby is supposed to be in the oral phase. Although there might be a Kleinian case based on stressing the unconsciousness of the supposed fantasies, this does not, I think, advance the argument very much. One still has to presuppose some way in which these fantasies are represented, even though unconscious.

Now what happens to Jungian theories of development in the light of these researches? Although I think that certain aspects of Jungian thought also need revision (and babies can never be thought of in the same way again by any discipline) I find, curiously enough, that Jungian theory is not only more compatible than Klein's but is actually given strong support by the new findings.

Without invoking an early fantasy-life of images in infancy, what can be seen is the emergence of patterns. Patterns can gradually be discerned by the developing infant which have certain of the characteristics of archetypes and I am tempted to regard them as the first manifestations of the archetype. Stern describes early patterns as aggregates or assemblies of percepts, actions and affects (Stern 1985, pp.97–99). This description closely resembles the complexes which Jung described before he elaborated his theory of archetypes (Jung 1906). One need only add that they are innate, universal and unknown to complete the notion of the archetype. They are un-imaged patterns at first and they remain un-imaged till the second year of life. They are therefore pre-symbolic. They form the core of the complex which is only later 'clothed in images', to use Whitmont's phrase (Whitmont 1969, pp.23–31). So the baby is truly 'unconscious' in Jung's sense (Jung 1912, p.235) and remains unconscious until he or she becomes quite old in Kleinian terms, i.e. a whole year old. One has to be careful to retain Jung's sense of unconscious as meaning unreflective because the baby is by no means unaware during the first year, as I have indicated.

Unconscious fantasy and the internal world

Because infant research is casting doubt on Kleinian notions of fantasy, analytical psychologists need to reconsider their own notions of the beginnings of fantasy formation and the start of the 'internal world', particularly where Kleinian ideas have been used to supplement or amplify Jung's. Unconscious fantasy, according to Klein, exists from the beginning of life. This implies a fantasy life of which the infant is unaware, and superficially this concept seems close to Jung, who stresses the unknowability of the archetypes. Though it is difficult for researchers to disprove the claim that something unbeknownst to the baby is going on in his or her mind, the evidence, as I have indicated, suggests that infants in the first year do not have internal representations in the sense that Klein assumes. Although they are shown to have the most amazing capacities in the early months of life, they do not appear to have images that are independent of perceptual cues. This does not start to happen until the end of the first year, and it is only then that one can reasonably begin to speak of an 'inner world'. But this does not mean that the infant in the early months is not having extremely rich subjective experience. In fact, the evidence supports the notion that the experience is actually much more rich and differentiated even than Klein thought. At the same time, her notions of unconscious fantasy do assume that the infant has images which have some existence independently of direct sensory stimulation. The issue is not whether the infant sees the breast: it is whether there is an image of a breast which begins to occupy what could be called a representational world.

According to Kleinian theory, a pleasurable feed would evoke an image of the 'good breast'; and such an image would exist independently of a 'bad breast', which would be evoked as a projection of the baby's destructive impulses. These would constitute for the baby the so-called part-objects. Even if we modify the theory so that whole objects exist first and are later split into part-objects, the whole object would have to give rise to some sort of image which is internally perceived in the absence of the actual breast. The kind of evidence Kleinian observers use to show that this is so, is that the baby is sometimes seen to be behaving as though hallucinating a breast. At three months, babies are observed to stop crying and to smile contentedly after putting fingers into the mouth. But there is no reason to assume the baby is then having a hallucination even though it can be reasonably assumed that there is a memory of previous good feeds. But the memory does not imply an *image* of the breast. It is more likely that the sensation of hunger has become associated with sucking. It acts as a stimulus and it is known that the motor activity of sucking produces a reduction in tension accompanied by the signs of pleasure-affect.

As with memory, so with expectation. Much has been made by Jungians of the idea that the rooting behaviour of infants means some built-in expectation of a breast. This is then thought to be met by the actual breast. But here again, there is absolutely no reason to think that the rooting baby has an *image* of a breast. Innate expectations might be simply bodily, i.e. there might be innate neurophysiological patterns without representation in the form of an image. Though it cannot be proved that babies in the early months do not have images, there is no evidence that they have. In the second year this is not the case. For instance, a crawling baby meets what looks like a cliff painted on the floor. It hesitates and then looks round at the mother who is seated nearby. If the mother is smiling encouragingly it will continue the journey. This could not happen without some internalised image of the mother which is available for checking. To have a stable image of this kind, the infant must have had a good deal of experience of the mother, but the experience, however rich, is not imaged in the first year. A repeated pattern of experience forms the basis of images later.

In fact it is this formulation, of a pattern rather than an image, and not Klein's, which supports Jung's concept of archetypes. The archetypes are unknown, but there are symbolic images which indicate their existence. They may be related to deeply unconscious bodily activities of, say, the autonomic system. The archetypes form our experience, but we cannot directly experience them. They are according to Jung unknown.

Christopher Bollas, following Bion, speaks of a similar situation but suggests that things can be known without being thought, the 'unthought known' (Bollas 1987). It would make a Jungian perspective clearer if we imagine that at first there is an un-imaged archetypal form to experience, an 'un-imaged known'. Images in this formulation do not provide knowledge; they make a bridge from what has previously been known to what we more usually call knowledge, which depends on *reflective* thought. Archetypes form, also, the experience of lowly animals, but nobody suggests that these animals are capable of symbolically representing them.

This must be what Jung means when he calls children, along with animals and 'primitives', 'unconscious'. He must be referring to the stage when the self and others, as well as objects, though differentiated, cannot be symbolically represented. If so, he may be wrong about the higher primates, who seem to show some primitive powers of symbolisation but he is wrong about primitives, who we now know are not at all primitive, and he is wrong about children in general. What I want to stress here, though, is where Jung is right, or at least where his theories and those of the infant researchers agree, but do not agree with those of Klein. All the evidence is that the infant does not have an 'imaging capacity' until the last trimester of the first year. This means not that the younger infant has no images, but that he cannot use these images outside the action sequence in which they occur.

We are all familiar with patients who interest us with the richness of their imagery, but have no capacity to respond to interpretations as to the meaning of their imagery. They cannot imagine (Plaut 1966). They have no internal image, which can be used as the infant does of its mother in the cliff experiment. Kleinian thinking makes quite an opposite assumption about the first months of infancy. It assumes that the baby attributes meaning to a bad feeding experience in the form of a bad breast. By projecting its bad feelings on to the breast, the approaching breast is understood to be attacking it. The resultant image of the bad breast is then supposed to account for the rage the hungry baby is thought to have when the breast is presented too late. The paranoid-schizoid position is one in which the breast is construed in a particular way (Klein 1929, pp.249–50). In the adult who is paranoid, we do, to be sure, recognize that the paranoia is an attempt to give meaning to the world. Paranoid delusions in schizophrenia, in which good and bad experiences are sharply divided, are secondary to a threatened sense of chaos, an attempt to give an ordered meaning to the patient's experience.

The baby, on the other hand, does not at first derive meaning from violent contrasts of good and bad. In the early interactions, the mother provides a sense of order through the regularity and repetitiveness of her play with and her handling of the baby. Memory traces are gradually built up in the baby of these interactions which form the pattern for later symbolisation. Although this may rely partly on the baby's experiences of contrast, there is no violent separation of good and bad which could be designated the good and bad breast. If this is the case, the paranoid adult has not regressed to the early months of life but to the same period after the end of the first year. His original experience will have been organised by the regulations of the mother and the paranoid fantasies would be a secondary attempt to organise his experience, i.e. splitting and projective identification might still be the earliest defensive mechanisms to appear, but they do not occur before the second year when early primitive forms of symbolisation are possible. Part-objects such as the breast would therefore play no part in the fantasy of an infant, even the unconscious fantasy of the infant, at the time it is having its important experiences of the breast, as weaning, at least usually in our culture, is complete by the end of the first year.

To illustrate Kleinian theory I have been referring inevitably to the breast because this is said to be the first object for the baby. Nobody would question that feeding is of central importance in infantile life and yet psychoanalytic theory has concentrated on it to such an extent that it has ignored practically everything else. I have in mind principally the early experience of being in the womb and then of the mother's face, her voice and her unique ways of relating to her baby, which we now know to be the medium through which socialization takes place. The breast-bias, of course, dates from the earliest of Freud's formulations of drive-theory centred on the erogenous zones.

A further bias has been the pathological one. The problem is Klein's tendency to regard adult pathology as being the normal state of affairs in the infant. Although it is true that babies in the first year can be very distressed, this does not mean that they are disturbed in the same way as adults. A great deal of this bias stems from Freud's early emphasis on infant trauma. Traumatic experiences were also dramatic events and the focus on the dramatic has made it difficult for the psychoanalyst to consider that for most babies highly dramatic events are rare and the greatest development occurs in the relatively quiet times when the infant is both contented and alert. The psychoanalytic observer may see these times as uneventful. But it is these relatively quiet times in which the infant mostly lives. The infant manifestly has a keen interest in many things other than the breast. It has a distinct preference for the mother, particularly her face, but also her feel, her voice, her smell and her ways of doing things. Even when feeding, it is usually the mother's face on which it gazes and which gazes back. Dramatic events are, for the infant, bad events and the main function of the mother is to so regulate the baby's life that it does not experience sudden changes.

Melanie Klein was, I think, deceived by drawing conclusions from patients who, whether adults or very young children, were treated in conditions of deprivation resulting from Freud's original rule of abstinence. In addition, the child-rearing practices of her day, as horribly exemplified by the advice to mothers given by Truby King, led her to reconstruct a deprived infancy so that she built up a totally distorted view of the early months and saw this as a normal state of affairs to which one regressed. Splitting and projective identification have therefore come to be thought of as the order of the day in the very young infant. Infant research would suggest the opposite, that they do not occur at all in the first year. They may occur in the second year, but even then are likely to be excessive only in the absence of satisfactory mother–infant interaction.

A great deal of attention is paid to the degree of attunement between mother and baby. If they are badly out of tune the baby and mother may become distressed, but even then a distressed baby is not necessarily an angry or sadistic baby. A further problem is particularly taken up by Daniel Stern. This concerns the timetable. Splitting according to Klein is supposed to precede differentiation of self and other and self and other can only be distinguished after the joining up of good and bad. Stern on the basis of all the evidence reaches the opposite conclusion which is a much more logical one. The good or bad object and the good and bad self require differentiation of self and object first (Stern 1985, pp.240–242). He does give a great deal of evidence that in the interactional matrix the infant can make the distinction of self from other from the very beginning and that there is at least an emergent sense of self in the first three months (Stern 1985). At that age, when everybody agrees there is marked change in the baby, the baby appears to have a sense of a core-self. Stern is here understanding that the baby has a sense of self without invoking an *image* of the self, an important distinction when considering the self archetype. He concludes that merger fantasies do not represent an early symbiotic phase, as Mahler postulates (Mahler 1969), but can only arise later, after this differentiation of self and other has taken place. Differentiation is, of course, not the same as splitting.

I should like to return, for a moment, to splitting, because this is one of the great links made between Jung and Klein. The good and the bad breast are easily equated with the mother-archetype as imaged in the bountiful and terrible mother. Jung does not use a term like 'splitting' when discussing the archetypes. When he speaks of bipolarity, he envisages one unit with two poles, or he speaks of the two aspects of the archetype, e.g. when discussing the horn of the unicorn (Jung 1944, p.471). He sees symbols as reflecting the two sides, e.g. the snake is both destructive and life-renewing. It is precisely the splitting-off of one aspect, as in Christianity, which he sees as pathological, i.e. as not respecting the primal unity of the archetype. I have been very struck, on re-reading the Jung–Freud correspondence, by the extent to which their break-up revolved around Jung's seeing everything as united and Freud seeing everything as divided (McGuire 1974). This was the source of Freud's pessimism. Jung was no pluralist and his belief in a pre-existing unity was the source of his optimism. I think that in this fundamental difference, infant research supports Jung and not Freud and certainly not Klein.

In a passage which gives great weight to the theory of archetypes, Stern states:

> Infants appear to experience a world of perceptual unity, in which they can per-
> ceive amodal qualities in any modality from any form of human expressive be-
> haviour, represent these qualities abstractly, and then transpose them to other
> modalities. This position has been strongly put forth by developmentalists such
> as Bower (Bower 1974), Moore and Meltzoff (Moore and Meltzoff 1978) and
> Meltzoff (Meltzoff 1981, Meltzoff and Borton 1979) who posit that the infant,
> from the earliest days of life, forms and acts upon abstract representations of
> qualities of perception. These abstract representations that the infant experi-
> ences are not sights and sounds and touches and nameable objects, but rather
> shapes, intensities and temporal patterns – the more 'global' qualities of experi-

ence. And the need and ability to form abstract representations of primary qualities of perception and act upon them starts at the beginning of mental life; it is
not the culmination or a developmental landmark reached in the second year of
life. (Stern 1985, pp.51–52)

In this passage, representing the work of several researchers, we have the idea of
perceptual unity, of abstract representations in the form of shapes or patterns to be
found at the very beginning of life. This is despite the conclusion that the imaging
capacity does not begin to appear till nearly the end of the first year. These then
are surely the archetypes, the shapes and patterns which give form to our
experience and to our behaviour but which are not images even though it is
possible to 'image' them. To image them we have to be at least a year old. If this is
true, then analysing a child even as young as eighteen months can work through
what imaging capacity is there, but it does not provide evidence of earlier images,
only of earlier archetypes. There is no great difficulty in seeing these archetypes as
innate, as existing for thousands of years before the birth of the infant and being
somehow remembered in the sense of being recognized, though if we speak of a
'racial unconscious' or of racial memory, we must be careful and must bear in mind
that we are using somewhat rough metaphors.

Stern provides a good deal of evidence for cross-modal perception. Blindfold a
baby, give her two dummies, one smooth and one with knobs on, ask her which
one she prefers by recording the rate of sucking on each and later show the baby
the two dummies and she will preferentially gaze at and show interest in the
previously preferred one (Meltzoff 1981). This is just one of hundreds of
experiments showing that a pattern detected in one sense-modality can be
recognized in another; in this instance, what is felt in the mouth can be recognized
by the eyes. In fact, there is usually a close mutual support from all the
sense-modalities. If a baby sees the mother's face and she is speaking to him but
her voice is not synchronized, the baby shows distress even if the time lag is only a
fraction of a second. A baby from a few weeks old can thus be shown to have
split-second timing, but what interests us here is the pattern, the 'pattern that
connects', to use Bateson's term (Bateson 1980, p.16). What is found
experimentally is not just the cognitive ability to perceive the pattern but a cluster
or assembly of a percept, an action and an affect. The combination, as I have said,
seems to correspond to Jung's early description of the complexes. These patterns
are archetypal in that they have universality, innateness and numinosity and
though not imaged at first they are nevertheless shaping the baby's experience.

The vitality affects and interactional patterns
Before we go on to consider clinical implications, I would like to make a
distinction between form and content. Regardless of *what* is experienced by the
infant (the content), there is also the question of *how* it is experienced (the form).

In so far as the baby's experiences are influenced by the mother, what the baby picks up is not only what the mother provides but how she provides it, her way of doing things. Whether feeding, changing, rocking or talking with her baby, the mother has her patterns and these are conveyed to the baby as invariants. These have certain universal characteristics, if satisfactory communication is to take place. There is also the mother's special way which the baby quickly learns to recognize, but these are only variations of the universal patterns. Archetypal forms from the beginning are accompanied, if not by imagery, by numinosity – a powerful affect which it is not easy to describe in the absence of the archetypal pattern which evokes it.

It is interesting therefore to find in infant research the idea that certain abstract patterns not only form affects but actually *are* affects. Stern, following the work of Tomkins (Tomkins 1962), has made a useful distinction between what he calls 'category affects' such as anger, sadness, joy, fear and disgust, and 'vitality affects'. These are by no means the only patterns underlying the infant's experience. They are a special case which, I consider, has a special relevance to analysis because they deal with emotions which are not usually considered. The vitality affects cannot be classified in terms of these readily recognizable emotions and they do not have names, but they can be described in terms of their kinetic qualities such as 'surging', 'exploding', 'fading away', 'accelerating'.

An example he gives is that the father gets out of his chair 'explosively'. This explosive action might mean he is angry, but might not. He may always get up in this way. What is picked up is the explosive quality, the vitality affect, his particular form of being alive. Vitality affects seem to me like the musical signs that are not of the notes to be played but indicate how they are to be played. The musician learns the shape of a *crescendo, diminuendo, sforzando, calendo, subito piano, accelerando, con fuoco, allegro man non troppo* and even *con amore*. These are the 'forms of feeling' of Suzanne Langer which Hobson used in his conversational model of psychotherapy, though I do not think that he gives them the archetypal significance that I am suggesting (Langer 1967; Hobson 1985).

Technique

Now it may be that the Kleinian, on hearing all this, would say: 'What does any of this matter for the practical business of analysis? Our patients do exhibit splitting and projective identification. They do seem to have fantasies of good and bad breasts and they do move, with our help, from the paranoid-schizoid to the depressive position. All is speculation about what is going on in pre-verbal babies. Perhaps we need to make a few amendments in the light of all this research, but they are largely academic and have little practical importance.' This objection concerns the relevance of theory to technique, and to answer it I now turn to questions of technique.

By technique I simply refer to the means by which the insights of the analyst are conveyed to the patient to produce change. Technique seems to me to be divisible into a circular, interactional model often called 'dialogue', though Jung preferred the word 'dialectic', and a linear model of the analysis and interpretation of the patient's material by the analyst, who is, at the time, standing back from the patient as a person. These modes may be combined or separated (Zinkin 1974). In the light of infant research I can see that the division can be according to whether the patient is seen to be communicating as an infant does with its caretaker in the first year of life, which is only understandable as part of a two-way communication, or to be capable of the symbolic interaction which occurs later. It is at this later stage that sequences of ideas can be formed and communicated to another, or they can fail to be communicated; that is, they do not require to be understood by the analyst in order to exist in the mind of the patient. The message does not have to be received in order to exist. This is in marked contrast to circular interaction where what the baby transmits has no real existence until completed by a response from the mother being given back to the baby. The later possibility of the unreceived message being held on to by the baby cannot obtain without symbolic representation requiring imagery. In the pre-symbolic stage, so often seen with borderline patients and other patients who are highly regressed, the analyst cannot interpret, in the sense of translating, symbolic material to what is symbolised (the usual nature of analytic interpretation). He can nevertheless participate and respond like a mother does when she gives meaning to what the baby expresses, and is concerned, at the same time, with the regulation of affects and levels of arousal and the transitions between them as well as the satisfaction of basic bodily needs. This requires her sensitive interaction with her baby and maintained attunement between them. She 'interprets' only in the sense of tuning in and picking up the 'patterns which connect'. Specifically, she connects the patterns with the feelings, percepts and actions which they arouse in her and she can only transmit these back to the baby in a slightly altered form which, if they stay attuned, the baby can then respond to with a further slight alteration of the pattern. The pattern is cross-modally transmitted. The resulting dialogue is pre-verbal and depends on the sharing of patterns.

If the patient, in spite of using words, is in this pre-symbolic state of the first year of life, then the analyst, whether or not he or she is using words, also has to communicate pre-symbolically. The words will not be attended to, since the analyst's meta-communication is what is being picked up. The only means available to the analyst at such times is the interchange and sharing of patterns. These will emerge from an interactional matrix similar to the mother–baby one and although these modes of communications are archetypal, they are also highly interpersonal, as they will transmit the vitality affects. They are circular rather than linear because the patients' communications, like the babies', are not complete unless received and passed back in a slightly altered form. It is not that the patient has a thought, or even an image which she or he can choose whether or not to tell the analyst. There is some sort of pattern which can only exist if completed by being recognized and shared in the interaction between patient and analyst.

This gives rise to the vexed question of when to give what Michael and Frieda Fordham have called 'tokens', which are often regarded as a last resort to be used by the analyst when interpretations are no longer useful because of the depths of the patient's regression (Fordham 1964). But I am suggesting that, in these situations, what is being given is not a token like a book token, given when one does not know what book to give and is therefore rather impersonal. If you hold the patient's hand it is not, strictly speaking, a token for holding the whole patient. Although this might be a correct symbolic interpretation, it is not one which can at the time be understood by the patient. It may, nevertheless, work as an action because the way the hands are held has the same pattern as the way that the whole person would be held and it is the pattern that is important. Such interactions are very frequent in analysis, even if interpretations are being given. The patterns then lie in the timing, the pacing, the tone and inflection of the voice. Whatever words are used the important interaction is pre-verbal and pre-symbolic. A pattern is exchanged and shared, with feelings which can be recognized but not categorised. The pattern is a combination of a percept, an action and an affect and is very finely graded and regulated in its quality and intensity. Again, as in the mother with her baby, it all depends on being attuned.

It should also be recognized that if the patient is using the couch, and is in this pre-symbolic interaction, he or she is denied access to the richness of facial expression. This may not matter too much as infant research has shown the existence of cross-modality. What is expressed in one sensory modality can be recognized if expressed in another. But this means that everything may depend on the voice and the way it is being used and there is no cross-checking with the face. Although I think that while the whole question of the couch needs to be reappraised in view of the centrality in importance of the mother's face for the infant, we should still recognize that the essential patterns can nevertheless be transmitted by the voice alone.

Clinical vignettes

I shall now give three clinical vignettes. These have been chosen as typical everyday examples where I think the conditions obtaining in the analytic situation are the same as those in the early infant–mother situation. In all three I cannot effectively use interpretations to produce change, but change takes place through an interactional pattern. This is often attributed to some kind of intuition on the part of the analyst, but can be usefully conceptualized if we alter our picture of infantile development away from the Kleinian one.

Many years ago I had a patient called Amy, who wanted to train as a therapist. She had not originally come for that reason, but for a sexual problem. The trouble was that I simply could not see her as a therapist, but it was not easy for me to explain why not. The reason, which gradually became clear to me, was that, throughout all her sessions, for many years, she was always alert. Whether sitting or lying on the couch, she had a manner of communicating which was direct and open. She spoke fast and was not evasive or cautious and she talked quite readily of intimate matters, including some quite complicated feelings about me. This meant that she did not give an impression of defensiveness in any obvious way. What worried me was her manner. Whatever she said was always said to me in a way that seemed more suitable to talking to a dinner party companion than to an analyst, even though the content was different. This did not mean she was unable to provide lots of associations, and it did not prevent her from taking a keen interest in her dreams; she did and she also took a keen interest in my interpretations. Indeed, her general manner was keen and sharp, and of course she was very keen to be a therapist. She was not someone who found it difficult to express a wide range of feelings. Also I could not, in the well-worn phraseology, say she was 'not psychologically minded'. She was able to symbolise and could be extremely perceptive. How, I wondered to myself, could I possibly have doubts about her being a therapist? Although I could not formulate it to her effectively, it was, in fact, all this brightness and keenness that was the trouble. To some extent I could and did try to interpret this in terms of a manic defence, but I think the difficulty was that, for defensive reasons, she remained in a particular state of consciousness, one of alertness or high arousal.

We know from infant research that babies are not just either awake or asleep any more than they are either happy or distressed. Five distinct states of consciousness have been described, and the mother helps to regulate the transitions between them. These are: drowsiness, alert inactivity, alert activity, REM sleep and non-REM sleep (Wolff 1966). My patient could relate only in the mode of alertness. She could never be dreamy. I believe, incidentally, that the main purpose of using the couch is to provide a setting in which the patient has the opportunity to experience all these states. Patients who go to sleep on the couch deserve a paper all to themselves, but there is a case for saying that the experience of REM and NREM states in the presence of the analyst may also be therapeutic. But certainly a great deal of productive work can take place only when not only the patient but also the analyst is allowed to enter a dreamy state. Though there might be problems if the analyst actually falls asleep, there are advantages in being drowsy as well as quietly alert.

As a technical aside, I prefer, if seeing the patient more than once a week, to see them at different times of day. This is more than a question of whether they are just about to go to work or able to relax afterwards but of whether the light is bright, or in a twilight state of dawn or evening or whether it is dark outside. We see quite differently with our rods and our cones. Sometimes we need sharp central vision and sometimes the gentler but vaguer peripheral vision. Though I am not speaking here about actual physical vision, the time of day and the light seems to affect, at least in some patients, the kind of insight they have. This is not so much 'looking at' as 'gradually becoming aware of' something.

It was this latter state that was missing in Amy. She seemed to live in a world of perpetual bright sunlight where everything was bright and uniformly illuminated. At times her dreams did reveal another world, a twilight underworld she dared not enter and her word for depressed was 'gloomy'. As I came to realize that my difficulty was that she always also induced an alert state in me, a change took place. Perhaps it was that I could understand the need not to be clear, not to clarify my interpretations, that I could help her to become aware of the presence within herself of a 'lost child'. It was this lost child who was not ready to be a therapist even though she might do well at interviews and have been accepted as one. The figure of the lost child later emerged in the form of a painting which she saw at an exhibition. The painting was different from the paintings she usually liked and filled her house with. Those were bright, lively and colourful, while this one was neither bright nor gloomy, but there were pale colours, and a bleakness which she associated with my room. In the picture there is a young girl standing alone in this room. She has her back to us and there is an open door. It is quite unclear whether she is about to go through the door or is just standing there. There is no knowing what lies beyond the door. The little girl has an air of being 'lost'. She also seems to be alone and one feels there are no other people in the house at the time. This exactly described a hidden part of Amy which I had not seen before.

In this case, what eventually seemed to work was my recognition of the pre-symbolic state which had for years prevented us from working with a healing symbol. This arose out of a pre-verbal interaction which had a shape. Perhaps, using the musical analogy, it was a case of *molto piu lento* or the sign for an indefinite pause. In Amy's infancy, as in that of so many others, this interaction had been bypassed as she entered the second year.

My second example is of a woman who spent a whole session talking about clothes and hairstyles. This may sound like a similarly highly defended session in which she chatted brightly throughout but it was nothing of the sort. In fact she was musing about her self-image. She was recalling what she had worn at different times of her life, talked of how her mother did not wear clothes, but how the clothes 'wore her' and about the difference between 'looking nice' in her mother's terms, and feeling good or being herself or being sexy. This was a patient who clearly had images and fantasies throughout the session. But as soon as she left, she felt bad about what she had spent her session talking about. She had enjoyed the session herself, but now felt sure that I had been bored and irritated with her for this feminine chattering. I could see that the content of the session had been of the sort which a woman might have had with a woman friend rather than with a man. She was apologising for not really talking to me or even thinking about what I might be feeling. On the other hand, she did not feel she had been simply talking to herself either. As we recalled the session together and I could let her know that I had not been bored, but had enjoyed the session too, she gradually felt better about it. The paranoid fantasy had occurred to her only in my absence. In my presence we could once again restore the shape of an interaction which had taken place in a state of quiet alertness that I had tuned into.

My third example, Cathy, has been chosen to illustrate how, even when using the model of the mother–infant pair in the first year of life, it is not always appropriate to be soothing and comforting, but that surprise and confrontation may be the necessary vitality affect. In so many games with babies the sudden rise or sudden unexpected fall of tension or change of direction plays an important part and can be a source of joy. Cathy always managed to invoke in me a countertransference in which I took on a gentle and protectively reassuring manner, as though she were a shy but rather appealing child. But she had what she called 'a drinking problem'. This had been confided to me with great shame after sufficient trust had been built up between us. She never drank socially but drank when alone, just small quantities at a time, so that she never got noticeably drunk but still consumed a good deal of alcohol in the course of each day; but as she said: 'It's not how much I drink, it's the way I drink'. At a certain point I decided to tell her she was an alcoholic and would never get better unless she stopped drinking. It would be no good trying to reduce it, she would have to stop completely. If she could not manage this, and I thought it extremely unlikely that she could, she should go into hospital and be dried out. The next session she told me that she had stopped drinking and she never drank again. So here, what worked was *sforzando*. It would not have worked if there had not been a good deal of empathic listening first. A long time later, she told me that the reason she had been able to stop was that when she told me she had not had a drink for twenty-four hours, she saw on my face a look of surprised pleasure and she knew I was genuinely pleased for her. I had no memory of expressing this, but it was another important example of a non-verbal communication, which she was able to pick up because she was sitting and able to see me.

In all these examples what worked was not interpretation but the sharing of a vitality affect or shape or pattern of interaction. In each case interpretation later was possible with appropriate imagery, but even in the last case I never referred to the drinking simply in terms of a good or idealised breast. Rather than these part-object images, I understood her to be providing herself with a pattern of interaction which she could give up trying to have in my absence because she could have it with me, not of course by our having a drink together but by finding another interaction with the same 'shape'.

Summary and conclusions

The argument of this paper has two strands. They are interlinked in my presentation, but the reader may accept one without necessarily accepting the other. One is the importance of contemporary infant research, which challenges not only psychoanalytic, but all our previously held, notions of infant development. In so far as the Jungian reader, who may be an analyst, feels it important to have a theory at all on infant development, the way in which the archetypes, or awareness of the archetypes through their images, develop, needs to be reconsidered in the light of the new discoveries. Especially important in this regard is the development of notions of the self, the focus of Stern's interest in his seminal volume, *The Interpersonal World of the Infant* (Stern 1985).

The second strand is the influence of Klein, which is particularly marked in the London School. This has occupied a great deal of this paper, because it is Klein and her followers whose theories can most easily be brought to bear on Jung's. In some cases they can be regarded as repeating much of Jung's ideas but using a different language. In some ways they complement or fill in the gaps left by Jung. In other ways they can be seen to represent views which go further than Freud did, in directions to which Jung made the most strenuous objections.

To conclude then, I shall deal first with the Kleinian influence and then with the new way of understanding the origin of the archetypes.

Although there has been much to criticise in the Kleinian view of infants and their development, I have not attempted a systematic critique of this view but have limited myself to certain questions which are posed by the new research. The clinical usefulness of Kleinian theory remains formidable, however. It is useful because it is based on much careful and clinical observation in analysis. But this does not mean we have to accept Klein's *explanation* for the presence of these phenomena by accepting her theories on what babies are like and how they develop, even though she and most Kleinians tend to regard these as inseparable. Particularly valuable is the distinction between persecutory and depressive anxiety, with their associated defence mechanisms, particularly the defences of splitting, manic denial and projective identification. It now looks as though it is wrong to see these as the very early events which occur as part of the normal emotional life of the very young infant. What may need revision, therefore, is the order in which these events occur and we need to reconsider the differences between normal and pathological mother–baby interactions.

The inner world, an essential notion which Jungian and Kleinian theory has in common, may not, after all, be present until the second year, when it becomes more proper to speak of a fantasy life because the distinction between fantasy and reality can be made. However, the first year is all-important in laying down a rich and subtle *unified* world and splitting and projective identification may represent a defensive breakdown of this world, which occurs later (and not necessarily during infancy but at any stage of life where severe trauma takes place).

In other words, the existence of the 'inner objects' of object-relations theory, as opposed to the independent existence of outer objects making up an inner world, has to wait until quite late in development, until the beginnings of symbol formation. Both merging and projective identification may occur only after self and other are differentiated and there is some experience of self *with* another. Furthermore, both merging and projective identification are likely to be excessive or thought to be pathological where there are insufficient early satisfactory experiences of shared patterns of interaction. This, I am sure, was the case in all three of my clinical examples.

Theory and practice go hand in hand. Not only do clinical preconceptions influence one's technique, but one's way of working helps to decide which out of various rival theories seem the most credible. My clinical examples show a departure from an interpretative approach towards one which seeks to modify the patterns of non-verbal interaction. This does not, of course, mean abandoning analytic interpretation. But it does mean paying more attention to the overall framework in which it is given. This is a framework, often disregarded or left in the background, of a continuous series of affective and cognitive interchange of actions between the partners. This works therapeutically more through supplying a corrective emotional experience than through the insight provided by verbal interpretation. This is the dimension which is being so thoroughly studied by infant researchers. It is early faulty experience with the other, such as failures in attunement, which may be subject to correction in the analytic interchange. This need no longer be seen as depending on the intuition of the analyst. It can be studied and learnt, and watching mothers and babies together is one of the best ways of learning how to (as well as sometimes how not to) do things.

The implications for Jungian theory and practice are also considerable, but the situation is complicated by the great variety of approaches used by analytical psychologists. There is much less consensus than there is among the Kleinians. The generally held idea that the archetypes, being impersonal and collective, dominate our early experiences so much that they need 'personalizing' and 'humanizing' in the process of individuation, as we proceed from primitive to more civilized beings during the process of normal development, has always seemed to me to be at least a gross simplification. My suggestion is that infant research can help us to be aware of definite patterns which are the manifestations of the archetypes *before* images exist in an inner world. The patterns which can be discerned do not need to be thought of inside an individual. They are made by two individuals through their need to communicate with each other. Though they make use of innate (inherited) patterns, they are subject to infinite variation. This partly depends on the culture in which it takes place but ultimately depends on the individuality of the mother and baby (and later other individuals) who are expressing them. This is what makes the patterns so highly personal from the start.

My emphasis, therefore, is on the priority of a two-person system over a model of one person plus an 'environment'. The two-person system is one in which both partners are exchanging information, about themselves, about their common culture and their common history, but doing so through the way they relate. The relationship is primary, or in Martin Buber's more biblical words: 'In the beginning is the relation' (Buber 1970, p.69).

'It ain't what you do' should be amended to: 'It's not so much what you do – the most important thing is the way you do it. That's what gets results.' If there is any truth in this for babies, it must have some truth for analysis. It will continue to be necessary to study the patterns which emerge in the analytic relationship, whether or not we regard them as archetypal. But it is not sufficient to learn only the note-patterns. These are meaningless without the expression-marks, of which perhaps the most important one is *con amore*.

References

Bateson, G. *et al.* (1956) 'Towards a theory of schizophrenia.' *Behavioural Science 1*, pp.251–264.

Bateson, G. (1980) *Mind and Nature.* London: Fontana/Collins.

Bollas, C. (1987) *The Shadow of the Object: Psychoanalysis of the Unthought Known.* London: Free Association Books.

Bower, T.G.R. (1974) *Development in Infancy.* San Francisco: Freeman.

Buber, M. (1970) *I and Thou.* Trans W. Kaufmann. Edinburgh: T & T Clark.

Fordham, F. (1964) 'The care of regressed patients and the child archetype.' *Journal of Analytical Psychology 9*, 1, pp.61–73.

Fordham, M. (1968) 'Individuation in childhood.' In J.B. Wheelwright (ed) *The Reality of the Psyche.* New York: Putnam.

Fordham, M. (1988) 'Some historical reflections.' *Journal of Analytical Psychology 34*, 3, pp.213–224.

Hobson, R. (1985) *Forms of Feeling: the Heart of Psychotherapy.* London: Tavistock.

Jung, C.G. (1906) 'Experimental researches.' *Collected Works 2.*

Jung, C.G. (1912) 'Symbols of transformation.' *Collected Works 5.*

Jung, C.G. (1944) 'Psychology and Alchemy.' *Collected Works 12.*

Klein, M. (1929) 'The importance of symbol formation.' In *Contributions to Psycho-Analysis.* London: Hogarth.

Klein, M. (1932) *The Psycho-Analysis of Children*. London: Hogarth.

Klein, M. (1946) 'Notes on some schizoid mechanisms.' In *Envy and Gratitude and Other Works*. New York: Dell.

Klein, M. (1952) 'The behaviour of young infants.' In *Envy and Gratitude and Other Works*. New York: Dell.

Langer, S.K. (1967) *Mind: An Essay on Human Feeling*. Vol I. Baltimore Md: John S. Hopkins University Press.

Lichtenberg, J.D. (1983) *Psychoanalysis and Infant Research*. New Jersey: Analytic Press.

Mahler, M.S. (1969) *On Human Symbiosis and the Vicissitudes of Individuation*. London: Hogarth.

McGuire, W. (ed) (1974) *The Freud/Jung Letters*. London: Hogarth and Routledge & Kegan Paul.

Meltzoff, A.N. (1981) 'Imitation, intermodal co-ordination and representation in early infancy.' In G. Butterworth (ed) *Infancy and Epistemology*. London: Harvester Press.

Meltzoff, A.N. and Borton, W. (1979) 'Intermodal matching by neonates.' *Nature 282*, 403–4.

Moore and Meltzoff, A.N. (1978) 'Object permanence, imitation and language development in infancy.' In F.D. Minifier and L.L. Lloyd (eds) *Communicative and Cognitive Abilities: Early Behavioural Assessment*. Baltimore, Md: University Park Press.

Plaut, A.J. (1966) 'Reflections on not being able to imagine.' *Journal of Analytical Psychology 11, 2*, pp.113–132.

Stern, D. (1985) *The Interpersonal World of the Infant*. New York: Basic Books.

Tomkins, S.S. (1962) *Affect, Imagery and Consciousness: Vol I. The Positive Effects*. New York: Springer.

Whitmont, E.C. (1969) *The Symbolic Quest*. New York: Putnams.

Wolff, P.H. (1966) 'The causes, controls and organisation of behaviour in the neonate.' *Psychological Issues 5*, 17.

Zinkin, L. (1974) 'Flexibility in analytic technique.' In *Technique in Jungian Analysis*. Library of Analytical Psychology, Vol 2. London: Karnac.

Zinkin, L. (1986) 'Some thoughts on deintegration.' *Journal of Analytical Psychology 31, 3*, pp.297–305.

CHAPTER SIX

The Hologram as a Model for Analytical Psychology

PART I
Introduction

In the hologram, the whole is contained in each part. Dividing it into two produces not two halves of the whole but two wholes. This remarkable fact, which sounds like a miracle performed by some semi-divine religious figure or fantastic delusion, defying all our commonsense notions of reality, is an invention that all can see, demonstrating an advance in science. Any tiny fragment of the hologram will still reproduce the whole image. This invention may be seen as a clever new toy, a new art form, or as having uses such as protecting the identity of credit cards. But some have taken it as exemplifying a new paradigm in science, a new way of understanding the universe. They believe it to be a model, not only of the physical world but of thought itself, meaning by 'thought' the whole of mental life, memory, emotion, perception, imagination and intuition as well as cognition.

Such claims should not go unnoticed by analytical psychologists. Jung, in his association with Pauli especially, was alive to the developments in physics and quantum mechanics which led to this new paradigm. I think Jung, had he lived to see it, would have been delighted with the hologram, perhaps much as he was by the world clock dreamed by one of his patients. Jung, on the whole, confined himself to using the findings of modern physics as analogies for psychic processes. At the same time he could see that, in dealing with subatomic particles, the physicists were dealing with entities which could not directly be represented, just as ultimately the archetypes could not be represented. At the same time, his hope was that, increasingly, physics and psychology would come closer together and be shown to be, if not proved to be, alternative descriptions of the same reality. Out of many references in his writings, I should like to quote from his 1954 essay 'On the nature of the psyche':

> When the existence of two or more irrepresentables is assumed there is always the possibility – which we tend to overlook – that it may not be a question of two or more factors but of one only. The identity or non-identity of two irrepresentable quantities is something that cannot be proved. If on the basis of its observations psychology assumes the existence of certain irrepresentable psychoid factors, it is doing the same thing in principle as physics does when the physicist constructs an atomic model. (Jung 1954, p.214)

Later he says:

> Since psyche and matter are contained in one and the same world, and moreover are in continuous contact with one another and ultimately rest on irrepresentable transcendental factors, it is not only possible but fairly probable even, that psyche and matter are two different aspects of one and the same thing (Jung 1954, p.215)

In this paper I shall try to give some account of what has come to be called the holographic paradigm (Wilber 1982) presenting, in considerably abbreviated form, the idea of its main proponents, Karl Pribram and David Bohm, which may already be familiar to some readers. The sheer breathtaking sweep of these new ideas should caution us to be careful, critical and scientific. Certainly the ideas generated by the hologram are by no means new: the idea that all is flux, that the world is not many but one, that the microcosm mirrors the macrocosm and the whole world can be seen in a grain of sand. These are similar statements to those made in modern physics. What is new, however, is the claim that a new paradigm is emerging which gives greater explanatory power to the detailed and painstaking observations in that 'hardest' of sciences. This model is replacing the causal-mechanical reductive paradigm of the last few hundred years which has been regarded as 'natural science'. It is this which makes it of importance to Jungians. In making our own judgement of its scientific status, we can review again our own scientific status.

My own belief, which I shall try to convey, is that the hologram provides a new way of clarifying the most confusing and contradictory concepts in Jung's thought, the nature, the nature of the psyche, the self, the collective unconscious, the archetypes and individuation.

I can, in this paper, do little more than indicate some of the possibilities that have occurred to me in the short time that I have been familiar with the holographic paradigm, in understanding and refining these very large concepts, but I would also try to focus on the way I think it might illuminate our ordinary day-to-day working with patients. This is usually called 'analytic work'. I hope it will become clear why I hesitate to use that description.

The hologram

Although its general principles had already been worked out, the invention of the hologram by Dennis Gabor had to await the invention of the laser beam. The laser beam, unlike an ordinary beam of light, is coherent and highly ordered. In the hologram, the beam is directed to an object, say an apple, by way of a half-silvered mirror, part of the beam going directly through the mirror to the apple, the other part being reflected by the mirror. The rays which strike the apple are scattered in all directions and in this process they cross the rest of the laser beam which has been reflected. The highly scattered rays and the deflected coherent rays eventually cross, interfering with each other and thus producing an extremely complicated pattern known as an interference pattern. If this pattern could be looked at it would be quite unintelligible but, if a photograph is taken of it and if this photograph is illuminated by a laser beam, it reproduces or reconstructs the original object. It is this reproduction which seems miraculous. It does not look like a photograph, but has the three-dimensionality of the original object. The apple appears to stand in space, quite separate from the photographic plate, and one can look around it. What one sees is almost indistinguishable from a real apple. In this sense, it is not even an optical illusion, as the eye receives the same information that it would from the apple itself. What is most remarkable and most pertinent to this paper is that, if only half the plate is illuminated, we see, not half an apple but the whole apple; no matter how small the area of the plate we choose, we always see the whole apple. The only qualification to be made is that as we reduce the size of the plate exposed, the image becomes less clear, less distinct, but it always retains its wholeness.

To understand how it is possible for a small part to contain the information of the whole it is helpful to use another analogy. Imagine a pebble thrown into a still pond. A few moments later, a second pebble is thrown in. As the waves of the two pebbles radiate outwards across each other the water is suddenly frozen. Any piece of ice contains the complicated wave patterns made by the two pebbles so that the whole pond, the exact place in which the pebbles fell, and the time interval between them can be read off from this small piece, provided the patterns of crossing curves can be decoded.

The brain, the mind and the universe

Psychology has to address itself to problems which have always been difficult for psychology, of mind and matter as well as of mind and body. A psychology such as analytical psychology assumes the reality of mental events (the psyche) and rejects the purely materialistic description attempted by behaviourism. The psyche is, of course, the proper object of study in psychology, but what we mean by it depends to a large extent on whether we think there is anything which is not psyche, and, if so, what we think it consists of and how it is related to psyche. Most would agree that there is external physical reality and that the brain, though not external to the body, is part of that reality. It seems to me to be important, therefore, to keep abreast of developments in both physics and brain research. These disciplines should act as constraints to our theorising. Some might argue that such matters lie outside our province both as psychologists and as clinicians. The most extreme form of argument used is one that claims that we deal only with the 'inner world'. This begs the question, not only of how we understand the nature of the 'outer world' but of what kind of distinction we are making.

There is, however, a more urgent reason to attend to other disciplines. There needs to be a universal alteration in consciousness such that no discipline pursues its interests in isolation. Both physics and brain research are now acknowledging the reality of mental events. Physics can no longer separate the observer from the observed and it is also noteworthy that Roger Sperry, a leading neuroscientist, now declares himself to be a 'mentalist', having begun as a materialist (Sperry 1983). It is strange though gratifying to a psychologist to see mentalism revived as a respectable scientific concept.

The holographic brain

The idea that the brain may function like a hologram was first advanced by Karl Pribram, who, like Sperry, also began as a staunch behaviourist and only gradually came to accept the primacy of mental life (Pribram 1971). His holographic model has gradually developed, so that it is no longer restricted to an account of the brain in isolation from the world around it, although to begin with it was put forward as an explanation of memory storage. Pribram was interested in the fact that discrete memories survive even after very extensive brain damage; it occurred to him, therefore, that perhaps it was stored not in one small bit of the brain but that, as in a hologram, any bit could store the whole memory. In other words, memory was not like a photograph depending on point-to-point correspondence of image and object through a lens, but holographic; not focused by a lens, but scattered over a wide area in a complex pattern which could be decoded, even if only a small bit of brain survived. Although this idea has not been accepted by all neuroscientists, there has been a good deal of evidence to support it from a number of different laboratories.

The holographic method of sorting memory has now been used in constructing computers, vastly increasing the richness and detail as well as the sheer quantity of memory stored. Holographic storage is thus a special form of information processing, involving complex mathematical operations. Although beginning with memory, Pribram has suggested that all perception or comprehension (prehending) of the outside world is dependent on a 'frequency domain' which, like the ripples in the pond, needs to be decoded. The frequency domain can be regarded as an intermediate zone between the object and the image:

[Object —— Frequency Domain —— Image]

In this formulation the brain is an object, part of the outside world. But physics has reached the stage where it no longer speaks of objects as being outside the observer and Pribram quotes Wigner as making a statement (which might also apply to analytical psychologists) that microphysics studies the relationships between observations, not between observables. Pribram suggested therefore that both images and objects have to be 'read out' of the frequency (like the holographic blur) so that there is a reciprocal relationship between the frequency domain and the image–object domain:

He then takes the further step of suggesting that the frequency domain, in which time and space are collapsed, is both primary and mental. He considers that mind is not emergent from the interaction between the organism and its environment with the brain constructing mental events through its input from the physical world, but that mental events are primary, the pervasive organising principle of the universe, which includes the brain.

The implicate order

David Bohm, a physicist, but also a far-ranging thinker, considers that the findings of quantum mechanics lead to a new order in which the universe as a whole is to be understood, which he calls the implicate order. This idea is not easy to present in an abbreviated form and the interested reader is referred to his *Wholeness and the Implicate Order* (Bohm 1980). I do not think that any Jungian could fail to resonate to Bohm's ideas once he has encountered them.

The hologram for Bohm is only an analogy and he points out that like all analogies it is limited, and that if this were not so it would not be an analogy. The pattern on the holographic plate, which is normally invisible, is only a static record of the movement of light. What is caught is light waves of movement. He states: 'The actuality that is directly recorded is the movement itself in which information about the whole object is dynamically enfolded in each part of space, while this information is then unfolded in the image' (Bohm 1985, p.11). This enfolding and unfolding is regarded by Bohm as the primary reality and this is called the 'holomovement'. Object and image, therefore, result from an unfolding into the explicate order. In this folding and unfolding of the holomovement, there are no absolutely fixed or separate entities, though there are relatively stable and autonomous entities, which are like the vortex, which is a stable form though a result of the movement of a fluid.

As far as parts and wholes are concerned, Bohm always asserts the primacy of wholeness. He emphasizes that both the theory of relativity and quantum mechanics indicate an unbroken wholeness of the universe, that the whole does not simply consist of parts in interaction, but that the whole organises the parts and that the whole is enfolded into the parts. The universe is imagined as a net, as woven together. The network of indivisible quanta can compel us to see an underlying order which is no longer a mechanistic order, in which parts are only externally related, but an order in which everything is interconnected. The connections are not necessarily by local continuity, by communication through time and space or by cause and effect as would be the case in classical physics.

Reductionism, causality and mechanism

Jung's principal concepts, the self, the archetypes, the idea of the collective unconscious and individuation, could not have been incorporated in the causal-mechanistic-reductive framework which Freud tended to use in accordance with his ideas of the requirements of a natural science. In psychoanalytic circles there has been a great deal of divergence between those who wish, in the names of orthodoxy, clarity and precision, to retain this framework and those who have modified it in order to do justice to psychological events. In analytical psychology there has been a similar divergence, and what has come to be known as 'the London School', under the influence of Michael Fordham, has made many modifications in analytical psychology in the direction of psychoanalysis.

As I am trying to show that Jung's anti-reductive and anti-analytical stance can be more fully justified in the light of a scientific paradigm shift, I must at this stage give some attention to Fordham's position, particularly as his approach has been highly influential in my own work. Through his teaching, I have become totally convinced of the value of trying to elucidate in my patients the genesis of their present difficulties in their infantile past, especially in the first year of life. This does not in itself necessitate taking up the extreme position in favour of reductive analysis that Fordham does. In his book *Jungian Psychotherapy* (Fordham 1978), particularly at the beginning of part two, where he sets out his own views, he proposes a very narrow definition of analysis in terms of 'the resolution of anything complex into its simplest elements' (*Oxford English Dictionary*). He goes on to make a very vigorous and forthright statement in support of this basic conceptualisation, suggesting that Jung as well as Freud thinks reductively in arriving at 'a number of primary entities called archetypes' (Fordham 1978, p.57).

He suggests that 'full analysis means, then, that the primary entities have been reached and the patient's psychology explained in terms of them'. He also picks up Jung's observations that the analytical-reductive method should be given up when 'things become monotonous and you begin to get repetition', or 'when mythological or archetypal contents appear' as meaning that Jung thought he had reached a complete analysis at this point. But this account does not seem to me at all what Jung meant. He did not see the archetypes as simple entities and their appearance indicates not that analysis is complete but that a quite different and non-analytic approach would now be fruitful. It seems unfortunate that Fordham is driven to such an extreme position in favour of analysis in order to counter Jung's attacks on it.

Jung strongly opposed reductionism all his life. At first, this can be seen as a reaction, perhaps even an over-reaction, to Freud's 'nothing but' tendencies, but later it developed into a revised view of causality, culminating in the notion of synchronicity. An early statement of his views is to be found in his definition 'reductive' in his work on psychological types:

> Reductive means 'leading back'. I use this term to denote a method of psycho-
> logical interpretation which regards the unconscious product not as a *symbol* but
> *semiotically*, as a *sign* or *symptom* of an underlying process. Accordingly the reduc-
> tive method traces the unconscious product back to its elements, no matter
> whether these be reminiscences of events that actually took place, or elemen-
> tary psychic processes. The reductive method is oriented backwards, in contrast
> to the *constructive* method, whether in the purely historical sense or in the figu-
> rative sense of tracing complex differentiated factors back to something more
> general and more elementary. The interpretive methods of both Freud and Ad-
> ler are reductive, since in both cases there is a reduction to the elementary pro-
> cesses of wishing or striving, which in the last resort are of an infantile or
> psychological nature. Hence the unconscious product necessarily acquires the
> character of an inauthentic expression to which the term 'symbol' is not prop-
> erly applicable. Reduction has a disintegrative effect on the real significance of
> the unconscious product, since this is either traced back to its historical antece-
> dents and thereby annihilated, or integrated once again with the same elemen-
> tary process from which it arose. (Jung 1921, p.459)

There are many difficulties in Jung's opposing reductive to 'prospective or synthetic'. Briefly, the problem is that the 'prospective' suggests final causes which, even though they lie in the future, could still be identified and limited by some kind of analytical process, and 'synthetic' suggests the building up of complex structures from the simpler ones, as in the formation of chemical compounds. Neither does justice to Jung's real intentions, which are towards wholeness and unity, and which imply a *holistic* standpoint as being in true opposition to the analytic one. If we make a division into parts and wholes, then defining the parts leads one also to attempt to find the wholes of which they are part. The difficulty is that if they are defined as clearly as the parts, i.e. with very distinct boundaries, they then appear to be 'entities' or parts themselves and we are still left with an analytical-reductive method (which is what Fordham picks up in Jung). However, Jung deals with this problem by being deliberately vague about the wholes. He suggests that they can never be defined because they can never be fully known. The ambiguity of such notions as the self can never finally be done away with. There is always a conflict in Jung's wish to be conceptually clear when he knows that such clarity was not part of the experience he was describing. For example, all the archetypes (not just the self) are infused with the idea of totality. By this I mean that each demands total allegiance, that everything is understood within its domain. The shadow is total darkness and the *puer* is *aeternus*. Unfortunately, when put into a theory, it looks as though each is a limited concept. Patients who talk of 'the child part of me' or analysts who talk of the 'shadow part of you' are not talking about the archetype. Archetypes cannot be part of us. In a sense we can say that they are within us or we are within them. Nevertheless, in spite of their totality, the archetypal figures can all be arranged, like the gods of Olympus, in a system of conceptual thought and they then become parts of that thought, but in doing so they become rather empty abstractions. Jung was always struggling with this problem, appealing to the reader to ignore contradictions and at the same time attacking theory itself.

This is the point where the hologram helps. The *discrete* memory is spread all over the brain. Though the memory appears to be a limited thing it cannot be localized. Most of the brain has to be destroyed (and the animal killed) before this one little memory can be erased. The memory is therefore both small and infinitely large, both limited and total. If we think of the human psyche in this way, how can it be analysed? I raise this question here somewhat rhetorically, but I will consider some tentative practical answers in Part II.

What is at stake here is the very existence of discrete entities and we can be helped by Bohm's conclusion as a physicist that they do not exist in any absolute sense.

Wholeness and individuation

The fundamental difference between Freud and Jung might be expressed by saying that Freud believed in the absolute existence of individual entities while Jung did not. Freud worked on the level of the organism as a discrete individual entity each with its own mind, its own unconscious, which was a part of its mind (comparing it on one occasion to an abscess to be drained), each therefore having a clearly defined boundary which separated an inside from an outside. Much of the psychoanalytic literature (e.g. Winnicott's notion of unit status; Winnicott 1931) implies that an important stage of development is reached when the individual *realizes* that this is the case. In psychoanalysis, even the word 'individuation' has been appropriated to mean just this and it has been coupled with separation in Mahler's use of the term individuation-separation (Mahler 1963). One even has the impression that being separate, having an inside and an outside, is the summit of mature development.

For Jung, on the other hand, individuation is always described paradoxically. Wholeness is its unattainable goal (Jung 1954). This suggests that everyone is always incomplete. Many patients do complain of feeling incomplete and by this they do not necessarily mean fragmented, 'in bits', but that they feel like a part-person. Sometimes this is expressed as an internal defect, or as being empty inside, but often it is a sense of being not all there, a common colloquial expression for madness. Usually this symptom is found in people who do feel themselves to be separate and in fact very often complain of being too separate, cut off, isolated and alone.

Now Jung always took a positive view of the most distressing symptoms and my understanding of individuation is that he regarded this state of incompleteness as having value in leading to growth – not just growth in the sense of getting bigger, a concept which Hillman attacks in his criticism of the desirability of growth (Hillman 1975). In other words, the absence of the sense of incompleteness could be pathological, just as any kind of self-satisfaction or contentment can be pathological.

Individuation, though a noun, refers to movement – a movement towards a goal which is never reached and never can be reached. If Bohm is right, movement is primary and the appearance of forms as they emerge from the movement is secondary, objects or images never being entirely autonomous but only relatively so. They appear only in so far as they unfold and the process of unfolding or explication constitutes the explicate order. It would be better understood if the movement of the psyche in individuation is taken as primary, not the structures such as the archetypes, the ego and the self or the unconscious, which are only comparatively stable and autonomous forms. There has been a good deal of criticism of our tendency to hypostasize, of treating psychic events as things. Rycroft, I think, reveals some misunderstanding of Jung when, in reviewing the Tavistock Lectures, he attacks him, admittedly alongside Freud, for this hypostasizing tendency (Rycroft 1985). The very ambiguity and self-contradiction we have struggled with in the self results from Jung's never seeing it as a fixed entity with a constant boundary and definite size or as having an inside and an outside. Bohm often gives the example of the vortex, or the ripple in the water, as an analogy for this kind of relatively stable entity which is indivisible. The water is in the vortex and the vortex is in the water. Perhaps like the vortex the self unfolds, and is then folded back, which is the holomovement which is primary. Jung was using a very similar analogy when he spoke of consciousness as arising like an island from the sea of the unconscious.

PART II

In Part I, I introduced Bohm's notion of the holomovement and suggested that in our theoretical writings the movement or activity of individuation might be regarded as primary and the entities of the self, ego and the unconscious as secondary structures, which have only a relative autonomy and stability. Now I should like to apply the same model to the analytic procedure, and to suggest that in this, too, movement is primary, and that various entities which can be distinguished are secondary. Such entities include states of mind, insights, transference and countertransference phenomena, dreams, sessions, and 'objects' whether inner or outer, and also images and phantasies, whether archetypal or personal. They unfold and become enfolded again, appear, disappear and reappear and have certain varying degrees of autonomy and stability in the explicate order.

I know that I have taken a series of nouns which apply to different areas of discourse and varying levels of abstraction. I acknowledge freely the need to distinguish, separate and order these areas and levels when we try to think about them. Though it may be useful to talk *as though* we are dealing with separate entities, they may in reality not be separate but indivisible, like the vortex, not having a separate existence from the fluid in which it arises. It is particularly when dealing with rival systems, each claiming to be more useful than others, that we need to consider whether there is some underlying order to which we can turn. Science has always relied on there being such an order, but its appeal to objective fact in a world 'out there', independent of the observer, is useful only up to a point.

Bohm posits a more fundamental order, the implicate or enfolded order, to account for phenomena, particularly those involving subatomic particles, where these assumptions no longer hold. In Bohm's vision of an unfolding and enfolding universe, everything is connected with everything else to form one indivisible whole. Such interconnections do not depend on local proximity in time or space. It has been shown that the behaviour of one particle can be predicted from the behaviour of another, without there being any possibility that one particle is *causing* the behaviour of the other. Such causation would have to depend on communication and such communication, if it occurred, would have to be faster than the speed of light, which so far as we know is not possible. In other words everything is interconnected through an acausal principle, just as Jung proposed in his notion of synchronicity. Jung of course worked very closely with another distinguished physicist, Wolfgang Pauli, in elaborating this idea. The hologram helps us to understand that interconnections are not simply between events but that every apparent part enfolds the whole.

Although I shall continue to refer, for at least the rest of this paper, to analytical psychology, the analyst, the analysis and the analytic procedure, this is now for want of better words. Although we may at times analyse in the sense of reducing complex phenomena to simple elements, this now seems to be a subsidiary procedure, a small part and not the most important part of what goes on in the analytic process. More importantly, analyst and patient are together assuming everything is interconnected. They are establishing connections between astronomically separate events and trying to agree on what are true rather than false connections. If archetypal images, for example, emerge from this process, these images are *not* simple discrete primary elements but are rather wholes of parts which unfold and become enfolded again.

A personal experience

As I was writing this paper and reached this point, sitting on a beach, I looked up to watch some windsurfers on the water. Previously I had noticed them with a certain contempt, not only for the beginners who kept falling in the water and then began laboriously hauling their craft upright again only to collapse once more, but also for the experts whizzing backwards and forwards, rather pointlessly, as it seemed to me, showing off their skill. I expect I had been quite envious and cut off from them all. Now I suddenly saw them in a new way. They were no longer competing with each other for one thing. There now seemed to be a gradual transition from the beginners close to the beach, to the experts far out at sea and I marvelled at the effort and struggle, not simply to master nature but to become part of it in graceful harmony with the wind and the sea. Moreover, I too was in the scene, I was no longer a voyeur but a participant, sitting in a chair writing this paper (another kind of struggle). I was at one with them and with everybody else. I could encompass the whole beautiful seascape which encompassed me. This feeling of being at one with what lay outside me was a way of feeling whole while being part of a greater whole. I could acknowledge now my own inability to windsurf without minding. I knew this was not 'manic denial' although no act of mourning had taken place. Nor do I think I had overcome my persecutory anxiety by making an act of reparation arising from my phantasied attack on the envied objects. I was simply aware of one harmonious world to which they and I both belonged. We did remain differentiated so I did not 'fuse' with my objects.

Such a state is not easy to maintain and it was not easy for me to maintain it when, the next morning, I found my car window smashed in by vandals, though I did with some effort just manage to include them in my unified world. I do not think any reductive interpretation is possible that would account for this (not so very unusual) situation. It requires a model of interconnectedness, much as is provided by the holographic paradigm, the brain acting as a whole perceiving and also creating the reality of the universe as a whole, even if it was just one brain and just one beach. At such moments it does not matter if the self has a small or large 'S'. It really simultaneously needs both.

On reflecting on this experience, I began to make new sense of Jung's writings on individuation. My sense of balance and harmony, my state of mind, while it made me feel more whole was also clearly not just something inside me. I was simultaneously becoming more of a part, a tiny part, of a much greater whole, which perhaps partly because of my internal preoccupations while writing, I quite suddenly became connected with. This could be synchronicity, which I had previously regarded as a somewhat rare event, mostly experienced by other people. It was the realisation that, in the outer world, there already existed the wholeness I was seeking in my thinking and that had included me. The next step, unfortunately, was to realize that though my hatred and envy had been replaced by love and benignity, when I discovered next day that my car had been vandalized I realized that I was part of this world too, part of the world which contained hatred and envy. It would not have been right for my analyst to have interpreted this as my projection and to have disregarded my protests that it really happened *to* me, but I did need to incorporate this 'shadow'. My own rage could be overcome only by seeing myself as part of a yet greater whole (seeing myself as an invader in a territory which was not mine, and that this was part of being a tourist) and seeing that my 'whole' was only a part.

Thus, although it is true to call individuation the search for wholeness, it would be no less accurate to call it the search for partness. This, though, enabled me to see more clearly why it is that illness, mutilation and death and even blindness (one of my personal fears) could be individuating, to see more clearly how the blind can be miraculously cured and see again – more clearly. Of course I could still see that they might not be individuating, but then so might feelings of wholeness not be. What was essential to individuating was seeing both partness and wholeness together.

Time and space in analysis

Time. Analysis usually goes on for years and is divided into so many sessions per week, each session customarily lasting for fifty minutes (though personally I prefer regular forty-five minute sessions with occasional ninety-minute sessions on special occasions). Of course, these sessions are much smaller than the periods of time in between, as some patients are inclined to point out. Nevertheless, it is customary to regard analysis as though it were part of a continuous process, in which weekends and holidays are called 'breaks'. The sessions themselves, perhaps like quanta, are indivisible, not to be broken, even by the telephone.

Space. Analysis takes place in a room, the patient usually being confined to the territory of the chair or couch and the analyst to a chair. There may or may not be other objects of interest in the room and there is also another room, the waiting room, which is not just for waiting but serves as a transition to and from the world outside. Often an illusion is created that no other patient uses either room, although the analyst, if challenged, will readily acknowledge that this is not really the case. There are also toilet facilities, which have their own functions but are also excellent grist for the analytic mill. All this is a part of what is called the 'setting' and is usually referred to by both the analyst and patient as 'here' to distinguish from the world out 'there'.

Roughly the setting and the session are referred to respectively as the 'here' and 'now'.

These facts are very well known, but perhaps we are not always aware of the extent of the contradiction created by the seemingly arbitrary boundaries we impose, while at the same time we try to help our patients to be less fragmented, more whole. Of course, there are many ways in which analysts justify these arrangements. They are often presented as not at all arbitrary and convenient but as intrinsically meaningful, analogous to feeds, for example, or to the baby leaving and returning to the mother's womb. Although these analogies may indeed be useful, we are making use of arbitrary elements in the same way that elements of a language may be arbitrary and conventional and acquire significance only in their combination, as Saussure has shown (Saussure 1915). We should be aware that, in a sense, we can never satisfy the needs of our patients and that, at least to some extent, we are really asking them to accept our arrangements as simply arbitrary and conventional. The patients are always complaining about this and I will here quote just one patient who, after ten minutes' silence, explained that he was not going to start the session as I would end it only at a prescribed time. It did not seem to me very helpful to point out that he had already started it and indeed that the session had actually started ten minutes previously. This could clearly only make matters worse.

We would not persist with these arrangements if we did not know that each session can be a whole and that even in one moment everything can be experienced. It is the hologram which gives a solid theoretical base to this knowledge. We find, over and over again, that quite a small part which seems like a fragment can be illuminated to reveal the whole. It may be said that such thoughts are by no means new; the alchemists, for instance, perhaps thought in the same way about what went on in their retorts (the alembic container), to take an analogy often used for the analyst's setting. Bohm expresses this idea by regarding mind as a subtler form of matter than body. The 'session-setting' then, is more than a container or *temenos* like the alchemist's retort or the mother's arms holding the infant. These contain what is inside them, but just one session in its familiar setting can be also the whole analysis, the whole patient and analyst and the whole world and the whole of time.

A quotation fromWilliam James is apposite here:

In the pulse of inner life immediately present now in each of us is a little past, a little future, a little awareness of our own body, of each other's persons, of these sublimities we are trying to talk about, of the earth's geography and the direction of history, of truth and error, of good and bad and of who knows how much more? (James 1902)

Patients who crave instant satisfaction may know this. They crave, not instinctual gratification as such, but this experience of wholeness which they know is possible but which they do not always know how to bring about. It seems that energy is required to achieve this, such as is provided by the laser beam for the holograph.

The session-setting is a time-unit, but the holographic paradigm enables us to see that we should not consider the analysis simply as a string of such units. Nor need we think of every session as being different or as part of a jigsaw puzzle which can gradually be put together. Each one gives a picture of the whole. Session 75 may give a clearer picture of the whole than session 203, but it is the whole as shown by any session which we are interested in.

The analogy I am making is not simply that between the session-setting and the holographic apparatus, but includes the human beings making and using the apparatus. Despite the emphasis on sharpness, clarity and the detail, there is no lens as there is in the telescope or the microscope. Such lenses, though they facilitated enormous advances in science, rely on a point-to-point correspondence of object and image whereas the hologram captures the holomovement.

The importance of detail

In my description of myself and the windsurfers, I made the point that the whole was differentiated. Though feeling part of the whole, I did not lose myself. I did not, for example, have omnipotent phantasies that I was a windsurfer myself. Thus the differentiation of the elements was clear. I have mentioned also that if only a small part of the holographic plate is illuminated, it is, though whole, not very clear. This fact goes against our usual assumption that to see more detail the field has to be a restricted one. That assumption is derived from our experience of the lens and does not apply to the hologram. In fact there may have been vandals among the windsurfers, but this perception could have come not by scrutinizing the windsurfers one by one but by including my knowledge of vandals in my perception of the windsurfers. It is true that, once this knowledge exists, it would be possible to do a statistical analysis, to discover that, say, 0.5 per cent of windsurfers are vandals. But this is beside the point. In fact, I would have come to the wrong conclusion if it so happened that none of these windsurfers were actually vandals.

Vandalism needs to be added to the concept of 'windsurfer' in the sense that we are all vandals whether we vandalize or not. This is the essence of the individuation concept as exemplified by the idea of the archetypal shadow rather than the personal repressed one. (This is recognized in the Jewish Day of Atonement, where a congregation collectively acknowledges a list of sins collectively committed regardless of whether or not any particular individual has actually committed a particular sin.)

This brings to mind a common problem in 'analysis'. Patients, in their need to be understood holistically, often reject detail. They fear that attention to detail would detract from what they want to express, whether in reporting a dream or a phantasy about the analyst or recalling some past event. The analyst, wishing to clarify or illuminate the 'material' (whatever is reported as material for analysis) starts to analyse; the patient gets angry or distressed and the analyst analyses further. By now he is drawn into analysing not the patient's dream or whatever, but the patient's distress. Jung actually advocated, in working on dreams, a non-analytic attention to detail. 'What colour was the table?', 'Who did that man look like?', 'What sort of knife was he holding?' This helps to build up a picture which is a more whole and detailed one of the dream. The analyst, when he does make an interpretation, is thus paying attention to a detailed whole. Though Jung was speaking of dreams, this does not apply only to dreams.

A good deal of the analyst's interpretative activity is non-analytic. Instead of looking for elements, the analyst is often making analogous links. The remark, 'That reminds me of what you once told me about what your father did when you were five', clearly does not reduce the patient's material. It can usefully be compared with the deflected laser beam which interpenetrates the direct beam in a hologram. The analyst has recognized a pattern he has seen before and adds to it. There is no limit to the number of times he may do this as the same pattern recurs in different forms as the hologram takes shape.

Gendlin's focusing and concentrating techniques in analysis

The enquiry by the analyst into detail, as described in the last section, contrasts with Freud's ideal of the patient's free association and the analyst's evenly hovering attention. It interferes with the examination of the material which the patient produces in his own way. Both analyst and patient may concentrate, rather than suspend conscious control, though perhaps the concentration is more akin to that used in meditation techniques than to that required, for example, in playing chess. It is as though a concentrated, coherent beam is used to bring out the image or object from the holographic blur.

Gendlin, though trained in the classical psychoanalytic method, has described an elaborate technique which he calls 'focusing'. He believes that this is a powerful technical tool for producing changes. Focusing is a way of helping the patient to do what is often loosely called 'getting in touch with feelings', particularly bodily feelings, often missed if the patient is allowed to free-associate as he follows Freud's basic rule. He is helped to experience what Gendlin calls the 'felt sense' of an experience rather than a feeling because it has a precise content. This method is described in a number of papers, but is conveniently presented in popular form in his book *Focusing* (Gendlin 1981). The holographic implications of his work are well discussed by John Welwood in his contribution to *The Holographic Paradigm* (Welwood 1982). I am drawing attention to it here because, as with most of the newer forms of therapy, its basic principles were understood by Jung in his approach to individuation.

Transference and countertransference in the here and now

Whatever the material brought up by the patient, one important aspect is its function as an expression of the relationship between the patient and the analyst. Many analysts regard this as the most important aspect and some consider that only interpretations which bring this in are effective in producing change. See for example among the psychoanalytical literature Strachey's influential paper with its concept of the 'mutative interpretation' (Strachey 1934).

Here again, analysis will analyse and identify elements so that the relationship is divided into two and called transference and countertransference.

This, like all such analyses, is useful, but only up to a point. The relationship between the two partners in the dyad is complex, and the suggestion that transference and countertransference are two distinct entities is not easy to sustain. Not only are their boundaries indistinct, but it is never possible satisfactorily to understand one without the other. Again, these entities become further classified and sub-divided: negative and positive, syntonic and neurotic, concordant and complementary and so on. Like Jung's typology, these divisions have their uses, but at the same time they do not conform to the richness of the actual experience. Jung's writings on the transference, unlike his work on psychological types, relies less on classification and dissection and more on the use of alchemical analogue.

Although we freely recognize the subjective feeling of being fused with and mixed up with the patient as Jung has described, we tend to assume that this is due either to a kind of failure or to phantasy, and that in reality it is to be taken for granted that there are actually at all times two separate individuals in the room. A holographic revision would question both the sharp division between phantasy and reality and that between the two partners in the analytic enterprise. In fact the word 'partner' means a sharer even though it implies parts. The sharing emphasizes the whole of which a partner holds a part, but the holographic paradigm makes it clear that each partner holds not just a part, but the whole because each part contains the whole.

Since there are no objective events that can be observed outside, no independent 'observables', the relationship (following Wigner – see Part I) is not between the observables, but between the observations. Thus, all material has to be understood within the totality of the analyst–patient pair. If the patient is talking about her husband, for example, the husband that is spoken about is not to be understood simply as an object outside, but as one that is experienced by both analyst and patient in their relationship with each other. It is true that each may have a different view, but a proper description would be of a holographic image which both partners could look at from various directions so that different viewpoints would be recognized as being of the same object. This process again is not analysis.

Infantile roots of the analytic relationship

In the above account of the analytic relationship, I have tried to present it not as an interaction between two individuals who, like machine parts, are externally interrelated, but have emphasized their intrinsic and internal connections with each other. This forms a kind of interpretation which creates something like the interference pattern of the hologram.

The inadequate and sometimes misleading interacting-entity model is often projected backwards by the analyst, who wishes to reconstruct infancy, to the mother–infant pair. In doing so, it is often assumed that so-called fusion is always a phantasy or even always an illusion which may be shared by mother and baby. Although this *may* be the case, it should not be assumed that it must always be so. Fusion need not be *confusion*. A sense of being simultaneously one *and* two rather than one *or* two is, in my view, the normal and usual state of affairs, not only for the mother but also for the newborn baby. I cannot here go into the evidence to support this belief, but my purpose is served if the holographic model shows that it is possible.

It has been suggested by Merleau-Ponty (following Wallon's description of infantile development) that one of the earliest sources of distress is a sense of incompleteness when the mother goes away before the baby can distinguish the mother as separate (Merleau-Ponty 1964). The incompleteness gives a sense of 'partness'. But there is a distinction between the partness which all babies experience and that experienced by the kind of separation brought about by mothers who, for example, put their babies out of earshot. In many cultures the mother never 'parts' from her baby, and in all cultures the sensitive mother recognizes that she and her baby are true 'partners' who are never really 'apart'. Both recognize that though each is part of the other, each is also whole while being a part of the greater whole. In other words a holographic model, while retaining the importance of connecting the analytic relationship to that of the mother and baby, sees holographically the mother–baby relationship also. Again, the greater detail I have mentioned can be seen to be present in infancy. The mother's smell, the details of the mother's handling, of her face and in the way she talks, all help the baby to feel complete in her presence without being confused about what belongs to him and what to her. There is no need to imagine, under normal conditions, that the baby over-identifies or too sharply divides the two individuals, as both participate in the holographic-like pattern which involves them both.

Conclusions

There can be no easy or definitive conclusion to be drawn from all these reflections. I hope rather that the hologram will have emerged for the reader, as at least an invention that can help to break old habits of thought. I am not wishing to suggest that any Jungian actually thinks in an exclusively reductive or deterministic way. No reading of Jung could possibly justify that. On the other hand, the task of developing Jung's attempt to provide an alternative paradigm, which reached its highest point in his remarkable essay on synchronicity, is a daunting one (Jung 1952). Jung hoped that one day it would be possible to integrate his psychology with physics just as Freud hoped to integrate his with biology. Perhaps this dream can never come true. The biggest obstacle is the sheer difficulty of understanding what the physicists are talking about. Not only is their science rapidly developing, but they themselves are struggling to grasp all the implications of their own discoveries when they conflict with our existing view of the world, and they by no means agree among themselves about these implications. The least that analytical psychologists can do is to try to communicate with each other when they think they have got hold of something which grips their imagination or which provokes them to think freshly about what they do. This I have endeavoured to do, in my own way, with the hologram. Simply having it as an image hovering around sometimes in the back, and sometimes in the front, of my mind has given me a new way of looking at old problems. Perhaps there are others for whom it will do the same.

References

Bohm, D. (1980) *Wholeness and the Implicate Order*. London: Routledge and Kegan Paul.

Bohm, D. (1985) *Unfolding Meaning*. Mickleton, Glos: Foundation House Publications.

Fordham, M. (1978) *Jungian Psychotherapy*. Chichester: John Wiley.

Gendlin, E.T. (1981) *Focusing*. London: Bantam Books.

Hillman, J. (1975) *Loose Ends*. Dallas: Spring Publications.

James, W. (1902) *Varieties of Religious Experience*. London: Fontana Books.

Jung, C.G. (1921) 'Psychological types.' *Collected Works 6*.

Jung, C.G. (1952) 'Synchronicity: an acausal connecting principle.' *Collected Works 8*.

Jung, C.G. (1954) 'On the nature of the psyche.' *Collected Works 8*.

Mahler, M. (1963) 'Thoughts about development and individuation.' In *The Psychoanalytic Study of the Child*. New York: International Universities Press.

Merleau-Ponty, M. (1964) *The Primacy of Perception*. Evanstown: North-Western University Press.

Pribram, K. (1971) *Languages of the Brain*. New Jersey: Prentice Hall.

Rycroft, C. (1985) *Psychoanalysis and Beyond*. London: Chatto and Windus.

Saussure, F. de (1915) *Course in General Linguistics*. London: Fontana Books.

Sperry, R. (1983) *Science and Moral Priority*. Oxford: Blackwell.

Strachey, J. (1934) 'The nature of the therapeutic action.' *International Journal of Psycho-Analysis 15*, 1.

Welwood, J. (1982) 'The holographic paradigm and the structure of experience.' (ed K. Wilber) in *The Holographic Paradigm and other Paradoxes*. London: Shambala.

Wilber, K. (ed) (1982) *The Holographic Paradigm and other Paradoxes*. London: Shambala.

Winnicott, D.W. (1931) 'A note on normality and anxiety.' In *Collected Papers*. London: Tavistock Publications, 1958.

CHAPTER SEVEN

Correspondence Between Louis Zinkin and Michael Fordham

After hearing Zinkin's paper on the hologram, Michael Fordham wrote to take issue with him over references to his own work, and so initiated the following exchange of letters clarifying their respective positions on the origins of the self and other theoretical points. Fordham had been Zinkin's supervisor during his training and his mentor thereafter. Fordham had hoped at one time that Zinkin, because of his long experience in child psychiatry, would be an active participant in the Children's Section which Fordham had set up in the Society of Analytical Psychology, but Zinkin's interests were moving by then in another direction. These letters demonstrate the ongoing respect these two men had for each other in spite of some divergence of their paths.

✠ ✠ ✠

Jordans, 8.1.87

Dear Louis

I want to try and express something about your papers which I find tantalizing. You seem to be expressing your debt to me and then start sniping or misrepresenting my views. James Astor has corrected you in the *Journal* and I am not sure whether I should not write there too. I prefer to write to you first.

I dislike it when you say, on the subject of analytic reduction, that I am launching an attack on Jung. That was not at all my aim and it is very doubtful whether Jung would have agreed or no. His *Problems of Modern Psychotherapy* suggests that he would have agreed. I intended to define analysis in this way in order to give the word a meaning that is comprehensible and has practical application. Today it has lost its meaning almost entirely. Analysis itself may be considered in relation to reduction so long as it is not confused with reductionism. Analysis well used does not 'reduce', i.e. it is not reductionist, and can more often enrich the personality by bringing to light aspects which have been split off and repressed or otherwise made inaccessible and so damaging self representations.

I do think that when you introduce a new word, i.e. 'hologram', you should say why and relate it to Jung's self, with which as far as I can see it is identical. I recognize that you may want to annihilate Jung's terminology because you cannot conceive of a self without a sense of 'I' or 'myself', but Jung persistently denies that his 'self' is that and he regularly distinguishes the ego from the self. It is psychoanalysts who do not do so and proceed as you do. I was quite horrified at the symposium on the self in the *Journal* to see how far our members had departed from Jung in that respect.

Coming to your recent and beautiful paper, I wondered whether you understood that your personal example was a beautiful example, taken from your own experience, of a deintegrate leading you to a simple and convincing experience of the self in Jung's sense.

I don't want to discuss your good discussion of psychotherapeutic procedures. It is very close to what I have been teaching for years but evidently not writing up adequately.

In summary, I think we can agree on most matters, though you evidently disagree with my Jungian notation.

I don't know whether these brief remarks will be of any use but there they are.

Yours

Michael Fordham

✠ ✠ ✠

15th January 1987

Dear Michael

Many thanks for your letter. First let me repeat that whatever criticisms I may have expressed of your views, I do feel a great debt to you principally because of your supervision while I was training (which has remained introjected) and also through what I regard as your pretty radical revision of Jung's theories.

What you call 'sniping' is meant to be a reasoned argument in which I am trying to say not that you are attacking Jung but that you are defending a position on reductive analysis which Jung himself attacked. It may only be from time to time but it does look to me that this leads you to a too narrow formulation of the analytic process. Perhaps the difficulty is, as you say, that the word has almost lost its meaning and it is then that we need to try to be more exact. When you go on to make a distinction between reductive and reductionist and suggest that analysis can be reductive without 'reducing' in well used analysis, you are into the very area of paradox which I have tried to address. I have tried to overcome Jung's opposition of reductive and synthetic (and both processes occur in a well conducted analysis) by using a paradigm in which the conflict disappears. I tried to show that this is not just 'mystical' but 'scientific'.

I am of course familiar with your very healthy objection to the introduction of new words when old ones will do. But by no means did I want to substitute the hologram for the Self. It was simply meant to be a model to help us to think about the Self as well as the analytic process or individuation. I was also intrigued at your horrified response to recent writings by members on the self. I had not anticipated that you would have such misgivings at our departure from Jung in the direction of psychoanalysis. I see what you mean and am still struggling with this question, particularly with trying to find a bridge between Kohut's ideas and our own.

I was also most interested in your description of my personal experience as a deintegrate leading to an experience of the self. I hadn't quite thought of it in this way. I suppose I would have said it was an integration. You see the deintegration as *leading* to an integration. In the actual experience these are not distinguished even though retrospectively I can analyse it in the way you do. In fact the notion of 'leading to' assumes a time sequence which may belong more to our thinking than to the reality we are trying to think about.

As you know I have great difficulty with your idea of the original self and your equally strong insistence on the idea of the infant being an individual from the start. I certainly agree with the latter but I still can't see how there can at the same time be an original self except in the sense that the baby experiences his own individuality (as opposed to say the mother experiencing it) which does not seem to be what you mean. I have tried to answer James Astor's remarks in a letter to the *Journal* which hasn't for some reason been published but which I now enclose. Have you read Daniel Stern's book on *The Interpersonal World of the Infant*? It's the best account I know of the findings of infant research in helping us get an idea of the infant's subjective experiences and I particularly like his notions of an 'emergent self' in the first three months. All this needs a lot of further discussion. I haven't yet read your own latest book on the subject but I hope to soon.

Finally I would like to say how much I appreciate your thoughtful comments on my papers. I doubt if we are fundamentally in much disagreement in these difficult areas. I am sorry that it is hard for both of us to join in face to face discussions nowadays as it might help to clarify this very question.

Please give my warmest regards to Frieda.

Yours

Louis

✠ ✠ ✠

23.1.87

Dear Louis

It is true that it is geographically difficult to meet face to face, but it gives me much pleasure that we can correspond.

Your second paragraph: we are I think in agreement. I have a way of deliberate overstatement. For instance in a paper which will be published in a book in the States, I wrote that to me reduction is beautiful. Such overstatements are intended. Of course, I know that the kind of depreciation of valuable elements in the self is deplorable and I believe that is what Jung was objecting to. All the same 'my definition' is not mine really – it is one which both Freud and Jung were wrestling with.

I hesitate before your last sentence because I would want to consider whether the mystics were not scientific. Were they not experimenting with religious experience. Is that unscientific?

Your third paragraph: my own experience with Kohut may interest you. I was invited to take part in a symposium on the self in San Francisco. The other discussants were one of Kohut's pupils, an existentialist and a Marxist. I knew nothing of Kohut so I bought *The Analysis of the Self*. It was not too bad, I thought, and I listened with some admiration to (I think it was Bernstein's) exposition. It was enormously enthusiastic and lucid. After that experience I started on *The Restoration of the Self* and soon returned it to my bookshelf. I thought, 'This man knows nothing of how to contain a negative transference. I can't be bothered with him' – another of my exaggerated responses you may say. But Kernberg I believe is more on the right track because he includes the destructive element.

I can I think clear away one difficulty about the primary self. It was an idea that grew up as a *hypothesis* derived from a number of data I accumulated and collected in *The Origins of the Ego*. I do not class that as a logical necessity. What results from logic is as follows: if you start from self contained closed system, something must happen to it since an infant clearly relates to its mother, i.e. it must deintegrate. I refrained at first from trying to date the existence of the primary unit and still do, but it must exist before birth. I made some notes about this which may help.

I would like to know what you think about it.

Yours

Michael Fordham

Notes enclosed with this letter

All these researches show that a foetus is by no means a passive agent but, like other human beings, interacts with his environment. There remains the subject of the effect of his mother's nervous and emotional states on him. These have often been doubted but mothers have proved right and paediatricians and obstetricians wrong. The effect of how a mother feels about her pregnancy and the baby inside her is often decisively important and, whilst short-term crises may not be damaging to the infant's development, long-term disorders in a mother's emotional life can produce lasting change.

Considering the accumulation of data it would now seem wrong to assert, as has been widely done and still is in many quarters, that a foetus has no mental life and so no ego even in the later part of gestation, say after five months when his brain is fully formed. Even before this it would be daring to assert that there are no physical elements from which mental life will emerge.[1] These are presupposed in theories of the self and its archetypes, which Jung already conceived as having a psychoid pole. I see no reason to suppose that mental and emotional functioning has not its structural potential from very early on and even in the genetic code.

A foetus engages in many activities which are responses to stimuli from outside and inside the mother's body, and amongst them some involve hearing. Indeed there is reason to believe that hearing is quite well developed. Music for instance can have a definable effect which is unlikely to be a simple reflex response. Mozart is soothing and foetal movement diminishes, whilst the loud music of the romantic composers, and even Beethoven, increases some foetal activity. If we assume that, for a sense organ to develop, stimulus to it is required, it is less surprising that hearing can mature: the uterine cavity is a noisy place with the pumping of the aorta, which sounds like an old-fashioned steam engine, and the mother's intestinal movements – the borborygmi are not silent. It is more surprising how sight, though less developed than hearing, is present at birth. Indeed an infant can see quite well up to a distance of eight inches, certainly after four days. The uterus is not absolutely dark, however, and it is known that a strong light can penetrate the abdominal wall and the uterus. If a strong light be shone onto a mother's abdomen, the foetus will turn away from it. Thus, if we include the

1   Handwritten marginal note: 'add re opening up of thought about foetal life' (eds)

proprioceptive, kinaesthetic, and touch, i.e. hot and cold and pain, all the sensory equipment of the foetus has reached a considerable development at birth.

As to the motor functions, arm and leg activity is felt by all mothers, though they will not know that spiral movement takes place, designed to increase the comfort of the foetus as growth makes the uterine cavity an increasingly restrictive place. Besides all these, there are a group of activities which would seem to prepare the foetus for extrauterine life: he sucks his thumb, ingests amniotic fluid and performs 'breathing exercises'. Thus disturbances of the unitary state occur whether they be initiated by sensory input or by discharges from within the organism.

As for the states of consciousness the foetus achieves, on the basis of infant observations I speculate that the baby is neither awake nor asleep for much of the time. That suggests that the two states have to be discovered or differentiated as a result of deintegration. The evidence from electroencephalographic studies shows, however, that REM sleep takes place, which suggests dreaming, as well as NREM waves (quiet sleep in later life). Whether the capacity to 'learn' by being conditioned, which has been shown to occur, requires consciousness is uncertain.

✠ ✠ ✠

In utero the primary unit is the fertilized ovum containing the genetic code (DNA). Given a good enough environment that code controls the development of the organism without disrupting it as a whole – in that respect the unfolding may be compared with deintegration with adjustments to integration, the main difference being that physical development cannot be reversed. Though we cannot tell whether anything like a mind attaches to early states of the embryo, it can be speculated that a rudimentary element, a protomind, is present in the genetic code or possibly pervades its chemistry.

A body develops interrelated structures, just as we find a mind doing later on. So it would be daring to assume, as is frequently done, that body parts have nothing protomental about them or that a new born infant has no mind nor sense of himself distinct from his mother (cf. Stein). All along he has been distinct from her, a separate unit in utero. He has, however, been in constant communication with her, at first through the cell membranes and later through the placenta, especially in that it transmits hormonal and other messages, also through the amniotic fluid and finally, when development has proceeded far enough, through sensory perception and motor action. The mother's primary function is, however, to protect the foetus and provide the raw material for growth. Given that provision the genetic code can initiate and monitor the form of the developing foetus.

In the past a number of assumptions have dominated and interfered with the study of infant life and infancy as a whole. One of them was that an infant's capacity for perception was virtually absent. That idea has now been refuted.

✠ ✠ ✠

1st February 1987

Dear Michael

I am delighted to continue our discussion by correspondence. I am beginning to see more clearly how our differences arise. They are beginning to seem more differences of emphasis than of fundamentals. I'm sure that I too may sometimes overstate my case, not always deliberately but through overenthusiasm.

First, let me comment on your view on Kohut. He does write in a rather tedious and inflated manner, certainly compared to Kernberg. On the other hand, I find what he has to say more congenial than Kernberg's adaptation of the British Object Relations theory. His most important contribution is, I believe, his use of the term self-object. This gets us away from the over-rigid distinction between self and object and their representations. I also like his description of the idealising and the mirror transferences and the way he sees these states as requiring careful nurturing rather than premature (and often insensitive and unempathic) interpreting in the narcissistic personality disorders. I find useful, also, his idea of the separate and simultaneous development of the ego and the drives and the development of the self with its own drive and stages. Having said that, I often find myself on Kernberg's side (and yours) at his neglect of the negative transference. He must have been aware of the intense underlying hostility and the often sadistic intent of these sort of patients, who can make our lives such a misery, but he does not bring this out much (though there is a good paper in his collected papers on 'narcissistic rage'). But I do think that 'self-psychology' comes near to our ideas of the self. Most analytical psychologists seem to feel that we must insist that Jung's use of the term is fundamentally different, which is, I think, your own position. Anyway I do think *The Restoration of the Self* might be worth a second glance.

What I am beginning to realize about your 'original self' is that it is indeed a useful hypothesis as you use it within a particular framework, i.e. it works well if we think of development as a linear chain (as suggested in the idea of developmental lines). This would be something original like: original self – deintegration – reintegration – self – further deintegration, etc. This way of thinking has a good deal of explanatory power and is useful clinically as long as we think of analysis as progressing in a time sequence and as long as we are remaining in the position of an objective observer of the patient. In your own writings I think you use this particular framework. Although you stress the need for the analyst to make full use of the syntonic elements in his countertransference, this is only after it has been processed, i.e. subjected to 'analysis' by the analyst. Your work in this area has been of enormous value and enables us to guard against 'wild analysis' as well as against a cold and unempathic attitude to the patient. Nevertheless there are still puzzling questions which arise which I have tried to address in my papers which I think are quite different from those raised by the Zurich analysts. How does your chain start? I don't think this is a silly question: like the 'chicken and the egg' it can only be dealt with by shifting the framework. In other words when you avoid dating the original self it is not simply that we don't know the date and one day we might find out, but that *it has no date.* In this sense I entirely take your point that it is an abstraction. The reason that I said that I cannot believe in it except as a fantasy was to indicate that there never is an objective entity which corresponds to it even though there is enormous evidence in the creation myths, as you observe, as well as patients' material. This is by no means to dismiss it. Jung of course often talks of the objective psyche in this sense but what I am struggling to establish is more than just resorting to a vague concept like 'psychic reality' but to a view of science which encompasses the paradoxes generated by a non-linear epistemology. This is not illogical but may use other forms of logic. Hence my interest in the holographic paradigm and the work of David Bohm. The arguments on reductive versus holistic approaches begin to disappear and they are seen to be complementary rather than contradictory.

In teaching and supervision, I still concentrate on interpretations, on the here and now, on the negative transference, etc., but have come more and more to trust a lot of the analyst's activities when reacting more spontaneously in his feelings towards the patient as a whole. I know this is generally accepted but it remains difficult to incorporate in theory. I think this can only be done by not thinking of the self as the property of the patient but as a product of the person with the environment at all times. Even with the most personal and individual characteristics of the self I believe it takes form only as such a product, e.g. the self as it evolves is produced in the baby as resultant of a particular baby and a particular mother just as any analysis develops between a particular patient and a particular analyst. Infant observation therefore ought to be renamed 'infant and mother observation' to do it justice. Winnicott's idea of the good enough environment is not really good enough. There are no ordinary mothers and no ordinary analysts, thank goodness. If this is true, the self even as an abstraction, unlike the ego, will always elude precise definition. We can never observe it without participating in it. Perhaps all we can do is have the kind of discussion we are having now.

It was very good to see you at your film. I enjoyed enormously your frank and forthright presentation of your views and of yourself. My only regret was that Roger did not more fully engage you when you really got going but switched to something else. Still I suppose he had to cover a certain amount of ground and all in all it was fascinating.

Yours

Louis

✠ ✠ ✠

9.2.87

Dear Louis

I much enjoyed your letter. My position in all this is pretty flexible, except for Jung's discovery. I certainly think dating the original self is not important and am struck and attracted to your idea that 'it has no date'. That seems the obvious conclusion now you have suggested it. If that is so, and I am persuaded that it is, then can we speak of the self as existing? Against that we put Jung's idea, and that of others, which covers cosmic experiences extending to the limits of space and time. That is what I am talking about, following Jung.

Your remarks about Kohut are apt, only I wonder who those analysts are who appear to be just bad analysts. The term 'self object' puzzles me. I use it and I don't think I got it from Kohut! Over in San Francisco the Kohutians certainly seemed to agree with the idea of the sense of transcendence which adheres to self representations. My main bone of contention is the one you mention in relation to Kernberg. An important characteristic of self representations is their dual nature.

About the 'fundamental difference' way of approaching the subject, I don't like extravagant terms, even when I use them (which I hope is rare). I think that the modern trend, i.e. in the *Journal* collection of papers, is to consider the sense of self being a branch, as it were, of the ego. That corresponds to the notion of the self as 'the property of the patient'. Classically that makes the self an attribute of the ego and certainly Jung was emphatic in distinguishing the self from that and I think he was right to do so. He would be wrong if he thought the two were unconnected. I am in the habit of thinking of the 'my self' category as a self representation. A self representation is the product of the self deintegrate coming into relation with the environment. I agree, however, though it seems for rather different reasons, that infant observation is better called infant–mother observation, and do so.

I suspect that I agree with you about the analyst's interaction with his patient. It looks as though you have not come across a paper I wrote on countertransference. It was published in the States but is now in *Explorations*. There I tried to open the way to a new assessment of analyst–patient interaction by restricting the use of the term countertransference so as to make space for projective and introjective identification as a constant element in the relationship. I would suppose your metaphor of the two stones dropped in the pond refers to what I mean.

After I had written this, I returned to your letter and was struck by your effort to extract yourself from something I could not very well identify, but which seems to be expressed by the term 'linear thinking'. It is not a term that I am familiar with – I imagine that it is what Jung termed 'directed thinking'.

I also have little use for a number of ideas like 'developmental lines' which according to me refer to ego psychology and the subject of 'stages'. These are conceptual tools that have had their uses and up to a point still do so, but I think that the persistence and growth of patterns from infancy throughout life does away with the idea that stages are to be superseded. Therefore Melanie Klein's idea of positions is the best formulation, especially as it seems to indicate the durability of the self.

Finally on the definition of the self, I incline to your suggestion that the self cannot be defined, it can only be experienced. None the less Jung did succumb in the end and added a definition to those in *Psychological Types* and I expect we shall make further efforts to 'trap' it with a definition. I do none the less adhere to the idea that its characteristics can be known and I think it was Jung's achievement to know (to borrow from Bacon).

I am glad that you liked the film. Such products are bound to leave out a good deal. They did the same when I gave an interview at Ghost Ranch. The producer has to produce a manageable document. I did get going at one point near the end but it was not in the final document. None the less I enjoyed doing it and am glad to find it was appreciated.

Yours

Michael

✠ ✠ ✠

28th March 1987

Dear Michael

I am sorry about the long gap since receiving your most interesting letter. I have such a busy time (why are therapists all workaholics?) that it's hard to give the time I would like to think over what you say and sort out to what extent I agree. I think we are both trying to be reasonably flexible in areas which can often seem like theological disputes.

To make a general point concerning the question of flexibility, I think a lot of the trouble is that, given that we want to link theory with clinical material, we actually need different theories not only with different sorts of patient but with different states in the same patient. Perhaps this might be better expressed as different states in patient–analyst interaction. This would apply not only to theory but to the technique used at any particular time. If we think of notions like 'support', 'confrontation', 'interpretation' etc., these terms have different meanings according to our understanding of exactly what is involved at the particular moment. As an example I was challenged by a patient the other day as to why I was silent and I explained that although a number of things had been going through my mind about what she had been saying, I couldn't put it in a form which I thought would add anything helpful for her. So far so good but I went on to say that I was afraid that if I said any of these things she would say 'Quite'. That bit turned out to be a bad mistake. In the next session she was able to let me know that she had been both angry and terribly hurt. I had been referring to a habit she has of saying 'Quite' after my most careful and, I thought, rather good interpretations in such a way that I felt totally dismissed. At the moment when she was questioning my silence and feeling abandoned this particular reference to something about her which annoyed me was an attack on what was at that moment a fragile self, though at another time would have been acceptable to her, perhaps even a helpful confrontation. It is this sort of mistake which one can often spot in trainee's material which it is so difficult to explain to them. If one criticises them they might, for example, pay one back next time by producing a session in which they hold back from making what to them seems like an absolutely necessary, confrontative type of interpretation. Different analysts might have different views on what I thought was right or wrong in my own material and the arguments might depend on their theoretical background. Some might talk of a weak ego and different ego defences being mobilized at different times according to the level (or infantile stage) to which the patient has regressed, while others might talk about her fragile self and the analyst's need to respect it. I chose to see it in the latter way and acknowledged to her that I had been insensitive. (Admittedly she was reluctant to agree because she idealises me in comparison with her previous analyst; who does sound as if he really was extremely insensitive!)

The point I'm making is that these are not ultimately matters of style or intuition or analysis being an art but can be discussed in terms of the theory being used. We are still looking for an adequate theory to account for these different states which require different ways of handling. So it's not a matter of whether Kohut or Kernberg is right in general but *when* they are right and when wrong. So even if that does lead to a sort of eclecticism, this is only because we are trying to be true to the clinical material as we see it at any one time. As we go on we can agree more and more about these manifold states which we can recognize in our patients. One reason we have such different ideas of the self is partly because our patients keep experiencing it differently, sometimes very narrowly and sometimes on a cosmic scale. Actually I am beginning to think that it is the word 'ego' which should be abandoned because it is distinguishing ego from self which misleads because it is too simple. That is a thought I don't suppose I'll do much with but it's there anyway.

I'm interested in your using the idea of self representations to describe the 'myself' category and that you see this as a self deintegrate coming into relation with the environment. This sounds all right but presumably you use self representation as distinct from object representation and this distinction belongs to ego psychology or object relations theory where it is assumed that the object is the object of an instinctual (libidinal or aggressive) drive. I think this is not the same as what you mean by the environment. This word sometimes seems to mean what an observer would see as surrounding an organism but sometimes (as often in Winnicott) means a person like the mother relating to her baby and of course Winnicott also talks of object-presenting. What I keep hoping, as I expect you do, is that as analytical psychologists we can extricate ourselves from some of the muddle that psychoanalysts such as Winnicott got into in an attempt to do justice to their limited original theory. I do think your idea of deintegration is a real contribution as I tried to say in my paper on it but as I also indicated, I think it applies at a different level of discourse from the psychoanalytical one. I don't think they can be easily reconciled in the sort of way that Kenneth Lambert put forward in his book but that a greater knowledge of systems theory is needed by all of us. This does help me to accept the idea of an original self, for example, as the initial state of a system even though it makes it sound much more abstract than you require when talking about the unique personality of the newborn baby.

As for 'linear' thinking I introduced this idea (not as my own creation) in my early paper on flexibility. I meant it in contrast to the circular processes seen in interactive systems. The family therapists have taken this up in a big way and argue endlessly about the correct epistemology in dealing with the family system. I find what they say also relevant in analysis because there we sometimes talk of the individual as a system, sometimes of the individual and his environment, sometimes of the individual as interacting with other individuals, these are *all* systems which can be thought of in terms of circular processes. So it is not the same as what Jung meant by directed thinking because both circular and linear processes are directed.

As for Melanie Klein, I agree that positions are better than stages. I still find her two positions very useful clinically but leave out an enormous number of other phenomena both in considering infants and analytic patients. I now feel like going on attacking her especially the technique and style she encouraged. But I suppose she was also a genius and anyway I really must stop for the moment. Before I do I will just mention that I have started a small study group on the influence of Klein on analytical psychology which I hope will help us get this whole matter into proper perspective.

Yours

Louis

✠ ✠ ✠

Undated but postscript dated 9.6.87

Dear Louis

Your last letter was very thought provoking. There is much that I agree with but it is couched, I surmise, in terms which seem to indicate a different background to me. I found that in your papers also.

So, with regard to theory, I will state the position that I have arrived at. I think it almost inevitable that each of us collects a number of general propositions of which we become fond, but these propositions, once they are formed, become themselves facts and so subject to analytic or other investigation. If they survive more or less unscathed, they tend to get published or made the subject of discourse. They may then become rejected, put on one side or become fashionable. They are seldom generally accepted.

When it comes to patients, I try to eradicate my theories as far as possible from any particular interview. This opens the way for new theory of what that interview contains and that I may or may not communicate to the patient. You will appreciate that I am in agreement with you in this.

With regard to your example, I have made rather a speciality of patients that make one feel totally dismissed. As a result I would not pay much attention to making mistakes. That is where I think Kohut is wrong, because he leaves his patient alone with his/her destructive capacities. I am also very suspicious of ideas that a patient is a poor patient with a weak ego, inadequate self representation, fragile self and the like. These tend to become grit in the analyst–patient interaction. Of course you may say that I hate this line of approach and you would be right. I think my attitude has arisen because a 'weak' ego has become a blanket term and I usually think that the person (analyst) does not know what he/she is saying. Of course D.W.W. [Winnicott, eds] did make it plain when he gave long and frequent interviews and acknowledged that the patient might 'need' to go into hospital for a period if he went away.

I am nearer Kenneth's [Lambert, eds] position about Melanie Klein and Bion and Meltzer.

As a practical distinction, I do find the distinction between self-objects and object representation useful, but I would not split off subject from object. I thought Marion Milner's book *On Not Being Able To Paint* was a beautiful illustration of the danger of doing so.

I do not think much of Freud's drive theory which you mention, though drives are empirically to be observed, so I am not able to think of an objective object as the object of a drive; it may be or it may not.

Coming back to systems theory, it seems to me that we are dealing with systems all the time and seek to discover the elements of which they are composed. To think like that is useful, at least I find it so. But that is not systems theory as proposed by Bertalanffy. He proposed the investigation of theoretical systems and started to construct a meta-theory – I am not sure whether you are thinking of systems theory in that way or in my more parochial way.

I find it intriguing that you don't like Melanie's technique and style, because it was just that which brought me into closer relation with children. I am not so interested in her theories but agree with you that the paranoid schizoid and depressive positions are valuable, though I regard them as facts of experience – there are difficulties here which I have not the energy at the moment to go into.

Yours

Michael

PS I wrote this months ago and did not think it worth much. Today (9.6.87) I went through my papers and found it not too bad to send.

MF

CHAPTER EIGHT

Is Jungian Group Analysis Possible?

I would like to start by sharing a personal problem, to do with my professional integrity. I call myself a Jungian analyst and am reasonably happy to tell patients that this is what I am when they come, as people are tending to do nowadays, checking up on my professional qualifications. When it is clear that they are coming to see me for individual psychotherapy or analysis. I do not use the term 'analytical psychologist', which is meaningless and confusing to most people, nor do I claim to be a psychoanalyst. At the very least, I tell them that I have had a Jungian training. If they are contemplating joining a group I can equally explain that I am a group analyst. As I have done both trainings, I am not deceiving them and so I do not worry about the Trade Descriptions Act. My worry goes deeper than that. The real truth is that in my individual work, Jung has only a partial influence. I by no means embrace all of his ideas. My way of working is markedly different from his. I put less emphasis on the importance of dreams, often analyse the transference in the here and now, try to imagine what it was like for the patient as a baby, make many interpretations which Jung would regard as reductive, do not often consider what type my patient is and only occasionally try to understand my patient's material in the light of myths or alchemical symbolism. All of these differences from Jung have been subject to close and continued self-scrutiny and I can live with them. My work is still greatly influenced by most of what Jung had to say when he was protesting about Freud. But I have always tried to limit my own protest, tried not to take Jung's objections to the point of a wholesale neglect of psychoanalysis.

The psychotherapy field is confusing in its nomenclature and professional theorists can be as confused as the lay public. Group analysis is called 'analysis' to distinguish it from group therapy. There are, of course, other forms of group therapy with a psychoanalytic orientation, often called analytic group psychotherapy. Group Analysis is Foulkes' term and it should be reserved for a particular method or approach developed by him. I think it is right to call it analysis because the group conductor does indeed spend a good deal of time in analysing the material, and does regard the stream of undirected talk in the group in the same way as the stream of associations from the couch. It is true, also, that Foulkes developed his theory as an extension from the dyadic psychoanalytic one and this explains why it has retained some of the features of psychoanalysis. But Foulkes was at pains to point out that he did not mean that the individual receives psychoanalytic treatment in a group, the therapist being the analyst. He meant that it was analysis of the group by the group and the group, both analysing and being analysed, included the group conductor. This distinguished it from all other forms of group therapy, including others based on psychoanalysis, such as the Tavistock model, pioneered by Bion, Ezriel, Sutherland, Turquet and others, all of whom saw the therapist as the analyst whose main task was the analysis of the group transference in the here and now (Bion 1961).

Whatever differences there may have been between Foulkes and Jung, the role of the conductor or analyst can be seen to be strikingly similar. Jung's idea of analysis, as is well known, was that the analyst (or 'doctor' as he preferred to call him) was just as much inside the process as the patient and was also changed by the patient. In fact in the myriad forms of psychotherapy to be found nowadays, I know of no other which makes a clear statement of this sort. Foulkes and Jung seem to have shared a unique idea. It is possible, of course, that Foulkes got the idea from Jung. Certainly Jung was a great influence on him, although he was himself trained as a Freudian psychoanalyst. He understood the processes taking place in the group as being on four levels and the fourth, or deepest, level he called the 'primordial level'. At this level, he said, were the archetypes of the collective unconscious (Foulkes 1964). This again is an almost unique event. Although it is common for analytical psychologists to incorporate Freudian ideas, it is very rare for psychoanalysts to adopt Jung's, or when they do it is either not acknowledged or else a fortuitous coincidence.

But the idea of the collective unconscious is, for me at least, fraught with difficulties. It has always seemed a rather unwieldy notion, suggesting as it does, something outside the vagaries of an individual human existence, something which exists *outside* any one particular human being, to include the whole of humanity. It is also quite impersonal, because Jung makes an opposition between personal and collective, and so the collective unconscious, being collective, has to be impersonal. It has always seemed to me that, although Jung's descriptions of the archetypes do indicate a quality of inhuman otherness, figures which have somehow to be 'humanized', there is no logical reason why this should be so. After all, the opposite of collective is not 'personal' but 'individual' so that there could be four variables rather than two. We could then envisage a personal collective as well as an impersonal individual.

Another great source of difficulty is that the archetypes are supposed by Jung to be innate (Jung 1912). This seems to follow from his insistence that they are not culturally transmitted, and therefore he has to invoke some kind of genetic inheritance. This has led many to accuse Jung of Lamarckianism. Lamarck believed in the inheritance of acquired characteristics, and this was for Darwin an unlikely and unnecessary hypothesis. Although there has been recent criticism of Darwinism, on the grounds that it is difficult to account for the development of birds' wings or the eye by natural selection, and some form of Lamarckianism is having something of a revival, Jung did not mean to imply the possibility of acquired characteristics of the personality being passed on by the genes. He always made a careful distinction between form and content. He claimed that it was only the pattern of the archetype that was innate, common to all humankind regardless of time and place, and that whatever culturally determined ideas or images there might be that were contained by these patterns, the archetypes in themselves were unknowable. They could only be apprehended through symbols and he distinguished symbol from signs accordingly. A sign referred to something known, e.g. a road sign indicating there was going to be a bend in the road, pointed to the known fact that there was indeed a bend in the road. A true symbol, on the other hand, could only point to something whose precise nature could not be independently established and whose existence could be established only through the symbol. This idea of the unknowability of the thing in itself closely followed Kant who distinguished between noumena and phenomena and unknowability of the *ding an sich*, the thing-in-itself (Jung 1953a).

Be all this as it may, why was it that Foulkes, who seems much more down to earth than Jung, embraced, in his primordial level, an area of group functioning which was archetypal and expressed the collective unconscious? Foulkes was trying to look at group processes as being independent of individual processes. He did not quite say that there was such a thing as a 'group mind'. It is hard to speak of a group mind in the way one customarily does about an individual mind. After all, there is an individual brain and despite all the philosophical debate on the brain–mind duality, we are all ready to agree that we have minds of our own. A group, on the other hand, has no brain of its own, only a collection of brains located inside its individual members, yet we have to deal somehow with the appearance of a group mind.

We are all familiar with the gestalt of the group being more than the sum of its parts, although Yvonne Agazarian claimed that a better expression is that it is other or different from the sum of its parts (Agazarian 1989). Every group therapist, to my knowledge, is fond of saying that the group seems to be feeling something or other, or has a fantasy of something or other, without in the least meaning to imply that this feeling or fantasy exists independently in the mind of any individual member of the group. What is often implied by this is the existence of some sort of mental entity, which is shared by the group. Being shared, it cannot be said to *belong* to any one person. Often, what is meant is that the group-collective constructs some sort of image, a kind of we-production rather than an I-possession. Not only do all group therapists find some such formulation as this indispensable but they view a group's capacity to elaborate and work with such shared images as a sign that it is developing in a creative way and that it is a therapy group. It is thus becoming an increasingly more therapeutic environment for its members. In the individual therapy tradition, the therapist is often quite content to view fantasies as belonging solely to the patient, whose unique individuality is thereby respected and fostered.

So far, I have been pointing out a convergence between Jung and Foulkes in that Foulkes, starting from Freud, came to invoke Jung's as an addition to psychoanalytic notions, to account for what he regarded as the deepest and most primordial level of group functioning. At the same time, I have been saying that I find Jung's idea of the collective unconscious not a simple idea but a highly problematic one. The trouble is that, while it solves some difficulties inherent in confining oneself to the individual mind, it only does so by introducing others, equally difficult to resolve. Jung was fond of an analogy for the development of consciousness. He could not agree with Freud's idea that the unconscious exists because it is repressed from consciousness because our instinctual impulses are forbidden and prevented from reaching their aim. Jung's analogy was that the unconscious arose like islands in the sea of the unconscious. It is easy to imagine an archipelago. Gradually the islands coalesce and become a single and firmly established bit of dry land forming perhaps a whole continent. The sea would continue to exist around it and the sea would represent the unconscious. In other words Jung saw the unconscious as primary and consciousness as secondarily derived from it. But by this, Jung also meant *individual* consciousness, so that, while the original unconscious was not only undifferentiated but did not recognize individual variants, consciousness on the other hand could develop only as the individual developed. While at the stage of being a small island, an individual could easily be engulfed by the sea, symbolising the power of the unconscious to obliterate human individuality. The weakness of the ego to withstand collective pressures made it hard for the individual to integrate the archetypes, even though no one could individuate without doing this. Individuation was, therefore, a task not to be lightly undertaken. One needed a strong ego first, and Jung had personal experience of the risk of psychotic breakdown which was entailed. *Memories, Dreams, Reflections* makes it clear that this was indeed a great danger in Jung's own development (Jung 1963). Most of us, however, would consider our patients with care to preclude this possibility before exposing them to a group.

It is possible to separate Jung's creative contribution from a certain bias against collectivity. He very often used the word 'collective' quite indiscriminately. Everything was either individual or collective and although he saw the possibility of these opposites being reconciled, the very fact that he saw them as opposites in the first place might have been mistaken. Suppose that collectivity, far from being a danger to the individual, actually creates the possibility of individuality. Suppose that individuality can exist only if it exists first in the culture and that only in this way can an individual conceive of such an idea. Paradoxically, Jung did regard primitive people as lacking consciousness because they had no idea of the individual. But he did not seem to see that a developing society might be the primary way in which individuals become differentiated. He seems to have imagined only that it was the individual who had to fight social pressures who could then develop society's idea of what it means to be an individual, to have one's own independent mind. I regard this as a sign of Jung's Protestant background, and one can certainly think of Luther as exemplifying what he had in mind. But it seems more likely that Luthers are rare animals and though society can develop under the leadership of an exceptional individual, it may be far more often that it is the whole society which fosters individual growth. As I have said, I think Jung used the word 'collective' in far too general a way. Collectivity for him referred to *any* collection of individuals. It was as though any collection of individuals exerted a destructive force on any one member's individuality. Collective forces could mean anything from the forces of a crowd, or the pressure of one's family or social group to the power of systematic propaganda or the forces of a blind and impersonal unconscious. Here is a typical example of Jung's way of writing on this topic:

> He (the doctor) is answerable only to the individual in the first place and to society only in the second. If he therefore prefers individual treatment to collective amelioration, this accords with the experience that social and collective influences usually produce only a mass intoxication and that only man's action upon man can bring about a real transformation.

In passages such as this (and there are many of them) we find Jung speaking with an intensity of feeling which leads him to use a rhetorical mode of speech. The general thrust of what he is saying is like a prophet warning of a danger which threatens mankind. He is speaking against mass intoxication but his style here is reminiscent of the very kind of propaganda which he is arguing against. We applaud the idea that only man can act upon man to bring about a true transformation but surely in a therapy group, where people are acting upon other people, this is precisely what is happening. It would be agreed too, in group analysis, that the doctor, or what we would prefer to call the group conductor, is indeed answerable primarily to the individual and only secondarily to society. But it would be emphatically denied that this was any kind of mass intoxication. It could be claimed that it is easier for a group member to work out his or her position when hearing several different views than when hearing only the view of an individual analyst. The analyst may be wrong but nevertheless has great power and authority in the eyes of the analysand. So it is curious to see Foulkes, the great pioneer of group analysis, incorporating apparently quite uncritically Jung's collective unconscious.

Here it is worth making a distinction overlooked by Jung. It is true that a collective attitude, which is sometimes referred to as the 'received wisdom', is an inhibiting force. It may be difficult to assert or even think something different. But these collective attitudes are not necessarily expressed by any given collection of people, that is to say any collection of people grouped together at any particular time or place. The attitude is called 'collective' because it is attributed to the majority but it is often the case that the majority have never even given it any thought. The distinction is between a collection, in the sense of a class, such as the class of white male adults, and people actually gathered together. As soon as we think of a collection of people gathered together, we have a group. The group may not be a very sophisticated one but there is always a purpose for which they are gathered. They then have a collective attitude which is of a different kind. Thus we may speak of an angry group, an attentive group or a deferential one; or one which believes in God. We can even have a group which meets to examine its own dynamics in the spirit defined by the Tavistock Institute of Human Relations, following the work group of Bion (Bion 1961).

The group-analytic group is, of course, small enough to think in fairly comfortably, at least for most of the time. Its members are encouraged to participate freely and to voice their own thoughts and feelings. Clearly, Jung was not thinking about such a possibility. He tended to think of all groups in the terms of crowd or mass psychology. Now I want to emphasize that this bias in Jung has been a great obstacle, not only to the majority of Jungians accepting the therapeutic value of group therapy, but to the development of analytical psychology itself.

If we follow Jung in thinking of individual consciousness as an island arising out of the sea of the unconscious, we are liable to think of the sea only as a danger to the continued existence of the island. It might sink into the sea, like Venice, or the sea can be seen as threatening to flood the land as in Holland, or erode the land, as in Norfolk. Jung himself spoke of the sea lapping around the island of consciousness (Jung 1934, p. 138). Of course there are no worries in Manhattan or on the Rock of Gibraltar about the lapping of the sea. But if we consider, as many group analysts do, that in the words of Donne, *no* man is an island, we are not, curiously enough, contradicting Jung. Jung said much the same thing. We have to recognize that we cannot ignore our collective heritage. We cannot split ourselves off from the archetypal patterns which have given rise to symbols from time immemorial. Jung, in fact is saying that the contradiction is a polarity, an opposition which has to be reconciled. Consciousness, in other words, is not only threatened by the collective unconscious but is nourished by it. The sea is also the Great Mother. It has both a nourishing and a destructive aspect. The task of individuation is not simply to assert one's individuality in the face of the crowd which wants to destroy it. It is just as much to acknowledge that no man can live in isolation, that our lives have no meaning in themselves. Meaning is derived from the collective, of which each of us is a part. So we must continually be reborn or transformed by going back to mother, so to speak, to be swallowed up in the dragon and come out again renewed. This is the great archetypal theme which Jung eloquently expressed in the first work which led to his parting from Freud, *The Psychology of the Unconscious* (later revised and republished as *Symbols of Transformation* (Jung 1912)).

Whereas Freud concentrated on the individual, Jung challenged the idea of the ego as the organising centre of the personality. He saw the true centre as being the self, which mediated between and reconciled the apparent opposites of consciousness and the unconscious. And the self, like the collective unconscious, transcends the limits of the individual.

Foulkes in moving towards group analysis, had to move away from an intrapsychic model to an interpsychic and transpersonal one where the individual was a node in a network. He did not mean a *mere* node, of no more significance than many other such points which could be located in something much more important, the group matrix. Like Jung, he regarded the doctor's duty as lying in the service of the individual. The group conductor may take care of the group but only for the sake of the individual members who will eventually leave it. In fact Foulkes was working with the same opposition that Jung was preoccupied with all his life: the human being and humankind.

Few group analysts in the literature refer to Jung. Those who do are usually Jungian analysts, attracted to Foulkes' work but regarded with some suspicion by the Jungian analytic community, which maintains that real analysis cannot possibly take place in a group. This is particularly true of those Jungians with a strong Zürich tradition, who are also most opposed to Freudian psychoanalysis. There are many aspects of this confusing phenomenon, but I would suggest that the confusion comes mainly for the two following reasons.

First, Jung is under suspicion for being unscientific, for being carried away by unfounded speculation, by obscurantism, by a lack of any clear framework to his thinking and by contradicting himself. He is often seen as so muddled as not to be worth serious consideration. Though I think these accusations unfair, there is some basis for them. Nevertheless, I think it misguided to take a dismissive attitude towards him.

Second, there is the criticism that while Jung does have a valuably broader picture of human psychology, his use of the archetypes and the collective unconscious rely on vague terms like 'racial memory' which conflict with accepted notions of evolution and imply a woolly Lamarckianism which is discredited. Even if universal patterns are acknowledged, there is the old dispute as to whether they arise through the spread or diffusion of cultures or independently, as Jung thought, because of more basic structures of the human psyche.

My view here is an intermediate one. In all this controversy, it seems obvious to me that there are basic structures which are culture-free. The most basic would depend on the human brain and the way it works. This sets constraints on the variations possible in individuals and in groups of individuals. The only question then is not an either–or one but the relative parts played by fixed patterns and those subject to individual variation. In this respect I have one major criticism of Jung. He tends over and over again to polarise the individual and the collective in terms of the single individual person on the one hand and the largest imaginable collection on the other. This large collection is expressed by some such description as 'Man in his totality' (Jung 1940). This leads him to neglect culture, so he does not talk of a social or a cultural unconscious. Henderson, a leading contemporary Jungian, has drawn attention to the need for the term 'cultural unconscious' (Henderson 1967). The term 'social unconscious' has been used by Foulkes in a very similar sense but the advantage of this expression is that it does not commit itself to suggesting that the social unconscious is either cultural or based on structures which are universal and unaffected by cultural variations (Foulkes 1964). French group analysts, such as Anzieu, Rouchy and Kaes, and the Belgian, Le Roy, have greatly widened the field of group analysis by speaking of identity as determined not only by primary but by secondary groups (Anzieu 1984; Rouchy 1990; Kaës 1987; Le Roy 1987). Following Rouchy one may speak of the primary group as the extended family network and of the secondary groups as all other groups to which we may belong: our local community, our church, school, country, professional organizations and so on. Rouchy calls these 'groupes d'appartenance' or 'belonging groups' (Rouchy 1987; 1990). In all this large body of French thinking, which makes use of anthropological evidence, no reference whatever is made to Jung. Even so, there are frequent references to the self, to individuation and to transpersonal forces, the very building blocks of Jung's theory. Much as I regret this, I feel that Jung's neglect of the importance of cultural transmission is partly responsible. It was not that Jung was not aware of culture, only that his emphasis was on the acultural.

Foulkes, as I have said, did not neglect Jung but found a special place for him in his fourth or basic level of group functioning which he called the 'primordial level'. Usandivaras has paid special attention to this level, in which are to be found the archetypes of the collective unconscious (Usandivaras 1985). He has given graphic accounts of the numinous collective fantasies that can occur in groups. It should be remembered, though, that the groups in which he describes these phenomena are especially constructed to evoke them and they have something in common with psychodrama. Also these fantasies arise much more readily in South American groups which are more closely linked with a so-called primitive Indian culture. All the archetypes described by Jung, e.g. the mother, the father, the shadow, the persona, the trickster, the eternal youth, the wise old man, the witch, the hero, the animus and anima, the saviour and the self are to be found in the ordinary therapy group, but in much less dramatic form. These figures are not necessarily projected onto or carried by individual members, although of course they often are, but appear as group figures. They may dominate the group or hover in the background determining the group process. Perhaps the most commonly recognized is the way the whole group symbolises the mother, though this is not usually called an archetype. But it also makes rules like the father, seduces with a mysterious fascination like the anima, deceives like the trickster or unifies onto a higher plane like the self. These archetypal figures do not belong to any individual member. They are as much outside the individual and between them and each other in their communications as they are inside the internal world of each member.

It seems to me that the special and most important place to locate them is in between. That is to say, the archetypes take their life from and are constituted in patterns of interaction, and should not be thought of as independent entities acting autonomously. When they do they are pathological products but they have a natural function facilitating communication rather than obstructing it, provided they are not cut off. I realize that Jung himself, if he were here, would possibly say that the individual risks being swamped by the archetypes in a group and, though I think he tended to exaggerate the dangers, they do exist. I believe that a knowledge of Jung's work, particularly on the archetypes and the primordial level, is essential for the group conductor because it gives another dimension to understanding what is going on in the group. He needs to be aware that sometimes a split-off archetypal content may be damaging to the group process.

In conclusion, I should like to make a special plea for dialogue. It seems to me that in order to arrive at the notion of an individual who can be said to have a self, we must begin the story with people relating, that is to say communicating with each other, and not with the solitary person. This is because I see relationship as a primary and the individual as a secondary reality. In psychological terms, one becomes an individual only when one has an inside and an outside. The idea of a psychological inside, an inner world, is a construction derived from communication that takes place between people. This does not diminish its richness or importance. We need to have found ourselves in dialogue with other persons before we can have a dialogue with ourselves, with our dreams or with archetypal figures. We have to be addressed as 'you' and learn to use the word 'I' in order to imagine a reality within. We do not start with it.

This leads to a realisation that in analysis also it is the case that dialogue is primary and the building up of self knowledge is secondary. Even when the analyst is interpreting a dream, he or she is helping the patient to create for himself a picture of his/her inner world and a richer sense of self through a dialogue in which the analyst is saying, 'This is what you are' and the patient is responding, 'Oh yes' or 'Oh no' or 'Well, perhaps, but…'. I do not think that there is any natural end to this exchange in view, any point where something is established as objective. (Here again I may be differing from Jung when he speaks of the objective psyche (Jung 1953b)). I think that the patient ends up with a picture of himself or herself which is a result of the interaction, and that it enables him or her to have better internal dialogues in the future.

The process is not then essentially different in group and individual analysis. Both are capable of producing the kind of change that Jung thought desirable in his idea of individuation.

References

Agazarian, Y. (1989) 'Group-as-a-whole systems and practice.' *Group 13*, pp.1302–54.

Anzieu, D. (1984) *The Group and the Unconscious*. London: Routledge and Kegan Paul.

Bion, W.R. (1961) *Experiences in Groups and other papers*. London: Tavistock.

Foulkes, S.H. (1964) *Therapeutic Group Analysis*. London: George Allen and Unwin.

Henderson, J.L (1967) *Thresholds of Initiation*. Middletown, Conn: Wesleyan University Press.

Jung, C.G. (1912) 'Symbols of Transformation.' *Collected Works 5*.

Jung, C.G. (1934) 'The meaning of psychology for modern man.' *Collected Works 10*.

Jung, C.G. (1940) 'Psychology and Religion.' *Collected Works 11*.

Jung, C.G. (1953a) 'Symbolism of the Mandala.' *Collected Works 12*.

Jung, C.G. (1953b) 'Psychology and Alchemy.' *Collected Works 12*.

Jung, C.G. (1963) *Memories, Dreams, Reflections*. London: Collins and Routledge and Kegan Paul.

Kaës, R. (1987) 'La troisième différence', *Revue de Psychothérapie Psychoanalytique de Groupe*, 9–10, pp.5, 30.

Le Roy, J. (1987) 'The cultural structuring of the personality and cultural relationships.' *Group Analysis 20*, pp.147–53.

Rouchy, J.C. (1987) 'Identité culturelle et groupes d'appartenance.' *Revue de Psychothérapie Psychanalytique de Groupe 9*, pp.31–41.

Rouchy, J.C. (1990) 'Identification et groupes d'appartenance.' *Connexions 55*, pp.45–56.

Usandivaras, R.J. (1985) 'The therapeutic process as ritual.' *Group Analysis 18*, 1, pp.8–16.

CHAPTER NINE

The Grail and the Group

Jung was inclined to see groups as destructive rather than creative, as potentially of great danger to the individual. This they certainly can be. Nevertheless, there is a growing number of Jungians who have discovered that they need not be. Jung formed this view before anyone had tried to develop a format for analysis in groups, a format which had to evolve, while paying full attention to the sort of danger to the individual envisaged by Jung. In this evolution the constructive possibilities of group dynamics were gradually appreciated. Everything was found to depend on such matters as the size of the group, the selection of the members, the role of the conductor, and the creation of a certain atmosphere; in other words, on getting the setting right. In doing this analysts bear in mind what can take place in the one-to-one arrangement and try to preserve these possibilities in the group. Some will argue that this is not possible, that the setting has been so changed that what they call 'real analysis' cannot take place in a group. While acknowledging that there are certain inevitable differences in the process, there are, in my view, sufficient resemblances to justify the claim that not only analysis but individuation takes place in the group setting. I would not make this claim for group psychotherapy in general. My claim is based on my experience of training at the Institute of Group Analysis, using the methods of S.H. Foulkes (Foulkes 1964) and having worked for many years as an analytical psychologist.

In considering the potential for creativity in group analysis, I will not argue in defence of this claim. I hope you will bear with me if I take group analysis as providing a different setting for the same process, an activity roughly called analysis leading towards individuation in the individuals taking part. One of the difficulties in accepting this formulation is that the word 'analysis' itself immediately conjures up an image of two people: one the analyst and the other being analysed. Group analysts often call this 'individual analysis', and in general, psychoanalysts working with groups have tended to go on seeing the group in dyadic terms. Often this leads to an attempt to analyse the individual in the group at the expense of neglecting therapeutic group processes. This was true even of such notable group analysts as Bion and Ezriel, who saw the group as a whole but concentrated on the transference of the group to the conductor and on the conductor's countertransference to the group, thus retaining a dyadic framework (Bion 1961; Ezriel 1950). Foulkes, on the other hand, spoke of the analysis of the group by the group, including the group conductor and the group process, as taking place within a network of relationships which he called the 'matrix'. In this model there are multiple transferences and countertransferences as well as there being a notion of the group as a whole. This notion of the group as a whole is of something which is superordinate to and which contains the multiple dyads or groupings of individuals within it, which can be seen to be sub-groups. So, for the individuals and the sub-groups, the group becomes part of the setting.

In psychoanalysis, the importance of the setting for analysis has only recently been given attention, largely at the instigation of Winnicott (Winnicott 1965). Our notions of what constitutes the setting are, I believe, in need of considerable refinement, and groups which provide a dramatically different setting while retaining the analytic model provide a good opportunity to explore this question.

Groups can be highly creative, and the analytic group is set up to help it to be so. Creativity is on many different levels, and to simplify my task I am going to confine my attention to one area only, the creation of the setting itself. In one-to-one or so-called individual analysis, this is often seen to be a somewhat peripheral area, or a technical matter, something that needs to be thought about in the 'setting up' of the analytic situation, or in maintaining certain boundaries when they are threatened, as by the patient acting out. It is thought of as simply a framework in which all the creative processes take place. It is further assumed that it is solely the analyst who provides the setting, as a good host does for his guests.

This view has only a limited validity. It is a model that makes it hard for the patient to make changes in the setting or for the analyst to recognize his right to do so. The patient may feel bound to adapt to what has been provided, just as a good guest is supposed to do. As soon as we adopt Jung's model in which both partners change, the setting for the patient can no longer be constant, nor can it be simply the responsibility of the analyst alone. That is to say, we cannot exclude the analyst from his setting. His presence, his responses to the patient, his personality and his technique are inextricably bound up with what he provides.

At the same time the setting is more than the arrangements made by the analyst. For the patient, the setting is not just what is provided by the analyst but something that provides the analyst himself, the other person who occupies the room when he is in it. For the analyst the setting is again not just what he provides but the other person who is present in it. Once this is recognized, it is better to think of the setting as being a joint one for both the participants. Some elements may be given and may be determined by the culture or have archetypal roots, but others are highly personal, highly subjective and constantly changing. These subjective and personal elements continuously alter in subtle ways the way the two participants perceive the situation they are both in. By exchanging their separate perceptions, they continuously negotiate and renegotiate their agreement as to what the setting is or could be. They may or may not be aware that they are doing this. Usually they are only marginally aware, except when discussing quite gross changes such as the duration of holidays, the noise outside, or whether to alter the frequency of sessions. It more particularly becomes an issue when either partner thinks the other is acting out. Acting out means acting in ways thought to be destructive of the desired setting. This notion of destructiveness of the good conditions should be complemented by the notion of the creation of good conditions. The setting, instead of being thought of as given, should on the contrary be seen to be the continuous creation of the two participants.

Now let us return to the group. Let us suppose that we take a step that Jung would not have taken. Suppose we agree with everything he has said about analysis except with his insistence that there should only be two persons present. This step of disagreeing with one of Jung's passionate beliefs may seem a difficult one, but it is a procedure for which we have a precedent in child analysis. In that case, one had to disagree not only with the suggestion that individuation was specific to the second half of life, but with Jung's view that children were unconscious, before one could feel free to analyse children. Once this was tried, certain further modifications in the setting had to be made, such as the provision of toys, but these were not alien to the analytic process, to the analytic attitude, or to the way the material was understood. Just as working with children helped one to see adult analysis in a new light, so does working with groups help one to see the setting in a new light. In groups it is much easier to see that the group is being fashioned by the group. We are accustomed to numerous social groupings in which the group is continuously being changed by the participants. Although this process may not always be in the awareness of the participants, it is a more legitimate topic. It is easier too to see that the group is itself part of the setting for the individual and that it can be changed with the help of the other members of the group. We are also familiar with this process in our own families. As one gets used to being in and working with analytic groups, it becomes easier to see that the group is not merely an enlarged or diluted version of 'analysis', and then that dyadic analysis is really a group of two, a group which can be a rather limited and restricted version of the group of eight.

I have referred to the fact that the creation of the setting by the group is often outside awareness, and I should now like to consider why this is so. I think there is a general answer relating to creativity as such as well as a specific answer to do with the setting. In other words, we can be unaware that we are being creative and specifically unaware that we are creating our setting. I am using the word 'unaware' rather than unconscious because it is often unattended to rather than being unavailable to consciousness. In the general case of creativity, it is clear that most creative acts do not have creativity as their main conscious goal but emerge as having been creative when some other goal is attained. Group analysis pursues a therapeutic goal, and it is in the course of pursuing that goal that groups become creative. A conscious wish to be creative is almost guaranteed to inhibit creativity. In the special case of the setting, it is also desirable not to be too consciously preoccupied with it as the object of attention, and when I speak of the setting as continuously being created, I do not regard this as necessitating a conscious creative effort. Sometimes it does, but usually it does not.

As well as being unattended to, the setting may be unconscious in a deeper sense. I have elsewhere discussed my observation that the transference and countertransference in dyadic analysis is not confined to the unconscious fantasies of analyst and patient to each other but that there is also a play of unconscious fantasy of each to their setting. Sometimes, the transference to the setting is of much greater importance than that to the analyst (for example in prison), and the two are by no means always identified.

In group analysis, as in dyadic analysis, there are times when the members of the group wish the group they are in to be a different sort of group. This may be understood as a wish to avoid anxiety; in Bion's terms, this would be a wish for the group not to be a work group but it may also be a recognition that the group could indeed be a better one than it is (Bion 1961). At such times, the members of the group may become aware of their setting, and also that they can change it.

An example might be that the group discovers how to use humour. Rather than humour being indiscriminately permitted, they might make a fine distinction as to when and when not to see things as funny, when it is creative and when destructive to laugh. The group will then monitor humour, so to speak. To begin with, it might be simply establishing that it is all right to laugh *with* somebody but not to laugh *at* them. Gradually this might become more refined, recognizing times when any kind of laughter is out of place as well as times when one can be too serious. I am suggesting that these changes, which can be very subtle, are not just people changing within the group setting. They are, but in addition they produce an actual change of the setting itself, bringing about an evolutionary step in the group structure. This is in stark contrast to the idea of the structure as something which must not change. The group members never step into the same river twice. The group is not the same group once it has undergone a progressive change. The group has creatively altered its setting.

It might be objected that it is wrong to call this a change in the setting and that the particular people in that particular group have simply discovered greater potentialities in the original setting. In practice it may be impossible to locate who these particular people are who have made this discovery. It seems to be a group process. More importantly, one cannot go on making discoveries about the world one is in without changing that world. Newton may have been a solitary individual who discovered gravity, but once his discovery was accepted by the larger group, it was not long before this group was inhabiting a very different sort of world. In my particular group analytic example, the idea that is laid down for the group would simply be that there is no agenda and that they can talk about anything they like. This would make it seem different from any other group they had been in but would not deal with the use or misuse of humour. Every group does evolve rules of this sort, which are a great advance on Freud's basic rule, and the evolution of such new rules replacing the old one does rely on an understanding that the setting requires creative change.

A further objection might be that the original setting has not been altered at all. It still remains permissible for the group to laugh whenever it likes; it is simply that it chooses not to do so. The trouble with this argument is that it treats the setting as being a setting for a group which is not a group of any particular people. It is rather as though a jeweller were asked to make a setting which would do for any kind of jewels one might put in it. I would agree, however, that the very division into setting and what is set does pose some difficult problems.

In another paper I have discussed these questions with reference to Bion's formulation of the container and the contained and tried there to understand, while thinking of the group as a container, just what sort of container it might be (Zinkin 1989). In my ensuing sense of confusion, I was greatly helped by the fact that Bion himself noted that in the constant conjunction of container/contained there were similar contradictions in trying to separate out these two elements, neither of which had any meaning without the other; and that the two terms could be reversed, e.g. the word contains its meaning and the meaning contains the word (Bion 1961). Furthermore, in designating container and contained by the female and male signs, Bion brought up a lot of problems about masculinity and femininity which are of the same order – problems to which I shall return later. Rather than following Bion in his terse and condensed mathematical exposition, I am choosing, on the contrary, to amplify the material in the way Jung might have done, using myth, with its evocative rather than discursive logic, to show what is involved in regarding the setting as being created by the participants. For this purpose I shall make use of the Grail legends. Stories of this kind deal, of course, with imaginary events reported as though they are real events and real events as though they are imaginary and rely on the question as to whether they are real or imaginary not being too strenuously pursued. This uncertainty is not some unfortunate lapse in the art of story-telling but is absolutely necessary to establish the truth of what is being told. Although my paper is not meant to be a fairy story, it is equally important in following my argument to be aware that what I am calling the setting for analysis may be either what is objectively there or whatever is imagined to be there by the participants and that what I am regarding as a creative process actually depends on this uncertainty never being finally resolved but always being kept alive. This becomes possible in the logic of myth, and it is to myth that we now turn.

Of all the myths and stories which have attracted Jungian writers, there is probably none more studied than the legend of the Grail. Jung himself lived with this story in the sense that his wife, Emma, spent thirty years studying it, and her book was unfinished at her death. It was completed by Marie-Louise von Franz and there is a subsequent considerable body of Jungian literature. In all this literature, which seems to explore every conceivable psychological meaning of the story, I know none which addresses itself to the psychology of the group (von Franz and Jung 1986). Instead, the Grail quest is understood as a personal, interior and spiritual quest; an individual journey towards wholeness, towards the attainment and realisation of the self, the hero's journey towards individuation. The story is seen as the story of an individual, even though it is also seen as having a universality which means it applies to all individuals. Despite the vast richness of all this work and its undoubted value for the individual reader who can identify with the hero of the quest, this is a curiously one-sided account. All hero myths are also group myths. While it is tempting to identify oneself with the hero's amazing achievements, the hero is always fulfilling the needs of a group. Perhaps this is more obvious in some stories than in others, but it is exceptionally prominent in the Grail legend.

It is a long and complicated story. Just one of its many variants, Wolfram's *Parzival*, runs to over 300 pages in the Penguin translation and it is not possible to construct a composite version that contains and combines all the essential elements of the extended myth (von Eschenbach 1980). Nevertheless, in all the accounts the Grail has a past, a story of the origins of the Grail, a present in which the Grail is absent and an imagined future in which the Grail is found. The story is about the movement towards the ultimate realisation. Past, present and future depend, of course, on where one begins, but it is convenient to begin the story in the middle, at the stage where King Arthur and his knights are on the quest for the Grail. Although it is known that only one person will reach it, it is also known that this person will be a member of this particular group, the Knights of the Round Table. This is why Perceval (and for simplicity's sake I shall use this particular name for the hero) has first to get into this rather élite group. The Grail is some kind of vessel, or it may be a stone, but in any case can be regarded as a magic container whose contents will make the waste land fertile again. Its origins are not always certain, but most commonly the Grail is none other than a cup used by Christ and his disciples sitting round a table having a meal together, albeit a rather special meal. Where is the Grail eventually found? Again it is in the possession of a group, the guardians of the Grail. So there are three groups and each has a leader. Christ, Arthur and the Fisher King. In each case the leader is depicted as wounded, as suffering or as incomplete, and it is the mission of Perceval to bring about the healing or completeness. That is why we are drawn to him as the central figure of the drama, but without the group. Indeed, without the three groups he is nothing. He has no meaning. He is the 'Pure Fool'. He is ignorant and undifferentiated. It is not simply that the Grail is missing for him; it is that he is the missing member of the group and it is the group which is looking for completion and is incomplete without him.

This shift in perspective in our reading of the story is the shift of perspective which turns the individual analyst into the group analyst. It did not happen with Jung, or with Freud. But it happened with Foulkes and with all his Freudian and Jungian followers who began as individual analysts. The shift required is not one which gives precedence to the group over the individual, but is to see the group and the individual as two sides of the same coin. They are opposites like male and female, in that neither can be understood without the other. This has been most clearly brought out in a paper by Romano Fiumara on what he sees as a convergence between Jung and Foulkes (Fiumara 1983). In this paper Fiumara shows that in spite of all Jung's celebration of the individual, he did also at times have glimpses of the perspective I am advancing here. He gives one quotation from Jung which is worth requoting. Jung writes:

> In certain and not too uncommon cases...demand for individuation is against all adaptation to others. But in such cases the individual must bring forth values which are an equivalent substitute for his absence in the collective personal sphere. Without this production of values, final individuation is immoral and – more than that – suicidal. (Jung 1921)

This can be taken to mean that the individual cannot simply be seen to be on his own. When he is on his own he is missing from a group, and even if he is not missing the group, the group is missing him. In individual analysis it is the individual who is seen as being incomplete, but in the individuation process he restores his place in the group through grasping that his symbols are not his alone but belong also to the collective. In group analysis, the group has to learn that it has no function, no meaning, no existence without the individual. It is always incomplete and waiting for the individual who will complete it. This individual, like Perceval, has a moral duty towards it but also, as Jung says, it would be suicidal of him not to join it.

The group analytic group can be described as a model, as a way of working, but these descriptions never seem to do justice to the experience of being in one. Even as one tries to describe it, one is left with the impression of addressing the uninitiated as though they were initiated and trying to describe a mystery as though there were no mystery. It seems, in fact, as though the mystery cult is a better expression of what one is describing than any discursive or scientific account can be. I think the problem lies in attempting to avoid paradox, even though paradox plays an essential part in what one is trying to describe. Myth or dream thoughts then seem to offer a better form of description. One can approach the group situation only through metaphor. At least at this stage in my paper one can see one reason why this is so.

From the outside, the therapy group is seen as a place which contains some source of goodness, some Holy Grail, which the individual lacks. It is in this spirit that the single patient approaches the group. He expects the group to be led by someone who has the knowledge to make him better. He does not expect the leader to have an incurable wound, especially not in his genitals, to be virtually castrated and powerless. He does not expect the group to be suffering from the drought and famine of a waste land and least of all does he expect it to depend on his own arrival for the leader to be cured and for the waste land to flower again.

Inside the group it does indeed look like that. The leader is no magical provider. The members know that they have the Grail in their care and it does feed them, but at the same time they know that their leader can neither live nor die until a certain individual joins them. This individual is not a bringer of knowledge. He does not have an answer to their questions. On the contrary, he knows nothing, and what is needed is not his answer but his question. The situation resembles that of the incest taboo, of which Levi-Strauss has said that it is an answer for which there is no question (Levi-Strauss 1962).

Perhaps it is easier for the reader of *Parzival*, at this point of the story, to identify with the main character whose fortunes he has been following, than to imagine himself as one of those knights of the Grail, hanging on for dear life, not on Perceval's answer to a question but on his question to which the answer is already known. The question is a pretty obvious one. 'What ails thee, knight?' It's like saying to a crying child, 'What's the matter?' The answer is also rather obvious. It is essential to realize that this is not a story about problem solving. What is necessary is neither question nor answer but a conjunction of the two. Only a myth seems to be able to resolve the paradox because it moves and expresses itself through paradox.

The same paradox arises whenever we try, as Bion did, to see the constant conjunction of container and contained. A container can be conceived only with the contained; even an empty container has an absent contained. In the same way, no contained is conceivable without a container, even if the container is absent and has to be found. It is for this reason that one can say that the contained contains its container. Bion gives as an example the fact that although a word contains its meaning, this meaning also contains the word (Bion 1961). Fiumara arrives at the same conclusion when he says: 'The group "contains" the individual while the individual 'contains' the group' (Fiumara 1983). Perhaps, in our work as analysts, the realisation gradually dawns on us all that not only do we need the patient just as much as he needs us but that we need him for healing just as much as he needs us. We may often read that this is so, but it is really a mystery into which each of us has to be initiated. Individual analysis is a group of two. Analysis becomes a dream in which we not only reverse roles with the patient but each becomes a part of a conjunction whose existence is impossible without its parts. The comparison with dreaming lies in the symmetrical logic which combines opposites and which is used by dreams and is not questioned by the dreamer. The meaning is not reached by the asymmetrical logic by which we try to explain the dream from outside (Matte-Blanco 1975).

The Grail legend is a story that depends in its telling on the linear form of narrative. It moves from past to present to future. But it is also myth. The cup has a mythical past in the last supper; a mythical group, King Arthur's knights, seek it and it is found in the mythical Grail castle. Using it as a metaphorical or dream-like description of the group, it is better not to be too literal with the time sequence. All three groups can simultaneously apply to the analytic group. Even in the story, the first group is not really the first group. The Last Supper may have been a final transformed version of the Seder night, and Jesus was probably saying kiddush. The Seder night is itself a remembrance of a former group as well as looking forward to a future group in the words: 'Next year we shall be in Jerusalem.' The kiddush cup is itself a transformation of the life-giving cup of Dionysus which is in turn a transformation of the coffin of Osiris. The kiddush cup becomes the container of Christ's blood, which gushes from his side from which it is collected by Joseph of Arimathea. In a dream, while in prison it is returned to him by Christ in a blaze of light, taken by him to some place, perhaps Glastonbury, and zealously guarded until found generations later by Perceval, when its contents replenish the earth. At any rate this is what the legend says. What is being described in linear sequence is also describable as an endless cycle of birth, death and rebirth, as Eliot, having written *The Waste Land*, described paradoxically in his *Four Quartets*.

The analytic group sits in a circle, usually with a table placed in the centre, and it has an atmosphere of ritual and ceremony. In this respect it resembles all three of the groups in the Grail story. But it is never quite clear whether it is preparing for sacrifice, on a quest for a hidden goal or waiting for its redeemer. Sometimes one or the other image seems more appropriate, but it is always facing simultaneously its own incompleteness and its own longed-for completeness. For this, it looks to its past, to another unknown place, or to its future. As it goes through these cycles it hopes to individuate, to become a more differentiated whole.

If a group of people is continually changing its setting while remaining a constant group, the word 'setting' no longer implies something like the setting of jewellery, where the jeweller performs an act on static and inert objects. It implies a dynamic situation where there is a reciprocal interplay between the setting and its contents. In the analytic group, there is an interplay between the individuals and the group which contains them. Sometimes it is clear that an individual cannot change unless the group changes. Perhaps this is always the case. It is hard to think of movement in one thing without using another as a fixed point.

In the Grail legends, although there is a past, present and future, there are certain constant elements – the vessel, the group in a circle, the spear or lance, the table, the blood of Christ, the suffering leader, the hero – but all these elements undergo dramatic, sometimes magical, transformations. Are the three tables different tables, are the three groups different groups, or the same tables or groups transformed? Mythical stories leave these questions unanswered.

The analytical group, or indeed any group, has a similar problem. If it wishes to change, it looks back at some previous group and forward to the group it wants to become. If it changes, does it go on being the same group with changed individuals, a changed group of the same individuals, or are both changed, or neither? More specifically, does it have a Grail without a redeemer or a redeemer without a Grail? Of course, these are questions about the archetypes. It seems to me that their numinosity lies in not knowing whether we are looking at something very familiar, or totally new. This is what Freud said about the nature of the uncanny, but it is also true of the mystery of male and female. To each the other looks very familiar and also quite different and it is worth briefly considering the interplay of male and female elements in the Grail stories.

It is generally accepted that the Grail is a feminine symbol. This is not simply a psychoanalytic reflex response which regards all containers or vessels as representing the vagina. Jungian writers, from Jung himself onwards, point to the overwhelming association between magic or holy vessels and female deities in every culture, and Emma Jung is in no doubt that the Grail is an image of the mother archetype. It is in a similar spirit that Bion sees the container and contained as female and male, though not in a narrow sexual sense. In the cycle of Grail myths, as I have said, the Grail can always be seen in relation to a group who either have it with them or are looking for it. When they have it, the Grail container is itself contained. The group becomes the container within which the Grail container can do its work. The Grail castle is depicted as a rather closed group, highly inaccessible and protected by its guardians. When the Grail appears to them, it does so when the group is behaving in a solemn ceremonial ritual with an air of secrecy characteristic of a long tradition of initiatory mystery religions. The Grail is clearly not for public display but is hidden in the midst of a strange group of people in a mysterious and supernatural castle which is hard to find. It is a container within a container. If it is the womb, it is well hidden in the mother whose womb it is. A diagrammatic representation would be a circle within a circle, as is found in many a mandala. Wanting to get back into mother can be understood as the larger circle in the form of going back to the maternal country or home or being held like a baby in her arms; or the smaller circle, going right into her central, secret, inaccessible womb, where one once belonged, but to which one can never return except in the imagination.

The Grail in its different guise, whether it be a cup, a dish or a stone, seems to be a mythological way of expressing the ambiguous and paradoxical nature of the mother container, whether one can have it, be in its presence, or be inside it. Out of this problem there emerges the idea of serving it or being in its service and the ritual question that has to be asked is most often the question: 'Whom does the Grail serve?'

Returning now to the analytic situation, everybody agrees that it should be a containing or holding situation, but there is a similar air of ambiguity and paradox when one tries to describe exactly what it is that does the holding or containing. Is it the maternal capacity of the analyst, the setting in which the patient is seen, or is the setting something which they both need to be in so that they can interact? Although it is the latter case that I am advancing in this paper, it is not to the exclusion of the others and I do not think that it is ever possible to reach a final definition which says it is this and not that. I am far from regarding paradox as requiring a final solution and it is for this reason that I am using myth as the best way of illuminating a problem and as something whose main value is to help us to tolerate contradiction rather than to evade it through final solutions.

In the dyadic analytic situation, the container is often called 'the analysis' and in group therapy it is called 'the group'. In both cases the term is not clearly defined. Is the analysis, for example, something the patient is in, or something applied or provided by the analyst, or when the patient refers to it should it be taken up as an illusory substitute in the transference, for the analyst?

These questions are similar to the questions we may ask about the Grail story in considering the female symbolism of the Grail, where they are not so much answered as questioned. The questioner who transforms the feminine is himself unquestionably male and it is now necessary to consider the male elements in the story, because no change can take place in the feminine container without the masculine contained turning up. The situation is like that of the ovum, which cannot be fertilized until a sperm arrives to penetrate it. Out of millions of spermatozoa which seek it, only one is destined to find it. These biological facts were unknown to the authors of the stories.

In these, it is an all-male group which seeks the Grail, and its members' masculinity is greatly celebrated through their deeds of knightly valour. The sword, lance and spear are as clearly male as the Grail is female and the apotheosis at the end is brought about by the conjunction of these male and female elements. As in a mature sexual relationship, neither the male nor the female dominates the other but reach or touch or meet or contain the other. Needless to say, both male and female elements become transformed and spiritualized in the Grail stories and I am not suggesting that a purely reductive interpretation into sexual part-objects would be in order. But in the mature sexual relationship, or perhaps it is better to say the ideal sexual relationship, it is clear that both the containing female and the contained male are changed or, as I would prefer to say, created by the conjunction of the two. In many primitive groups, the infertility of the land is naturally associated with the impotence of the king and in the Grail myth the waste land is ruled by the castrated Fisher King. At this stage, the presence of the Grail is not much help except that it provides the company with as much food as they want. The wounded king can be released from his agony and the land made fertile only when the true knight with his sword, lance or spear arrives and asks his question. Until then neither the male sword nor the female Grail can do their real magic. Then it is that the group becomes transformed. Not only is the old king allowed to die and the hero becomes the new king but the group can be released, can separate and do good deeds elsewhere.

Jungian psychology has placed a great deal of emphasis on restoring the place of the feminine in the collective consciousness and the Grail legend has been amply used by Jungian commentators to bring out this need for the return of the goddess, particularly by Whitmont in *The Symbolic Quest*, where he discusses the Grail legend in a most illuminating way (Whitmont 1969). But what I am suggesting here is that it is not just a question of male consciousness needing the powers of the fructifying goddess, but that the goddess herself, if reached by the male in the right spirit, will change in the process. Only then does she actually become a fructifying goddess and in this form she does not simply change but a new goddess becomes created, not by the male but by the conjunction. This is a point not always appreciated by modern feminists, that women need not only to be freed from male domination, but to change themselves, which they can do only with the help of men.

The analytic group may be set up and its boundaries defined by the patriarchal act of the father, perhaps deriving from Foulkes himself. However, Foulkes recommended that, once set up, the authority of the conductor can gradually undergo a decrescendo and pass over to the group as a whole. This need not be an abdication of power from an individual person to a primitive archetypal force, as Jung feared. On the contrary, the boundary becomes subtler. It is not less distinct, but constituted by the group rather than being imposed on the group. Gradually, as new elements appear within the group, the group makes changes in the boundary, in what is allowed in and in what is kept out. In this process, the group as a container develops, just as the Grail becomes a fructifying vessel. Change in the container can be experienced as continuous or discontinuous. At times, there is a mysterious transformation and the whole group feels suddenly different as though a miraculous healing has taken place and the Grail is now in their presence and the waste land made fertile, or the reverse can happen. More often the changes are not dramatic but the group does gradually feel different. A good silence, for example, is not simply a silence taking place within the group but a silent group of which it feels good to be a member. The setting for all the individual members has changed through a creative act involving an interaction between the group as a whole and its members. Both the group and its members are of course people and they are the same people. This is why it is legitimate to call it a creative act at all. The group as a whole is not an abstract entity but a group of people. I find it difficult to think of the collective unconscious as being creative, though it is not so difficult to think of the unconscious of a collection of people becoming creative when joined or conjoined to the consciousness of the individual person.

It is time now to leave the Grail story, though there is a great deal more in it which bears upon my theme. I have used it as a description of the analytic process which, since Freud, has undergone changes away from the masculine idea of penetrating interpretations to an emphasis on its maternal holding function and the setting in which interpretations are made. Both are needed for a complete description. They constitute male and female elements, each of which is useless without the other. Taking analysis out of the context provided by its founder into the group has taught us a lot about group processes and about the relationship between the group and the individual. By taking this knowledge back now to the traditional dyad, we can begin to see the setting in a new light. It becomes possible now to see the dyad rather than the single individual and the dyad not simply as two individuals but also as being a group of two. If analyst and patient need to get mixed up, as Jung said was essential, they do not do so in the kind of fixed mixing bowl which Freud had in mind when he invented the analytic setting. In the group we can see the containing vessel as undergoing continuous change and sometimes the discontinuous changes which suggest that the cook has changed one vessel for another.

The study of alchemy, which, by the way, heavily influenced the writers of the Grail stories, has also shown the importance of changes in the vessel in the process of transformation. As with the Grail legends, Jungian writers have also treated alchemy as a solitary process rather than as the work of a group. In bringing alchemy to the attention of psychology, Jung was revealing, as best he could, the secrets of a secret group.

The shift in perspective from individual to group is long overdue. It does not detract from the individual and although in group analysis one sees the group as changing, group analysis is always for the ultimate benefits of the individual. However, greater weight is placed on the socialization of the individual than in

Jungian dyadic analysis. In the latter, there seems to be more acceptance of idiosyncrasy than in group analysis, where the group is taken to be the norm from which all the members deviate.

Although I think that individuation takes place in both, it is not surprising to find that group analysis leads to an individual who is better at belonging to groups, while dyadic analysis helps people to explore and realize their uniqueness as individuals. Although I am positing these as opposites, they are interdependent and Jung, who prized uniqueness, also considered it suicidal not to return one's unique discoveries to the group. Although one method of analysis may help a particular individual more than the other at a particular time in his or her life, it would be foolish to claim that one was 'better' than the other.

Conclusion

I have approached the problem of bringing together group and dyadic analysis by using a myth to illuminate it. Myths are so rich in meaning that it is hard to stop with some clear-cut conclusion. Myths do not solve problems, but they do address them. The Grail stories are about a precious and mysterious container and present the problem of finding it. They present also the opposition between individual and group, in that it is the heroic individual who is destined to reach it, but for the benefit of the group. Both the transformation of the group *and* the transformation of the individual is brought about in the course of the story. It is a story of the union and the transformation of both the container and the contained. It is a *coniunctio*, a bringing together of opposites. It is not an either–or. Group and dyadic analysis present the same opposition. In the group, the individual is seen to be a member, part of the group; in the dyad the individual is seen to be separate from the group, whether it be the group he comes from or a possible group he might join. But in both, the differentiation of group and individual leads to an enriched rejoining of group and individual. In both there is a container in the form of the analytic setting; and, in both, the setting as well as the contents require transformation. This, in turn, depends on a continuous or repeated joint act of creation in the imagination of the participants.

I should like to end, not with an answer but with a question. If the longed-for container has to be created, in what sense does it already exist? Is the Grail an object to be found or is it created by the imagination? 'Did you find it or did you make it?' is the question one must not ask babies, according to Winnicott. Even if he is right about babies, perhaps, as we grow up, we may dare to ask this forbidden question. In doing so we have the hubris of inquiring as to the source of numinosity, whether numinosity comes from the archetypes or from ourselves. In both group and dyadic analysis, we have a container which we call the setting. Is it a commonplace starting point, like a saucepan or a handbag, or is it the goal of the whole enterprise, a *vas mirabile*? Is it the *prima materia* or is it the philosopher's stone?

References

Bion, W.R. (1961) *Experiences in Groups and other Papers*. London: Tavistock.

Ezriel, H. (1950) 'A psycho-analytic approach to group treatment.' *British Journal of Medical Psychology 23*, pp.69–74.

Fiumara, R. (1983) 'Analytical psychology and group-analytic psychotherapy: convergences.' In M. Pines (ed) *The Evolution of the Group*. London: Routledge & Kegan Paul.

Foulkes, S.H. (1964) *Therapeutic Group Analysis*. London: Allen & Unwin.

Jung, C.G. (1921) 'Psychological types.' *Collected Works 6*, p.540.

Levi-Strauss, C. (1962) *La Pensée Sauvage (The Savage Mind)*. Paris: Librarie Plon.

Matte-Blanco (1975) *The Unconscious as Infinite Sets*. London: Duckworth.

von Eschenbach, W. (1980) *Parzival*. Harmondsworth: Penguin Books.

von Franz, M.J. and Jung, E. (1986) *The Grail Legend*. London: Coventure.

Whitmont, E.C. (1969) *The Symbolic Quest*. New York: Putnam's Sons.

Winnicott, D.W. (1965) *The Maturational Process and the Facilitating Environment*. London: Hogarth.

Winnicott, D.W. (1971) *Playing and Reality*. London: Tavistock.

Zinkin, L. (1989) 'The group as container and contained.' Chapter 10 of this volume; originally published in *Group Analysis 22*, 3, pp.227–234.

CHAPTER TEN

The Group as Container and Contained

When Bion first introduced the idea of the container and the contained he was providing one of the most fundamental concepts with which to think about thinking (Bion 1962). The change from elementary to more complex forms needs a container. So following Melanie Klein, Bion proposed that the baby's thought-fragments (or beta-elements) needed to be projected on to the mother's breast, which would act as a container in which they would be transformed into more complex thoughts (or alpha-elements) in which form they could be returned to the baby to be used subsequently as building-blocks for dream thoughts. Whether this account is a true or false description of how thinking starts, it is surely true that we cannot conceive of any evolutionary change, that is, any progressive change from a lower to a higher level of organization, as taking place except in some kind of container.

Starting with thought processes, Bion later (Bion 1970) saw the container and contained as a constant conjunction to be found in many other contexts. These included the group and group processes. An important example was the appearance of the mystic or messiah, either from within the group or from outside. Such a mystic was essentially an innovator – one who challenged the way the group was organised, who questioned, in some way, its basic structure. The problem for the group is to contain the mystic, who threatens to disrupt the group's organization. If the mystic can be successfully contained by the group, so that neither the group nor the mystic is destroyed, the group will change (and I would add that this may involve an evolutionary step to a higher and more complex level of organization). Bion cites the case of Jesus, who had to be contained by his followers in the establishment of the Church (Bion 1970). We can, however, think simply of an innovator who might have the same function for the group without necessarily having any mystical powers, and still retain Bion's formulation.

I believe it is a rich and fruitful application of this idea for the group therapist to see the group constantly as having the task of a container. To give an indication of how this may be, I present my thoughts on the group as a container in a series of conceptual steps.

Holding together

The first and perhaps the most obvious application is the holding function of the group. The therapist, in forming a group, provides a relatively fixed structure within which the desired changes in the members of the group can take place. This may be thought of in such terms as the provision of a suitable room, deciding the frequency and duration of sessions, the composition of the group, the arrangement of the chairs, the preparation of the members, the manner in which the group is conducted and so forth. This is 'setting the stage', the setting providing a safe, holding environment for the infant (to use Winnicott's terminology), or analogically it can be compared to the provision of cooking utensils before a meal can be cooked, or to the test-tubes and retorts in a chemical experiment. These containers have, as their most rudimentary function, that of holding the ingredients together so that they may productively interact. 'Holding together' is in fact what the word 'container' denotes – container being derived from the Latin con (together) and tenere (to hold).

Changing the container from without

A second step is to reflect that the container need not be fixed and unchanging while the contained undergoes change, but the therapist can alter the container or change containers, just as the cook may move the ingredients from mixing-bowl to saucepan or the chemist may pour the contents of the test-tube into a retort. The group therapist can make changes to the group structure by, for instance, the strategic introduction of a new group member, by subtle alterations in technique, and so on. Usually in making such changes, the therapist is mindful of the members' need for stability, consistency and reliability but may also see the therapeutic potential of novelty and surprise or even the occasional use of shock tactics in his or her departure from the usual psychoanalytic stance. This may take the form of self-disclosure, of direct confrontation of a group member or the use of paradox. Thus the therapist, instead of seeking change within the container, makes changes to the container in order to change the contained.

Change from within

A third step is to become aware that the container is subject to change from within. The group members themselves alter the group to which they belong. The group to some extent is responsible for its own container. The members are constantly determining the kind of group they are in. For this reason no two groups of the same conductor are quite the same and the conductor can never enter the same group twice. Even rabbits can extend and alter their burrows when they need to; and humans, of course, have enormous scope to modify their own environment. This applies to group members when the conductor does not tell them they are acting-out or acting-in.

Reciprocity between container and contained

In these three steps, we have moved from the idea of the fixed container, 'holding' the contained together, to the notion of the contents or contained themselves bringing about change to the container. We can now proceed to a model of circular interaction between container and contained. As the group members change, they change the group they are in, which then enables them to change further, which then changes the group, and so on. Such change, seen as the product of mutual interaction between the container and the contained, may be desirable or undesirable, controlled or uncontrolled. We are now in the realm of cybernetics, of positive and negative feedback loops, or runaway, as well as the re-establishment of equilibrium in relatively closed or open systems (von Bertalanffy 1968).

Male and female elements

A further step is to consider the male designation given by Bion to the contained and the female designation given to the container. It will be recalled that Bion (Bion 1970) liked to use the male and female symbols together to indicate the constant conjunction of container and contained. He did not mean that this conjunction should be understood purely in the narrow sexual sense of vagina and penis. The femaleness of the group container is evident in its womb-like function; but it seems to me important that in opposing the two terms we do not give undue emphasis to the container at the expense of the contained, but see male and female as equal and complementary. The male element called the 'contained' is not just passively contained, like the embryo. It has to get in and it has to get out. Getting into a group can be very difficult sometimes and so can getting out of one. The containing group boundary may need to be actively penetrated. The image of the phallus is not that of an object which allows itself to be placed within the female but is something possessed of a powerful source of energy, seeking out its target and competing with others in order to reach it and having to push its way in. I would suggest at this point that in group therapy, as in individual therapy, there is a recent tendency to overvalue the maternal values of holding, supporting, nourishing and promoting growth as a compensation for the previous male overvaluation of penetrating interpretations and overcoming resistance. In the same way, accounts of human development have been pushed back to start not with birth but with the foetus. Perhaps they should be pushed back even further to start with the spermatozoa and the winning sperm breaking into the cell membrane to enter the ovum. In other words, seeing the container and the contained as a constant conjunction and neither of them conceivable without the other it is a matter of punctuation whether we start with the female container or the male contained.

We now have a model of the group container as one which resists rather than facilitates change. Interpretations have to be made to alter a group which is stuck. They have to be put in by the therapist who sees the group as defended. The defences have somehow to be got through before the group can change. I am not suggesting that this needs to be violent, an act of rape. Guile or entreaty might be better ways of overcoming 'feminine' resistance. But we may have to recognize, as Bion suggests, the case of the mystic, where the issue for the group is to contain the new insight, if it is not to be disrupted by it. Again, of course, producing change through a penetrating interpretation is not the prerogative of the therapist but can be done by any group member.

Chance, accident and random variation

So far, our discussion of the container has rather assumed something round and symmetrical, like the uterus, the mouth, the breast, or the rectum. This is in keeping with a picture of the group as a circle. I have referred to circular interactions and to general systems theory as outlined by von Bertalanffy. This theory is based on the principle of systems which seek equilibrium in order to restore homeostasis. But a very different concept emerges from the work of Prigogine and his co-workers in Brussels studying thermodynamics (Prigogine and Stengers 1984). Prigogine has shown that discontinuous change with the appearance of novel structures of higher complexity arises when the system is *far* from equilibrium. Such principles have been used by family therapists such as Elkaim (Elkaim 1985). Evolutionary change results from random variations whose effects are essentially unpredictable. Such a model in the therapy group would lead the therapist to learn and make use of the peculiarities of any particular group arising from chance rather than from his or her efforts to maintain equilibrium and balance. In other words, the container can beneficially become distorted and asymmetrical. One common example is that of the missing member, the empty chair. The effects on the group can be very marked, even though unpredictable, especially if the empty chair is that of the therapist. Here is another example, in a group of mine, when one heterosexual man arrived drunk and in his disinhibited state expressed his love for another man in the group. He never again was drunk in the group but this episode produced an evolutionary change in the group, which thereafter could talk freely of homosexual feelings within it. The container had been permanently changed for the better by a random breaking of the therapist's unspoken rules, that is, that the members be sober. This depended on the group as a system being far from equilibrium, an asymmetrical container.

Muddle, confusion and dream thoughts

Finally, I believe that transformations of the group as a container can best be understood through dreams, fantasies and myths, even though this undertaking involves introducing apparent contradictions, paradoxes, ambiguities and other illogicalities. Anzieu (Anzieu 1984) has vividly described group fantasies of the group as a mouth, devouring as well as containing, or as a womb or as a 'toilet-breast', to use Meltzer's phrase (Meltzer 1986). All group fantasies, if the group is not a psychotic one, depend on the perception of the container and the contained as a metaphor for themselves and the situation they are in. Such fantasies may be original and personal, though they are usually based on collective archetypal patterns. Bion himself referred to the container–contained as an analogy without feeling any need to specify, except through illustration, what it was an analogy for. This enabled him to say cryptic or self-contradictory things, in which 'container' and 'contained' can be reversed or fused. For instance, the word can 'contain' its meaning or the meaning can 'contain' the word, according to Bion (1962). This reversibility is similar to that of figure and ground in certain optical illusions (Abercrombie 1981).

I believe too that our understanding of the group as a container can be enhanced by the study of anthropology and by comparative mythology, which is extremely rich in container imagery. Every mythology has a vessel which may be a sacred or a magical vessel, and we can think of Pandora's box, the genie in his jar or the fairy tale of the magic cooking pot, but perhaps the story which is the richest expression of the way a container can undergo transformation in its symbolic significance is the legend of the Holy Grail. A study of this legend can help to amplify the clinical study of group fantasies, as I have shown in another paper (Zinkin 1989). This is also true of alchemical symbolism, to which the Grail legend is closely related. In alchemy, the container, in the form of the alchemical vessel or *vas*, received a great deal of careful attention. According to one alchemist, Maria Prophetessa, the vessel is the most important thing of all (Jung 1944).

Here it is important to augment reductive analysis of the container to its instinctual infantile roots by adding to it the cultural transformation of the archetypal form. This may occur in the deepest level of functioning in the analytic group described by Foulkes, the primordial level of the collective unconscious.

Jung tells a story which is relevant to my theme of the container. It is of the Wachandi Indians who, as a fertilization ceremony, dig a hole in the ground, oval in shape and dance round it thrusting in their spears shouting 'puli nira, puli nira, wataka', which means 'not a pit, not a pit, but a cunt'. During the ceremony no one may look at a woman (Jung 1928). The illusion of the female genitalia is fostered, according to Jung, so as to transfer and redirect sexual energy as libido into the fertility of the earth. In this transfer, the container is transformed.

Myths and rituals are of the nature of primary-process thinking in Freud's terminology; C-category elements in Bion's; symmetrical logic in Matte-Blanco's (Matte-Blanco 1975); and undirected thinking in Jung's. In this kind of thinking, as in poetry, distinctions are blurred leading to ambiguities of condensation, fusion or identity. In this realm container and contained are not clearly separate. In group therapy, the group constantly generates this ambiguity when those who are the group talk of 'the group'. In doing so, they leave it unclear whether they are themselves the group, the contents of the group or the container of the group. Although this may be logically confusing, it allows for endless creativity. It is worth recalling that we begin and end our lives in a container. At times of crisis, we withdraw into a container or break out of one, or we change containers. Do we ever live outside one? If no man is an island no man can ultimately separate himself from his container. He can only undergo transformation of himself and his container together.

In the Grail legends, the Grail is the cup which feeds and nourishes. It is difficult to find, but when found the incurable wound of the wounded healer is healed and the waste land becomes fertile. Perhaps our efforts as group therapists to find, in our groups, the perfect container are our own quests for the Holy Grail.

References

Abercrombie, M.J.L. (1981) 'Beyond the unconscious – group analysis applied.' *Group Analysis* XIV/2, Supp 1–16.

Anzieu, D. (1984) *The Group and the Unconscious.* London: Routledge and Kegan Paul.

Bion, W.R. (1962) *Learning from Experience.* London: Heinemann Medical Books.

Bion, W.R. (1970) *Attention and Interpretation.* London: Tavistock.

Elkaim, M. (1985) 'From general laws to singularities.' *Family Process 24*, 2, pp.151–164.

Jung, C.G. (1928) 'On psychic energy.' *Collected Works 8*, p.42, para 83. London: Routledge and Kegan Paul 1960.

Jung, C.G. (1944) 'Religious ideas in alchemy.' *Collected Works 12*, p.225, para 338. London: Routledge and Kegan Paul 1969.

Matte-Blanco, I. (1975) *The Unconscious as Infinite Sets.* London: Duckworth.

Meltzer, D. (1986) *Studies in Extended Metapsychology.* Strath Tay, Perthshire: Clunie Press.

Prigogine, I. and Stengers, I. (1984) *Order out of Chaos.* London: Heinemann.

von Bertalanffy, L. (1968) *General Systems Theory – Foundations, Development, Applications.* New York: Brazillier.

Zinkin, L. (1989) 'The Grail quest and the analytic setting.' *Free Associations 17.* London: Free Association Books.

CHAPTER ELEVEN

A Gnostic View of the Therapy Group

Carl Gustav Jung is often an abstruse writer. This and the sheer volume of his collected works puts off all but the most determined readers, some of whom may then be drawn to more simplified popular accounts of his work. Unfortunately, these, including his own, tend to be either over-simple and therefore seem banal or, if they try to go deeper, become rather vague and general and thus difficult for the clinician to apply. In this essay (it does not fulfil the usual expectations of a scientific paper) I attempt to interest the group therapist in the more esoteric side of Jung, as manifested in his lifelong preoccupation with Gnosticism. This has not, to my knowledge, been a subject hitherto found in the group-therapy literature, but I hope to show that there are reasons to consider it. Jung kept his less obviously scientific interests fairly private but it is becoming clear that his published work cannot be fully understood if these more obscure areas, including also alchemy and the 'pansophic tradition' of magic, occultism and esoteric wisdom which involved him so much, are not understood. It is not simply a question of following Jung's wish to acknowledge a spiritual or religious aspect of psychology, which many others may do, but of seeking to understand Jung's unorthodox views on such matters. Whether these are considered relevant to psychotherapy depends on what are regarded as the legitimate aims or goals of therapy, and whether there is a specifically Jungian goal.

Comparing the different schools of psychotherapy is always a difficult undertaking. Each claims to be especially effective, but in trying to deal impartially with these claims one has to remember that their therapeutic aims may not be the same, that they may imply very different goals. A patient trying to choose what sort of therapy to have needs to consider not only which is most likely to be effective but what being 'effective' means. Such a patient might not find it easy to establish these differences by questioning a psychotherapist. If analytically orientated, the therapist might be reluctant to explain, or indeed be unable to, through ignorance of other schools, and would probably in any case want to evade the question and suggest that it is the patient's own goals which are of importance, not the therapist's, and certainly not those of any particular school. It might even be questioned whether there should be any preconceived goal at all and it is quite likely that by this time the therapist, if not the patient, would wish to be having another sort of conversation.

The fact remains that all the schools, though not usually explicitly, have a certain model of what is hoped for as a result of psychotherapy. Certainly, all the analytic schools have far-reaching aims compared with the more behavioural approaches, but there remain nevertheless considerable differences amongst the analytic schools too. On reading, say, Heinz Kohut, it may not always be clear that he is aiming for a somewhat different development of the personality than, say, Melanie Klein. The differences in aim may be both more subtle and more obscure when considering any particular therapist within the different schools. He or she has not only been trained in a particular way but has his or her own individual goals, both conscious and unconscious.

Group therapists, too, coming from different schools, may have different ideas as to what they would regard as a good outcome for the individual and there is also, of course, a good deal of uncertainty as to what extent the therapeutic changes which take place in a group differ from those which may be hoped for in an individual analysis.

Jungian group-analysts have a specially difficult problem. First, they have to square it with their consciences that they are conducting groups at all, in the face of the strong disapproval of an internalised Jung. This is not hard to do if they confine themselves to Jung's specific objection, a distrust of the group as being antagonistic to individuality, but it remains a question how to translate Jung's methods of furthering individuation, which he saw as a largely solitary and private matter, into the group setting. Some confusion may result from the fact that the term 'individuation' was not confined to Jung but also has been used by others, including Alfred Adler and, later, Margaret Mahler. Her well-known usage of the term, 'separation-individuation' as a developmental phase has something in common with what Jung meant but in some ways is totally different.

Individuation was, for Jung, a process towards a goal. It was the supreme goal of human development, involving a process of continuous movement, but in spite of its having a spiral-like motion in the direction of the goal of completion, was a process which could never be completely realized. Although Jung originally described individuation as a process of the second half of life it is generally regarded by his followers as taking place throughout the whole of the lifespan. The principal aim of any individual analysis, whatever the presenting problems, is always to further individuation. Separation from the mother, emphasized by Mahler, was certainly seen by Jung as necessary, but for him the individuation process was one of connecting to the mother in some new way just as much as in separating and reconnecting: a symbolically enacted form of rebirth was seen as a repeated pattern of renewal.

Individuation as a goal is one of those Jungian ideas which is not easy to describe briefly and it is often expressed in a kind of shorthand such as 'achieving wholeness' or 'becoming more who one is'. Put this way, individuation as a goal may seem readily compatible with the secular aims of group therapy, but for Jung individuation ultimately acquired a religious significance, and the psyche, the object of psychology and psychotherapy, has no real meaning unless one recognized in them a spiritual or religious need. This aspect of Jung's work contrasts strongly with Sigmund Freud's atheism, which was helpful to Freud in trying to keep psychoanalysis a respectable branch of science. Jung too, though not an atheist, struggled hard to maintain his position, which was that some sort of religious life was a *psychological* necessity, whatever might be the ultimate truth about the existence of God, which, he repeatedly said, as a psychologist he did not feel qualified to discuss.

Although there is a growing literature on group therapy from a Jungian standpoint this problematic question of the spiritual dimension in the therapy group is one which Jungian writers seem to have been shy of taking up. In practice the difficulty is much less than it might seem in theory, provided that one is prepared to learn group theory *from* the group as well as applying it *to* the group. An example of the latter tendency is the over-use of the idea of transference. There are many group phenomena not yet accounted for in theory where one sees an intensity of affect which should not be called transference because it relates to a true, not a distorted, perception and which has a numinous quality. One perceives at times a deepening of feeling involving the whole group, a sense of heightened meaning which cannot easily be defined but which can best be described as a sense of belonging to a greater whole, a sense that life in the group has acquired a new significance, somehow enlarging the individuals within it. Although there may be dangers of a group inflation, such experiences very often provide authentic evidence, to those willing to entertain the idea, of the spiritual growth of the group as a whole. They are often deeply moving to the participants, who have a sense of wonder or mystery or even of awe, which they cannot easily find words for, but feel they are participating in something akin to a religious experience.

In the group, then, even when it is set up as a therapy group, even where, in other words, its work is defined as being 'therapy' for its members, it becomes apparent that the group is pursuing an aim which, if therapeutic, is certainly not therapeutic in any narrow sense. In any case, what is significant to the group, and may be deeply moving, is not often to do with the neurotic symptoms of any individual. This has been noted by many non-Jungian therapists and has been well expressed by Caroline Garland who noticed that there was not much to be gained by the group's discussion of the patient's individual problem and that the group did better if work were done on what she called the 'non-problem' (Garland 1982). This is in keeping with the belief all group therapists have that the group is more than, or, as Agazarian and Peters (1981) have said, 'different from', the sum of its parts. But the non-problem may be not really a non-problem but a different sort of problem, a problem at a higher level, and the special efficacy of group therapy would be to subsume the problems of the individual members into this problem, a higher or greater one which all the group share, whatever their individual problems may be. It is in attempting to understand the nature of these higher-order problems that one begins to wonder whether to introduce something like a religious dimension into one's thinking about what is going on.

Here, a Jungian finds himself in familiar territory, knowing that this idea is of the essence in Jung's thought and was perhaps the most important single difference between him and Freud when they parted company so tragically. Jung felt he had to take note of a religious dimension and Freud would have none of it. To Freud, religion was not only a sublimation of sexuality; it was based on illusion. What I am hoping now is that we can at least begin to explore this difference, in the context of the therapy group, because the problem arises more readily there than in individual therapy; and what I am trying to point at may therefore resonate more with the experience of therapists who work with groups rather than with individuals.

Unfortunately, this cannot be attempted by a Jungian writer without taking the reader into realms which may evoke all the old anti-Jungian charges of being obscure, recondite, mystical, esoteric, magical, metaphysical, unscientific, speculative and of not being based on the hard empirical evidence of 'case studies'. These terms of abuse echo Freud's misgivings which in 1912 were understandable but are less so now.

Not without some trepidation then, I address certain questions which therapists often do not ask, on the grounds that they lie outside their frame of reference, but which are endlessly being asked by the groups we run for therapeutic purposes. They are quite big questions. What is the meaning of life? Is this all there is? Why should I care what you think of me? What makes us different from anyone else? Is there any hope for the world? These questions, and there are many more like them, all have in common that they go beyond the limits of what is usually thought to be the reason the group is there. Such questions might be thought to be more suitable for quite another kind of group, for a religious circle, a tutorial in philosophy or a political party. It seems to me though that these other groups differ importantly only in the way they endeavour to answer the questions and that the questions themselves cannot be excluded from psychotherapy, which is quintessentially a search for meaning.

It has to be admitted that these questions do go beyond the usual bounds of psychology, but, of course, no actual group can take these bounds for granted. They need, as they develop, to agree or disagree about the nature of man and the nature of the world and of the mind and the body *before* the psychological field can be delineated. What has emboldened me to take up this theme is the knowledge that if the therapist is taken out of his or her depth when the group approaches these big questions, no great disaster has taken place. The therapist's job is not to know everything, only to know something, and this largely concerns his or her acquaintance with individual and group dynamics. The group experience can be an enlarging one for the conductor as well as for the patients, but this cannot happen if the conductor's mind is closed by the limitations of his or her own field of competence. What I am proposing as necessary is not a glib set of answers but a theoretical framework which allows the questions to be asked.

The therapy group does not only ask these questions but, I am convinced, finds answers of its own. It does this precisely by virtue of being a group of strangers who are trying to get to know each other, to cope not only with their own but with other people's suffering, who have no agenda or creed and who gradually discover, in the group, that in spite of their differences they share more than they differ on, finding group forms of expression based on their common humanity and their common habitation in the same world. These conditions are perhaps found only in certain kinds of therapy group and I am assuming a group brought together and conducted with an analytical attitude, constituting group analysis as S.H. Foulkes has defined it, where the group analyses itself (Foulkes 1964). This requires an analyst whose style of leadership allows the group to find its own way through the free expression of ideas, feelings and fantasy as they struggle to communicate verbally with each other.

While the answers which each group finds are novel for that particular group, they tend to resonate with answers which others have found. They express themselves in symbolic forms which can be recognized as having a long history, not being confined to any particular individual or group. These forms lie behind the images which the group uses. They are similar to images which impressed Jung, by their universality in widely differing cultures, as the symbolic expression of forms which he regarded as being archetypal. As well as their universality, archetypal images can be recognized as having a quality of 'numinosity', a word introduced by Otto (1923) in his study of the sacred and the profane. The archetypes are not knowable in themselves and can only be apprehended through images and so, when I say the group finds answers, I do not mean philosophical, theological or political answers, nor even a greater knowledge of psychology. I am referring to a kind of knowledge called 'gnosis'.

Although I think it justifiable to speak of sacred and profane elements in the group (and it would be a fascinating exercise to try to distinguish them), the archetypes are by no means restricted to religious experience. They play a part in moulding everything that can be experienced. The recognition of archetypes or of a level in which they operate in group analysis, the fourth primal level of Foulkes, does not in itself imply any religious dimension in the group. In fact, it would probably be true to say that the recognition of archetypes with their numinous quality is quite compatible with a materialistic or even atheistic attitude. They are in themselves only the basis of a certain kind of symbolisation. If these experiences give rise to a religious attitude, it is because a religious attitude is one which pays a special respect to this symbolisation and not only regards it as an interesting psychological activity but as pointing towards a transcendent reality, an experience of divinity.

I have suggested that it is not always easy to distinguish psychology from other frameworks of thought, and in Jung's writings it is often not at all clear whether he was making religious statements, that is to say, statements of his own religious belief or, as he usually claimed, psychological statements based on the empirical evidence of what his patients experienced. This kind of distinction, incidentally, is often not clear in psychoanalysis either; terms like 'psychological truth', 'psychic reality' or 'internal reality' often leave it unclear whether some reality is being referred to which is more than psychological or psychic. But it has to be said that Jung's position is particularly vexing in this respect. His psychology has attracted the theologians but his way of dealing with this question usually ended by exasperating them, notable examples being for Catholicism, Father Victor White, and for Judaism, Martin Buber.

In his later life, however, Jung did make his personal beliefs clearer even though he continued to regard them as separate from his work as an analyst. In dealing with analysis, he continued to stress the need for neutrality and the absence of any prior suppositions when listening to or looking at the patients' material. The religious or spiritual dimension in Jung's work took the form of manifold references to every religion that one can imagine, from the great world religious systems to the most obscure and esoteric cults and the most primitive tribal myths and rituals. In general, after exploring Eastern religion, Jung turned his attention to Christianity, which he came to regard as no longer a relevant mythology for modern man. Though based on the archetypes, its symbolic images had become outmoded and stale, and in any case Jung found a better and more balanced expression of the psyche as he understood it to be not in the dogmas of orthodox Christianity but in the heretical Gnostic texts dating mainly from the first three centuries AD. Gnosticism has recently become more widely accessible since the translation and publication of the Nag Hamadi scriptures (Robinson 1977). Previously Gnostic ideas could mainly be gleaned from the early Church Fathers such as Iraneus who referred to them only to expose their wickedness and apparent absurdity.

So, although Jung seems to treat of practically every conceivable manifestation of religion, his deep inner preoccupation was with Gnosticism and any attempt to apply Jungian theory to group analysis should take account not only of Jung's numerous references to Gnosticism but of the fact that Jung was himself a gnostic. In the now famous 1959 television interview with John Freeman, 'Face to Face', Jung, when asked if he believed in God replied: 'I do not believe – I know!' This was a hint of his own Gnosticism, which in his published works he had never made clear. In fact it now seems that his writings are on two levels: a manifest level of scientific and philosophical discourse and a hidden one which, like the gnostic scriptures, makes only oblique and cryptic reference to a hidden world revealed through vision and prophecy. This was not a mere desire for secrecy. Jung did try very hard to put his insights into rational language and he kept calling his work empirical, kept on appealing to 'facts' which were certainly bits of his patients' material but were not easy to comprehend intellectually.

Jung's writings, then, on the psychological processes involved in individuation are inseparable from his own spiritual and religious development. This became more apparent after the posthumous publication in 1962 of his autobiographical work, *Memories, Dreams, Reflections*. It subsequently came to light that in the period following his break with Freud, between about 1912 and 1917, Jung went through a period of mental illness. In Ellenberger's (1970) terms, it can be described as a highly 'creative illness'. During this period, it is said, Jung, normally a voracious reader, read nothing. He did write, however, and during this period, in which he also carried on his clinical practice, he wrote in a book bound in red leather, in handwriting that was not his own but resembled that of a mediaeval scribe, with his own illustrations made of pigments he had prepared himself. This text, a personal record of his inner life, came to be known as the Red Book. The work, consisting of some 1300 pages, has never been available to the public. Only one little fragment has been translated and published, a curious but profound work called 'The Seven Sermons to the Dead', which had previously only been circulated amongst a few friends. It was signed with the name Basilides, a gnostic of the second century AD.

'The Seven Sermons', though very obscure, throws much light on Jung's interest in Gnosticism, which pervades his published writings. It would be out of place, in this essay, to attempt a detailed exposition of this strange text. The best account I have found is by Hoeller (1977) which includes Jung's text and adds an extensive commentary. Nor is it easy to describe briefly the multifarious movements which can loosely be called 'gnostic'. There is a growing literature on the subject and the interested reader is recommended the highly readable book by Pagels (1979) or the more difficult philosophical survey by Jonas (1958). All I can do here is to refer in briefest possible outline to a few of those elements in Jung's Gnosticism which can be fruitfully applied to the therapy group. The correspondences which can be made are only at this stage suggestive and require much more detailed research.

First, then, Gnosticism refers to gnosis. To translate this word into 'knowledge' is inadequate, because what is referred to is not intellectual knowledge but more what Pascal had in mind when he said that the 'heart has its reasons which the mind knows nothing of'. The knowing is more in the sense of 'acquaintance with', like the French *connaître*, than 'knowing about' or *savoir*. Orthodox Christianity and indeed most orthodox religious belief does not speak of knowledge of any sort, so much as of revelation based on faith. Though St Paul can with good reason be regarded as something of a gnostic himself, he left out knowledge when he talked of Faith, Hope and Charity. Even though these three are indispensable requisites in group analysis, and perhaps it can also be agreed that the greatest of these is Charity, few would deny that from our point of view as psychotherapists it is the acquiring of knowledge which is the most crucial. Usually we call this 'insight', again insisting that by this word we mean more than intellectual understanding. Insight usually comes in flashes but gradually these flashes become more coherent and carry greater conviction till they too can be graced with the name of 'knowledge'. Such knowledge usually means self-knowledge. Certainly this is true of individual analysis, but in the case of group analysis one can add knowledge of other people, knowledge of how people relate to each other, knowledge of the group as a whole, knowledge of the world outside the group. Ultimately, though here we are more hesitant, we might mean knowledge of God as Jung claimed to have. In spite of this hesitancy, the group does acquire knowledge in its search for the meaning of life and of death, and the purpose of existence – the big questions to which I referred at the beginning. God may or may not be dead in this context but perhaps what Jung preferred to call the 'god-image' might be more easily recognized in the group material, as we explore the gnostic conception of this.

The gnostic idea of God is a hierarchic one. There are a large number of gods and demons, all of which represent lesser beings when compared with the supreme deity, which is a hidden god, often called in gnostic terminology the 'pleroma'. This cannot be described and any perception of it is akin to all the inexpressible visions, the direct experience of reality called mystical. Among other paradoxical descriptions, Jung called it an 'empty fullness'. But the god who created the universe is not the supreme god and is often called a demiurge. In some accounts he is regarded as wicked, but usually (as in Valentinus) as ignorant; he is simply unaware, when he claims that there is no other god beside him, that there is the pleroma of which he is a mere emanation. The demiurge, together with the myriad lesser gods and demons, as well as all the created universe which we regard as our world, is a deception resulting from a breaking away from, or fragmentation of, the Unknown God, the pleroma. However the gnostic idea is that there are sparks of the original pleroma in all of us and indeed such sparks can everywhere be found hidden or imprisoned within matter, as has been beautifully expressed in the Gospel of Thomas (Robinson 1977) where Jesus says: 'Raise the stone and thou shalt find me. Cleave the wood and I am there.' The image of light is often used, the hidden light within man.

There is thus in Gnosticism a special way of dealing with the problem of the One and the Many, which was a major problem of early antiquity. Despite the vast number of lesser beings which are imagined, there is a fundamental unity of which they are all fragments. This is the pleroma and the sense of oneness is preserved in that we are all united through having within us this same originally undivided being. This may be trapped within us but our individual diversity is only on the surface. Gnosis consists of our awareness of this. In this sense we are 'fallen' not through being bad but through ignorance. Gradually, with gnosis, we can ascend through the hierarchic levels of the archons and restore the pleroma in its undivided wholeness. The ultimate godhead, however sublimely imagined, is therefore as dependent on us to acquire knowledge as we are dependent on it as the source of our knowledge and of our inner being. This bypasses the creator-god of the orthodox Judaeo-Christian tradition, who mistakenly considers himself to be the supreme god. The creation myth of Genesis, therefore, has quite a different meaning, the wise serpent enlightening Adam and Eve by getting them to taste the fruit of the tree of knowledge. There is no original sin, only ignorance or 'error'.

All this is, of course, quite heretical but perhaps to the modern group therapist it is a more cogent account of the state of affairs found in the group situation. The problem of the one and the many is of great concern here as we struggle to reconcile the claims of the individual with those of the group. The oneness, the unity of the group, need not be, as Jung feared, a loss of individuality in the mindless mob-like group but on the contrary is found in the formation of a superior mind, greater, higher and richer than any of the individuals' minds, including that of the conductor. The gnostic vision, although expressed in quaint and archaic language, can now be seen to be surprisingly modern. The 'invisible group' of Agazarian and Peters (1981), founded on the currently accepted tenets of systems and communications theory, is not very different from the 'unknown god' of Jung and the gnostics. In her 1988 Foulkes Lecture Yvonne Agazarian gave a beautiful description of how a Japanese group, whose verbal language she could not understand, gave at the end a moving physical representation of a mandala, a form which Jung regarded as a symbol for the Self which can arise spontaneously when the psyche is undergoing integration. Having passed through stages in which the group had divided hierarchically, with the students deferring to their professors, they united at a higher level as they all pointed to the centre, creating a timeless archetypal wheel-like pattern of wholeness.

In the same way Bateson (1972), using cybernetic and communications theory, has developed a similar idea of mind, and in his *Steps to an Ecology of Mind* pays great tribute to Jung. Bateson was deeply impressed with the 'Seven Sermons to the Dead' and with Jung's distinction between the 'pleroma' and the 'creatura'. Bateson considers that 'these are two words we could usefully adopt'. They refer to two different worlds, to which he gives two different levels of description. In the pleroma Jung says 'there are no distinctions' and this, in Bateson's terms, means 'no news of difference', which for the creatura is so important. It is from this idea that Bateson comes to define the individual mind, in his famous images of the man with an axe or the blind man with the stick, as being discernible sub-systems of mind (creatura) or units of evolution. He says: 'Now each step of the hierarchy is to be thought of as a *system*, instead of a chunk cut off and visualised as *against* the surrounding matrix ... It means, you see, that I now localize something which I am calling 'Mind' immanent in the large biological system – the ecosystem' (Bateson 1972, p.430). This seems to me essentially to be the same idea which group therapists have when they think of a group mind (in interpretations such as, 'The group seems to be thinking that ...') or of the invisible 'group-as-a-whole', where the differences between the individuals cease to be significant. But the group mind is itself a sub-system, the greatest supra-system being indescribable because undifferentiated, as is the pleroma.

We can no longer afford to ignore ecology and need to remember that the boundaries we draw around the individual in the group, as well as the boundaries we draw around the group, are simply for the creatura. They are only the boundaries which *we* draw. Useful though this is, we have also to regard the group, in its relationship to a larger environment or supra-system, ultimately in 'pleromatic' terms (Bateson's adjective). In the pleroma, these boundaries do not exist. In gnostic terms we are acquiring the gnosis to restore the pleroma. Intuitively we can all recognize examples in our group work, similar to that described by Agazarian (1988), moments when the group acquires a moving sense of unity. Not the primitive *participation mystique* of Lucien Levy-Bruhl, not a sort of lowest common denominator dreaded by Jung, but a higher level of awareness, a gnosis, which, when it experiences in itself an indescribable sense of wholeness which far transcends the *created* universe, might be rightly regarded as the true religious experience of gnosis. There is no need here for prayer in the usual sense and no need for any mention of any superior deity. The group remains a therapy group even though no longer considering neurosis. In fact, it becomes *more* of a therapy group because it is no longer considering neurosis.

Central to Jung's notion of individuation is that as it proceeds, opposites, constellated in the psyche, are united. Conflict, for Jung, results from opposition which could not be resolved at its own level because both sides of the conflict have to be given equal value. Only at a higher level could something new arise which represents the two apparently irreconcilable aspects of the psyche, conjoined. Typically, this can be seen in the male–female opposition and Jung repeatedly drew attention in alchemy to what is there called the *coniunctio*, the *combinatio oppositorum*, in which the androgynous figure of Mercurius appears. Jung treated many of the contra-indications appearing in the symbolism of dreams and myths in this way, stressing the need for a 'both–and' rather than an 'either–or' kind of thinking – for example, both large *and* small, high *and* low, spiritual *and* instinctual, good *and* evil, full *and* empty. Jung proposed that there is a special factor in the psyche, which he called the transcendent function, to account for the tendency within the individual psyche for opposites to be joined.

At this stage I can state more clearly my central thesis: that what I am here describing is an essential feature in the development of the therapy group, which also undergoes individuation. My thesis is that it is the individuation of the group, rather than of the individual, which enables the individual to experience a sense of belonging to a greater whole; that this can be regarded as the development of a group-self, a better term than a group mind, and that the group-self, in turn, provides the group members with some notion of a larger transcendent self, ultimately a sense of 'all there is', or in gnostic language 'the All' or the pleroma, as being undivided, and that this is a religious experience. As described by Jung in the individual, so in the group too oppositions are constantly being generated and only when these are combined or united in some way can the group reach a higher level of development. This does not mean a fusion, in the sense of a failure to separate or to differentiate, for things cannot be conjoined before they are separated. The process in which the opposites combine is reminiscent of Hegel's logic, the well-known dialectic of thesis and antithesis leading to synthesis. Although Jung was steeped in the German idealist tradition, his ideas on the opposite came more from his Gnosticism. The gnostics were constantly attacked by the orthodox for their dualism. While all the gnostic sects undoubtedly had prominent dualistic features (perhaps most obviously so in Manichaeism, with the forces of light and the forces of darkness), there was always an ultimate unity which transcended the duality.

It is in this field of morality that Jung's gnostic views have caused the greatest difficulty to theologians. Good and evil are opposites to be combined and are thus given equal status. Evil is not just the absence of good. Nor is evil simply to be overcome by goodness. The Shadow has to be integrated rather than disowned. it is hard to translate this idea into a practical morality. Therapists all accept the idea of projection, that 'bad things' should not be put on to others, but in their wish to be non-judgemental are inclined to avoid statements as to how their patients should, or should not, behave morally. In the group therapy literature there is very little to be found on moral development of the group, though, for instance Yalom (1970) does take altruism to be one of the therapeutic factors in group therapy.

But we do see in the group, from time to time, moral issues becoming an important theme. Such discussions cannot always be treated as defensive avoidance or as non-work, because at some stage the group actually has to decide what is and what is not acceptable to them. This, then, gives rise to an opposition which cannot be resolved. A typical example is when some group members are claiming they are in the group for themselves and not to help others, while others are saying it is more important to look after one's neighbour and if everybody did that the whole group would benefit. From the conductor's point of view, one can probably see some people getting better by becoming more selfish, or, at least, less self-sacrificing, while for others the opposite may seem to be true. It is in dealing with this kind of conflict that the group conductor may find a Jungian gnostic approach more helpful than a conventionally moral one. He or she will not then approve of 'goodness' and disapprove of 'badness' but will see that what are being labelled 'good' and 'bad' are both necessary to the group. Transformation takes place as these are integrated with each other. Like the wise serpent, the conductor will encourage the group to eat of the Tree of Knowledge of Good *and* Evil. The emphasis is, of course, on knowledge. As knowledge is acquired, distinctions based on simple opposition become more and more complex, until one stops saying 'this is good' and 'this is bad'. Such distinctions belong to the creatura but not to the pleroma, where all opposites are combined and all distinctions disappear. Jung in the first sermon to the dead says: 'In us the pleroma is rent in two' and, of the opposites, 'In the Pleroma they cancel each other out; in us they do not. But if we know how to know ourselves as being apart from the pairs of opposites, then we have attained to salvation' (Hoeller, 1977, p.47). Here Jung is saying we must separate ourselves from our thinking, and knowledge is not, in itself, thinking but requires control over and detachment from the thinking in which the opposites are irreconcilable.

A tentative conclusion

The starting point of this paper was that there is a spiritual dimension in group therapy which goes beyond the conventional aims of the medical model. This is seen in the sort of fundamental questions which groups ask and I suggested that the groups are looking for some kind of religious answer. This was put not as an assumption but as evidence which any group conductor can verify. The objection can still be raised that groups looking for religious answers are misguided and wishing to delude themselves, and it may be insisted the symptoms which bring people into the therapy group can be relieved without any such problems being raised, let alone answered. Or it may be said that the questions are indeed important to explore in the group but the answers need not be religious and can be dealt with within a scientific or otherwise rationalistic framework. Even if it is acknowledged that some religious form is needed, it may be asked: why on earth go to Jung with his muddling accounts of the obscure speculation of people living in the early years of the Christian era?

It may be that my account here of Jung and his Gnosticism has done little to answer such objections. Perhaps my only hope might be with those who ask the last question, that such readers might explore further some of Jung's gnostic sources, now that they have at last become so easily available in translation. They might find that these writings are surprisingly modern, in spite of their somewhat antiquated style. At least the writings address the questions of the perplexity of modern man in the face of a sense of alienation and what is now called existential dread. They give no simple optimistically comforting answers. They do not see the created universe in which we live as having any ultimate meaning, provided by some beneficent deity who loves us and is good, if we were only to realize it. Such beliefs, they would say, are indeed illusory. Such a god would be a wicked demiurge or at best a foolish, blind and ignorant creature who himself knew no better. Such notions, of course, led to the horrors of persecution, such as the Albigensian crusade, in which men, women and children were brutally put to death: these people, the Cathars, were themselves peace-loving and non-violent and men and women were given equal status.

It seems to me now that our therapy groups, as they develop in wisdom, are not very different from the Cathars. They too raise doubts about a beneficent creator, and see the need to rethink the roles of men and women, to agree that as individuals they feel alienated. In gnostic language, they are 'strangers in the world' and perhaps it is not for nothing that we call our groups 'stranger groups'. Like the gnostics, they feel they are strangers in an unfriendly or hostile universe. Such feelings, though correctly described as 'persecutory anxiety', should surely not, in Kleinian style, be treated as pathological or as signs of a primitive group mentality. As the groups progress, they have a growing experience of being connected in an ultimate unity; not just their own unity as a group but a sense of this unity reflecting some ultimate reality which goes far beyond their small circle. This does not deny their sense of alienation at a lower level.

In the group process the members gradually cease to be strangers. This can only happen, not through speculation and rational thinking alone, but through their devotion to knowledge of themselves and of others and of the world in which they try to live. This knowledge is different from belief. It is not the creatural news of difference but the pleromatic news of unity, and can be called gnosis.

Perhaps it would be best to leave the last word to the gnostics themselves by giving a few quotations with which I imagine most group therapists would agree. First, two further quotations from the Gospel of Thomas:

If you bring forth what is within you, what you bring forth will save you. If you do not bring forth what is within you, what you do not bring forth will destroy you. (Robinson 1977)

Let him who seeks continue until he finds, he will become troubled. When he becomes troubled he will be astonished, and he will rule over the All. (Robinson 1977)

Finally, what has become known as the Valentinian formula, which I think might be applied to the most important questions for the therapy group:

What liberates is the knowledge of who we were, what we became; where we were, whereinto we have been thrown, whereto we speed, wherefrom we are re-deemed; what birth is, and what rebirth. (Robinson 1977)

References

Agazarian, Y. (1988) *The Invisible Group: A Theory of the Group as a Whole.* Twelfth Annual S H Foulkes Lecture. Group Analytic Society (London).

Agazarian, Y. and Peters, R. (1981) *The Visible and Invisible Group.* New York: Routledge and Kegan Paul.

Bateson, G. (1972) *Steps to an Ecology of Mind.* St Albans: Palladin Books.

Ellenberger, H. (1970) *The Discovery of the Unconscious.* New York: Basic Books.

Foulkes, S.H. (1964) *Therapeutic Group Analysis.* London: Allen and Unwin.

Garland, C. (1982) 'Group analysis: taking the non-problem seriously.' *Group Analysis 15,* 1, pp.4–14.

Hoeller, S.A. (1977) *The Gnostic Jung and the Seven Sermons to the Dead.* Wheaton, Ill: Theosophical Publishing House.

Jonas, H. (1958) *The Gnostic Religion.* Boston: Beacon Press.

Jung, C.G. (1962) *Erinnerungen, Traume, Gedanken (Memories, Dreams, Reflections).* Reprinted in English, London: Collins 1963.

Otto, R. (1923) *The Idea of the Holy.* London: Oxford University Press.

Pagels, E. (1979) *The Gnostic Gospels.* New York: Random House.

Robinson, J. (1977) (ed) *The Nag Hamadi Library in English.* Leiden: E J Brill.

Yalom, I.D. (1970) *The Theory and Practice of Group Psychotherapy.* New York: Basic Books.

CHAPTER TWELVE

The Dialogical Principle
Jung, Foulkes and Bakhtin

To many Jungian analysts, any form of group therapy is unacceptable. Jung put his objections to it in no uncertain terms and they cannot lightly be set aside. Indeed, he wrote with such evident passion on this subject that, if one is persuaded by his arguments, it is easy to come to the conclusion that one should never see more than one patient at a time. Jung's objections depend on the observation that everybody is different and his belief that to treat people collectively would not take account of this undeniable fact.

However, there are many Jungians now practising some form of group therapy and they are not persuaded by Jung's objections. But they vary in the extent to which they are prepared to modify Jung's approach in order to deal with the complexities of group work. Having worked with groups for many years, as well as with individuals, my own belief is that there are important mistakes in Jung's theory of the individual which led him to an incorrect view of group therapy. Although a detailed critique of Jung's arguments on this subject would be well beyond the scope of this paper, I should nevertheless like to show how my own thinking has made it possible for me to work in a truly analytic way with groups and at the same time retain a Jungian orientation. This has been possible for me through using Foulkes' model of group analysis. There are a growing number of Jungians now using this model. Far from seeing it as antithetical to Jung's, they see a remarkable convergence between the two (see, for example, Fiumara 1983). One can, of course, look at the differences or at the similarities. In this paper, I am taking a dialogical principle as forming the salient link between this model and Jung's.

Group analysis is a method pioneered by S.H. Foulkes in Britain, and is now an accepted school with training bodies in many European countries. Foulkes was himself a psychoanalyst, a member of the British Psycho-Analytical Society, and was one of a number of analysts who sought to use the principles of psychoanalysis in the group setting. However, his method and his underlying theory did not evolve as a solution to the problem of how to psychoanalyse individuals in the group but fully took the group into account as having a therapeutic potential lacking in the dyadic setting of classical analysis. It was nevertheless designed to explore the unconscious, with less emphasis on the vertical dimension of tracing the patient's history and more on the horizontal dimension of exploring relationships in the here-and-now. This has been paralleled by a similar change of emphasis in psychoanalysis itself, particularly in the British object-relations school. But group analysts found that there was much greater scope in the group for exploring the richness of relationships with others than by the study of the transference and countertransference dynamics of individual analysis. An important shift of group analytic thinking lay in seeing the individual not in isolation but as part of group process.

Foulkes, in developing his model, stressed the essentially social nature of Man in contrast to the classical Freudian model which was based on the instinctual drives of the individual. In the group, he distinguished four levels of interaction; he called the fourth the primordial level, the level of the collective unconscious with its archetypes. There is therefore a close link between Freud and Jung, who both have a place in his model. It is unfortunate that so many analysts, both Freudian and Jungian, have shown little interest in these developments, both schools, for somewhat different reasons, being convinced that there is no need to depart from the one-to-one and suspecting that the process is either too 'dilute' or positively harmful to the analytic process. I would not altogether dismiss these objections. There is something in them but they are not usually based on a great deal of experience and often constitute an unexamined assumption. As in all disputes between rival schools, it is important to look at the differences and see what evidence there is to support conflicting claims, and it is not easy to examine the evidence. There are, of course, formidable difficulties in conducting outcome research in psychotherapy but a prior, and much easier, task is to look at rival theories or theoretical structures which, once the theoreticians are no longer alive, means a careful study of their texts. This often means assessing the background assumptions or premises on which the theories are built, as well as discerning contradictions or lack of coherence in the theories themselves. Often this comparative study can clarify whether or not strongly held differences of viewpoint can be, at least potentially, resolved.

The 'analysis' part of group analysis is derived from psychoanalysis and may be thought to be different from what is implied in the 'analytical' of analytical psychology. By emphasising that both methods are analytical I am not advocating analysis in place of synthesis but as being a necessary component of any method of exploring deep unconscious processes.

Analysis and individuation

The special characteristics of the Jungian approach to psychotherapy can be subsumed under the over-arching concept of individuation, which is at the same time both a process and a goal. Individuation, as shown in its many different formulations throughout Jung's writings, is, however, such a broad category that there is no ready agreement on its relation with analysis as a clinical method. In addressing the topic of individuation with different Jungian audiences I hear widely differing views about this. At one end of the spectrum it is regarded as a task or goal of the second half of life, and even then not for everybody, and at the other as a universal process from birth to the grave. In both groups, there are further divisions between those who think one can choose to pursue it and those who think one has to, whether one wants to or not, and between those who think it is necessarily a specific form of individual development, a sort of dialogue with the unconscious in which the archetypes are confronted in an orderly sequence, and those who think it can take a hundred different forms whether or not the individual undergoes 'analysis' (and all Jungian therapists seem to call themselves analysts). There seem to be some analysts who use Jung's model of individuation with all their patients and others who follow Jung's eclectic approach, recalling his suggesting that there are many people who could benefit more from a Freudian or Adlerian orientation.

Despite the notorious differences between Jungians, based on the many different strands in Jung's thought, it should be possible to agree on there being certain processes involved in individuation which Jung constantly stressed. These include the confrontation of the conscious personality with unconscious contents, their absorption or integration under the organization of the self rather than by the ego, the compensatory nature of these contents to a faulty one-sided conscious attitude, the religious or spiritual dimension of these experiences, the non-reductive synthesizing or prospective direction, the coming-together of opposites and the recognition of true symbols with their numinosity, leading to wholeness or completion rather than perfection.

Different methods of psychotherapy cannot be compared without taking into account the goal of treatment. When writing about his methods Jung was referring to the goal of individuation. Once Jung had articulated and proposed this goal, both therapy and analysis acquired new connotations. There was certainly an aim which went beyond the cure or alleviation of psychiatric conditions. It was more a recognition of a sickness of the soul whose healing meant a realisation and integration of parts of the self, so that it led towards wholeness. This wholeness was conceived as going beyond ordinary well-being, the rude good health that might satisfy some. Jung was advocating a path full of danger, and not achievable without suffering, to attain the 'pearl of great price', or the gold of the alchemists. His whole approach to patients was conducted in this spirit. He was inclined to be dismissive of other forms of psychotherapy, whose goals were more modest. He did acknowledge their usefulness at times but made it clear that they were not *his* way. This attitude has made it difficult for his followers. They may agree in general, but in their practical work do not always see the need for making such an absolute distinction.

One great attraction of the model underlying group analysis is that a place is found within it for both Freud and Jung. There is no question of one being right and the other wrong. Nor is it a question of one method being right for some people and not for others. Differences in group interaction are accommodated by placing them on different levels. These can be ordered as progressively deeper levels but they are all necessary and no one level is regarded as better or more helpful for the participants than any other.

Insight for any individual member at any time may occur in many different ways. It may, for example, simply be the realisation that one is thought by the others to be arrogant or aloof when one thought one was being modest or shy or quietly listening to the others. This example might be said to be quite trivial in insight compared to the revelations of a 'big' dream. On the other hand, the experiences which Jung considered to be conducive to the transformations of the individuation process can all occur in the group. These can indeed include the telling of a 'big dream' which powerfully affects the whole group, as well as other numinous confrontations with archetypal material. There can be the realisation of the compensatory effect of some quite small detail expressed by one member, which can transform the group when its true significance is understood, or the group may come to recognize the need to integrate the shadow in the form of one member who attacks the rest of the group or who may be scapegoated by the others, and so on. At times the group has a religious experience in the sense that Jung spoke of religion (cf. Zinkin 1989). As the group goes on, everybody is becoming more 'whole' in a way which goes far beyond the relief of whatever symptoms first made them seek therapy. Again, in Jung's terms each individual is becoming, not more perfect, but more complete. Of course, there are also dangers. It is always possible that the uniqueness of the individual can be swamped by the values of the group. But Jung never claimed that individuation was possible without this danger. He simply assumed that the best way to avoid it was for one analyst to concentrate on one patient. I would argue that the reverse is true, that the danger is considerably less in the small group (eight or nine participants) than in the one-to-one.

Dialogue

In *On the Nature of the Psyche*, Jung attributes subjectivity to the unconscious (Jung 1960). He does not merely say that the unconscious behaves *as though* there were an independent subject to the subject of consciousness but comes to the conclusion that this really existed. This seems difficult to reconcile with his use of the term 'objective psyche' which refers to the stark 'thereness' of universal contents of the collective unconscious. However, Jung regarded the archetypes themselves as unknowable, except insofar as the symbols could be related to as living for the individual, and therefore he thought it was not sufficient simply to study archetypal contents but that it was important to enter into some kind of dialogue with them. This we know he did for himself throughout his life. His principal technique for doing this was active imagination and he recommended this technique to his patients. Whether these contents be regarded as personal or archetypal, and whether or not they be regarded as parts of the self which needed to be integrated, Jung never meant one to identify totally with them. Indeed, in the case of the archetypes he tirelessly warned against the dangers of doing this. They were to be held in relationship with the consciousness, specifically with the ego as the centre of consciousness, and his notion of their being subjects as well as having objective reality is what justified him in having conversations, for example with his anima. Furthermore, he believed that dreams spoke to one. One had to listen to what they had to say, not of course to take them literally but to allow an interchange with the conscious mind. It is this interchange which constitutes dialogue.

Now, in saying that Jung, in various ways, was advocating dialogue with the unconscious, I am stretching the notion of dialogue. Although Jung left out the words 'as if', most people would think that he was not talking about a real dialogue but an imaginary one. They would understand 'talking to your anima' as being a metaphor as indeed they would contend that talking to yourself was not a real conversation. Really to believe one was actually having a conversation with oneself might be the first sign of madness.

In my own work, whether with individuals, with couples or with groups, I have come to place more and more emphasis on dialogue as being the principle which makes healing possible. In fact, experience with groups has very much influenced my work with individuals and this influence continues to be reciprocal. However, one should not use the term 'dialogue' loosely. It has unfortunately crept into psychobabble and is even used as a verb as in: 'I want to dialogue with you.' There is clearly a sense in which people in conversation are not in dialogue and, likewise, there is a sense in which one can indeed be in dialogue with one's dreams. I would like to draw out this distinction between genuine or authentic dialogue on the one hand and monologue or spurious dialogue on the other, because it is crucial to the link I want to make between analytical psychology and group analysis. I cannot do more here than indicate a few criteria in a field in which there is a vast and difficult philosophical debate.

First, it may be necessary to remind the reader that the word dialogue does not mean something restricted to two participants. Dia- is not duo-. It means 'through, during, across' and dialogue is 'a conversation carried on between two or more persons, a colloquy, talk together' or 'verbal interchange of thought between two or more persons, conversation' (*Oxford English Dictionary*).

This is important in validating group analysis. If dialogue involves two or more persons, a process which takes place in individual or dyadic analysis can occur also in the group.

In considering the nature of a true dialogue, Martin Buber's distinction between I–Thou and I–it is helpful, even though his language is evocative rather than precise. It is based on a distinction between ontology and epistemology and its appeal is to direct experience rather than to thinking. The I–Thou is always spoken from the whole being, from Man in his fullness, from the plenitude of being. 'The primary word I–Thou can only be spoken with the whole being. The primary word I–it can never be spoken with the whole being' (Buber 1937, p.3). Buber regards the ability to speak I–Thou as specifically human, though it need not be addressed to another human: it can be to a tree, an animal or even a stone. However, Buber dwells on the special province of the interhuman in his *Between Man and Man* (Buber 1947) and he addresses especially this dimension in his discussion of psychotherapy in *The Knowledge of Man* (Buber 1964). Interhuman dialogue requires (at least) two people holding separate positions but each affirming and confirming the other. Affirmation and confirmation are often used interchangeably but Buber makes an important distinction between them. This occurs in a discussion with Carl Rogers (Buber 1964) where he makes it clear that it is not sufficient simply to show acceptance of the other (affirming him) but to stand against him in confirmation. This implies that, in psychotherapy, it is not enough to be non-directive and to make it clear that one has understood what the patient is expressing, but to communicate that one is understanding *from a different perspective*. This makes room for the all-important function of interpretation, and thus of using a hermeneutic or exegetical approach to the utterances of the other.

It is unfortunate that Buber and Jung did not see at all eye to eye and this might itself be seen as a failure of dialogue. Buber spoke of Jung's 'panpsychism' (Buber 1957) and by this he meant that Jung failed to recognize being other than as existing within himself. Though I think this unfair to Jung, there is certainly a tendency in Jung to give precedence to the meeting with the unconscious rather than to the interpersonal dimension favoured by Buber. If one can have a dialogue with a stone, why not with an archetypal image? I have treated this problem elsewhere (Zinkin 1979) and here am simply drawing attention to some overlap between Buber's evaluation of dialogue and Jung's. In discussing dialogue, there are other philosophers than Buber, notably Marcel, Rosenweig, and Levinas.

More recently the 'Dialogism' of Bakhtin and his circle has attracted the attention of the West, having been published during the oppressive regime of the Soviet Union. Like Buber (who undoubtedly influenced him), Bakhtin stressed the 'in-between', not what is said but the fact that what is said is incomplete until it has met a response in the other. This he called the 'dialogical principle' (Bakhtin 1979). He has become something of a cult figure in the field of literary criticism, as his interest in language has anticipated post-structuralism and the now common idea that one cannot speak of a text without a reader. He regards dialogue as the meeting of two or more points of view. He takes Dostoevsky in his novels as exemplifying the interchange between multiple points of view and sees the author not as occupying some Archimedean point outside the characters from which he can objectively judge them, but as yet another point of view, though one with what he called a 'surplus of seeing' as his vision encompasses the separate visual perspectives of the characters. Even the author's viewpoint, though relatively full, is nevertheless incomplete. Bakhtin's explication of dialogue, unlike Buber's, is based on a contrast with monologue. Briefly, he defines monologue as speech which does not require, nor even expect, an answer. In contrast to the dialogism of Dostoevsky in a literary text, one could take epic poetry such as the Iliad as monologic. In dialogue there is an address and a response and the response too expects a response. One addresses the other and is answerable to the other, and 'answerability' (Holquist 1990) is Bakhtin's equivalent to Buber's 'responsibility'.

From a psychotherapeutic point of view, the dialogic principle can be stated as follows: neither the therapist nor the patient has the 'truth'. Each has *a* truth but in the interaction between them this is a point of view. If each can address the other (as a Thou) both benefit from the exchange as each point of view is developed in relation to the other. In the process each confirms as well as affirms the other. This can only happen insofar as there is mutual acceptance. Acceptance does not mean agreement but includes the acceptance of difference. From this view of psychotherapy, the understanding of the patient's material is needed in order to further the dialogue rather than the other way round. It is the developing of the richness of the dialogue which *is* the therapy.

This brief outline of the place of dialogue in psychotherapy has been necessary to make the link between individual and group therapy, but the special purpose of this paper is the more specific one of reconciling the style, the aims and the underlying theory of analytical psychology with those of group analysis, using the model proposed by S.H. Foulkes (Foulkes 1964). However well both models implicitly make use of dialogue, certain features of dialogue that are regarded as important to the philosophers of dialogue, the features of a 'dialogical principle', are problematic in both models. These difficulties need to be addressed if dialogue can be usefully regarded as a way of linking the two.

Dialogue in group analysis

Therapeutic group analysis is a method with certain differences, both from psychoanalysis and from other models of group therapy. Although much of psychoanalytic (Freudian) theory is used, it seeks, like Jungian theory, to 'go further'. The group functions in ways which cannot be understood as a simple aggregate or product of each member's individual psychology. It follows the gestalt principle that the whole is more than its parts. Moreover, its rationale involves a shift of emphasis towards seeing the individual as indissolubly part of society. Foulkes stated that Man was quintessentially social and also that, the notion of the individual being an abstraction, the individual in the group was like a node in a network. The network can be seen as a social or communicational network which Foulkes called the matrix. In the case of the therapy group, all the communications between the members which go to make up the complex network of interactions have to be borne in mind as a pattern of interaction in which the individual members act as nodal points. Locating the points within the pattern provides a context for them which gives them meaning. But it is not simply a matter of what lies outside the points. The matrix determines what lies within the individual as the lines of communication go through each one.

The communications need not be verbal; for example, a silent member is contributing to the pattern. His or her silence plays a part in determining the group dynamics but, seen as an individual, he or she may or may not be participating in the group and may indeed be benefiting from what is going on between the others. Interpretations or comments can be made which focus either on what is going on in the individual member or in the group as a whole, which is understood to contain that member as well as the group conductor. In addition it is often helpful, where possible, to link the individual and group processes. This shows the interdependence of the two, the relationship between part and whole. As the linking process goes on, both the group as a whole and the individual members can be seen to be developing. The members, of course, do not all develop in the same way or at the same pace and it is important to recognize these differences. Collectively the group recognizes and confirms both the uniqueness of the individual and the group process in which the individual is participating. Also, it should be stressed that the group conductor, though having a special role in the constitution and in the setting of boundaries, is by no means the only one providing interpretations. Although there may be much disagreement, each member is regarded as having a valid view on themselves, on others and on what they experience as group phenomena. This gives the conductor a relatively subsidiary role. Although at the beginning he or she is looked on as a leader, once the group is established he or she is rarely seen to be leading it at all. Transferences may be interpreted but are not thought of simply as existing between the group on the one hand and the conductor on the other, or between individuals and the conductor, but as existing also between the members, forming part of an interactive field.

Although the flow of talk in the group is often loose and unstructured, so that it can be treated as a flow of associations as in individual analysis, Foulkes has taken the exchange between members as providing one of the therapeutic factors which are group-specific (Foulkes 1964). In the usual structure of analysis, the patient talks freely in an associative mode and the analyst provides interventions in the form of interpretations (or, at least, if not formal interpretations, interventions designed to show what the analyst has understood of the patient's 'material'). In contrast, people in the group *address* one another. They respond to each other and there is a lively conversational exchange. Not all conversation can be called true or authentic dialogue in Buber's terms, but this does occur at times, when there is sufficient trust in the relationship. This dialogue can involve the whole group, and then to participate in it is a deeply moving experience sometimes akin to a religious one.

For the individual in the group the experience of being understood confirms him or her as both a whole and a unique person. This does not come easily and a good deal of the work of the group is in dealing with misunderstandings, due to transference distortions between the members, analysing resistances, etc., but in the process the individual members gain insight and are brought closer together. It is the mutuality of the understanding, the consequent sharing of a deeper and richer feeling for each of the members of the group which is therapeutic. It is difficult to describe but is easily understood by anyone who has taken part in it. The difficulty in description is largely due to a lack of vocabulary. Depth psychology has, in general, concentrated on the individual psyche and what is happening in the inner world. It is still hard to conceptualize what is going on *between* people rather than within them, even though the dimension of the interpersonal, the intersubjective or interhuman as Buber calls it, is gradually finding a place. It is easier to talk of object-relations than of subject-relations. The intersubjective takes place in the form of an 'utterance' which is not understandable except when it is responded to by another. In the dialogue there is always the sense of flow going backwards and forwards. As a result, even though one can often say what the dialogue is 'about', it gives no information as to how the interchange itself is experienced. This dimension is one which is more obvious in group than in individual analysis, and several group-analysts have written about it, notably de Mare, Pines and Brown (Brown and Zinkin 1994).

Dialogue and Jungian analysis

Much of what I have said so far will be regarded by Jungian analysts as true of their work also. In fact, Jung's opposition to groups can be understood as implying that *only* within the individual or with one other individual (the analyst) can true dialogue take place. Collectivity immediately associated with a non-insightful collective mind and groups of all kinds are then thought of as constituting the collective forces which Jung regarded as endangering the individual. His analytic model is based on the very special relationship between the experienced analyst and the patient, who accompany each other in a journey of self-discovery called individuation. This cannot take place unless the analyst is deeply committed to his or her patient. Almost everyone who met Jung can attest to his remarkable intuitive power to respond to the individual even in one meeting. Furthermore, Jung preferred the face-to-face position to using the couch, which he associated with the blank screen or 'opaque mirror' which Freud recommended. Instead he felt that the analyst should allow the patient to see his personal reactions. The analytic relationship was, furthermore, one in which the analyst changed as well as the patient. He called this relationship dialectic and this may sound very close to what I have described as dialogical.

Despite all these considerations, there seems to me to be an enormous difficulty with Jung in this area. His own development was largely a solitary journey. His Red Book was not for publication and is still kept secret. We have, of course, the massive Collected Works but really the main thrust of these is an appeal to *universality*. We are constantly reminded that the contents of the deepest levels of the psyche, in which the archetypes dwell, belong not to the individual, but to Mankind everywhere since time immemorial. Above all they are not personal. They are not the property of the individual, nor even located within the individual. They are impersonal and collective. This immense work, of the comparative study of archetypal material, relating clinical findings to esoteric disciplines such as Gnosticism and alchemy is, after all, Jung's great contribution. He left to Freud and his followers the task of working out the detailed study of what he regarded as the personal unconscious. For him, the collective unconscious was much more important. Consequently, dialogue for him, the important dialogue, was not that between people but that between consciousness and the unconscious. This was the kind of dialogue he himself had with figures which appeared to him in dreams or visions. However personal these figures may seem to the reader, however stamped they are with Jung's unique personality, they were, for Jung, not his but belonging to *other*. He regarded the personal factor as determining only the appearance of the archetypal images and he was careful to point out that however these images may change, the underlying structures, the archetypes themselves, were unchanging. They were ahistorical and acultural. I am not saying that he regarded the dialogue between analyst and patient as insignificant. On the contrary it was of the utmost importance, but one is left with the impression that this was only to help the patient better to conduct the more important dialogue with the unconscious.

Many Jungian analysts take this view. If there is a difference in point of view between them and the patient, they will say: 'Let's see what the dream has to say' and the dream will often have the last word. This is what is meant by the objective psyche. It means that there is no gainsaying what the unconscious has to say. It is vital to be in communication with the unconscious because it is trying to communicate something, to correct or compensate for the conscious attitude. It is true that, like the Delphic oracle, the message could be misunderstood. It is precisely for this reason that the patient needs the analyst, and the knowledge of the analyst of the hermeneutics of symbolism. Certainly there is a great danger if the symbolism is misunderstood but this only confirms the fact that, correctly understood, the unconscious is 'objectively' right.

Problems of the two halves of life

Now, it is not my purpose to belittle Jung's work in this area. Rather, I want to suggest that individuation as he saw it took too much for granted. What most therapists see as the development of a person as taking place in the context of other persons, Jung saw as something that should have been accomplished in the first half of life. Only after the achievement of what is usually regarded as maturity, the stage at which one has overcome youthful follies and has brought up a family, can the inner journey begin. After his separation from Freud, he regarded problems in achieving the aims of the first half of life as requiring a Freudian analysis, even though he saw Freud's method as over-reductive. In other words, he made a separation between individuation and the aims of psychoanalysis of a far-reaching, almost fundamental kind through his claim that life could be divided into two halves, the first half devoted to living more fully in the world and the second as a preparation for death. Roughly speaking, this can be contrasted as ego-growth until mid-life and a realisation of the self in later life.

Many, perhaps most, Jungians have rejected this division. Michael Fordham has been a major influence in effecting a revision of Jung's view (Fordham 1976). By adopting an empirical standpoint, he was able to demonstrate the process of individuation in very young children. Whether or not it is correct to understand the goals of life changing direction after mid-life, the process of individuation is generally considered to take place throughout the whole lifespan. But this is not a minor correction of a small mistake in Jung. It challenges Jung's neat way of dissociating himself and his methods from those of Freud.

The question we are left with is not 'How does a person individuate?' but 'How does one become a person *and* individuate?' Or, if we define individuation as becoming more what one truly is and becoming more whole, how do we combine the need for ego growth with a respect for the self as being the true centre of the psyche? In general the answer given by Jungians has remained an intrapersonal one; for example, the idea of an ego–self axis (Edinger 1960) implies a balance between the two which still uses Jung's approach for dealing with individuation. We look at dreams or other fantasy-products as being in a dialectic or compensatory relationship with the conscious attitude and once again we are dealing with a dialogue with the unconscious. It is tempting to call this 'talking to oneself' but this would not be the same as talking to the Self, because Jung's view was that the Self was not personal or individual in its essence.

I believe that Jung has left a legacy of confusion on these matters which continues to divide Jungian analysts and they cannot easily agree to differ because the issues are fundamental ones. By this I mean that they raise questions as to the nature of humanity: what it consists of, how it is formed; questions which rapidly become philosophical or theological, which Jung himself regarded as outside the sphere of psychology.

In this paper, I can do no more than suggest a possible remedy, one which has been consolidated for me in my work with groups (as well as with couples). A remedy has to be based on where one locates the problem. In my view, the recurrent problem in Jung's texts has been that no sooner does he make a useful distinction than he begins to polarise it. One glaring example is the way he has polarised the individual and the collective. In making a distinction, a logical opposition, he has treated it too much as 'a pair of opposites'. These opposites are like opposing forces which are seen as requiring a life's work to resolve or may indeed never be ultimately resolvable. Unquestionably this particular opposition was the focus of a lifelong struggle in Jung's personal life. I have said that I do not wish to belittle Jung's work on the archetypes, nor, of course, the value of introspection. On the contrary, I believe that where introspection shows that one is having the same fantasies as others have or that there is a common underlying structure it becomes evident that it is wrong to regard people as isolated and separate beings. It is the very sameness in the deepest roots of our being that provides the basis for human solidarity. But there seems to me to be an error in Jung's reasoning. Of course the individual and the collective can, at times, be at enmity. One can be at odds with one's group whether it be family, colleagues, one's country or the whole world. It does not follow that the problem lies in some basic incompatibility between individual values and collective ones. It is more reasonable to conclude that individuals and groups are interdependent and that when functioning well they benefit each other. One should not argue from the breakdown of a system that the system itself is fundamentally the wrong system. Such a conclusion would only be a last resort.

To return to group analysis: if a man complains that he cannot get on with people in groups, it seems sensible to see him in a group and see what goes wrong. This does not preclude hearing his account of how he experiences the group and himself, or listening to his dreams. In fact if one sees him first individually, it is extraordinary how what one sees differs from his description. As the other members not only react and respond to the way he behaves or attempts to deal with the situation, but gradually have access to his inner life, he gains not only insight but also understanding from others. In other words, the dialogue with others does not replace his dialogue with himself. It supplements it and he is gradually enabled to internalise it; in this way, his internal figures, despite their archetypal roots, become more humanized, thus enabling a better internal dialogue to take place.

I want to stress that this process is not an artificial one. Although one has to go to great trouble to construct the right setting, the right conditions for such a dialogue with others to take place, one is essentially *restoring* the normality of a healthy group–individual functioning. By healthy, I imply wholeness and what is being restored is what should never have been breached in the first place. The group is thus conceived as the natural environment in which the individual becomes himself. It is a harmonious and mutually enriching relationship like that between a plant and the soil.

There is a puzzling aspect to Jung's opposition to group therapy. It has often been pointed out that he was confusing group psychology with crowd psychology under the influence of Le Bon (Le Bon 1946). In a crowd, of course, the individual may readily panic or hold beliefs or behave in ways that are primitive compared with the maturity of the individual in private. It is then pointed out that this does not necessarily apply in small groups and certainly not in a carefully composed therapy group under the guidance of a sensitive conductor who is well aware of the dangers of mass psychology. The puzzle is that this objection is such an obvious one that Jung must have been aware of it.

Jung claimed to have a very broad picture of the nature of the human psyche going far beyond Freud's model. This claim, which all Jungians feel is justified, may produce a blind spot in Jungians similar to Jung's own. In a theory which includes so much, one may not be aware of what is left out. Jung seemed to me to have neglected or not seen as relevant the whole tradition of the social and political sciences, in which the relationship of the individual to society is crucial and the subject of intense debate. Although he was interested in cultural differences, he was much more interested in underlying structural resemblances in his unending quest for the archetypes. The general impression is that differences between even the smallest groups could be understood in terms of the differences between the individual and the group. His understanding of primitive groups was that they were primitive to the extent that they did not recognize the individual, but he did not go into the question as to how societies develop that recognition, except to appeal to the notion of a growth of consciousness. This always sounds as though it is an individual matter in the face of a group which opposes it. It does not allow for the possibility of it being more usually a two-way process in which social groups can enable the individual to be one.

Transcendence and containment

I have frequently referred to Jung's claim that his model goes beyond the limitations of other models and he particularly meant Freud's. I have also indicated that Foulkes' model of group analysis, including as it does both Freud and Jung, seeks to 'go beyond' both of them. These transcendent claims have their disadvantages. Not only do they give a suggestion of complacent superiority by exposing the limitations of others, but they seductively offer the prospect of a limitless or infinite perspective. There is a need then to contain them, to indicate the limits of the enquiry, in order to form a theory or method which has coherence and credibility. Jung, in particular, was so far-reaching in his field of enquiry that he frequently had to point out that he was not a theologian, not an anthropologist, not a philosopher but a mere man of science, an empirical psychologist simply concerned with elucidating certain facts within his chosen métier. In psychotherapy, too, the task of extending the depth of insight of the patient has to be balanced with the notion of 'containment', where the setting and the way the therapist relates to the patient act like the mother who 'holds' the infant (Winnicott 1971) or acts as a container of the contained (Bion 1984). Freud made use of a dialectical principle in which the opposites such as the opposition I have just brought about between containment within and transcendence beyond certain limits can only be reconciled, in Hegelian fashion, by some third term which both unites and reconciles them at a higher level.

I am using dialogue as a reconciling principle but not in this Hegelian dialectical way. Dialogue is not the same as dialectic and I would not accept Jung's suggestion that the relationship between analyst and analysand is a dialectical one. It is, rather, a dialogical one. It is not that something new emerges through the opposition of the two participants, something which then has greater validity or truth than either of them, but that the relationship shows each to have a relative truth because there are two subjects, each acting on the other so that the sense of self of each is enhanced precisely because of its incompletion without the other. The other need not be the alienated other of Marx or of Sartre or Lacan. In genuine dialogue there is a meeting, a sense of being addressed, which, while it confirms the existence or being of the single subject, also confirms the presence of other subjects. In other words the subject is decentred but not done away with.

This shift of viewpoint is a profound one because it moves from the quest for objective certainty to a realisation of the subjective being validated through the subjectivity of others. It is one which I have been helped to make through my experience with groups but, although there are certain advantages in the presence of more than one other person, the dialogical principle is realisable too within the dyadic framework, which also has certain advantages. But whether between two or more than two, dialogue is contained by the number of participants, by the setting in which it takes place, the conditions of time and place in which they meet and, above all, in the fact that language is used: a language which has to be common to the participants. I am stressing this last point because the knowledge or understanding which all psychotherapy pursues is that of the self-conscious subject and it is increasingly becoming recognized that, without language, the particularly human capacity for self-knowledge could not occur.

Conclusion

I have tried to address Jung's strictures[1] on group therapy and to show how Foulkes' model of group analysis is compatible with a Jungian approach. I have pointed to areas of common ground between Jung and Foulkes in the concept of the collective unconscious and in showing how the process and goal of individuation in analytical psychology describes also the process and goal for the individual in group analysis, the principle of dialogue being crucial to both. Jung focused on the individual's dialogue with the unconscious, an intrapsychic process, while group analysis depends on the dialogue which develops between the members of the group whose many strands connect variously and deeply with the individual in the group, an interpsychic process which places man as a social animal. The explication of dialogue by Buber and by Bakhtin has enhanced my work with both groups and individuals and I believe dialogue to be the principle which enables healing.

References

Bakhtin, M. (1979) 'The problem of text in linguistics, philosophy and the other human sciences.' In *Estetica Slovesnog Tvorchestva*. Moscow: Bocharov.

Bion, W.R. (1984) *Learning from Experience*. London: Karnac.

Brown, D. and Zinkin, L. (1994) (eds) *The Psyche and the Social World*. London: Routledge.

Buber, M. (1937) *I and Thou*. trans. R. G. Smith. London: T.& T. Clarke. Original German edition 1923.

Buber, M. (1947) *Between Man and Man*. Trans. R. G. Smith. London: Kegan Paul. 1964 new edition with introduction by M. Friedman and afterword by author, trans. M. Friedman.

Buber, M. (1957) *The Eclipse of God*. Trans. M. Friedman. New York: Harper.

Buber, M. (1964) *The Knowledge of Man*. Trans. M. Friedman and R. G. Smith. London: George Allen and Unwin.

Edinger, E. (1960) 'The ego-self paradox.' *Journal of Analytical Psychology 5*, 1, pp.3–18.

Fiumara, R. (1983) 'Analytical psychology and group-analytic psychotherapy: convergences.' In M. Pines (ed) *The Evolution of the Group*. London: Routledge and Kegan Paul.

---

1   Louis Zinkin's draft of this paper, which was found on disk after his death, ended at this point and his widow wrote the rest of the conclusion.

Fordham, M. (1976) *The Self and Autism.* London: Heinemann.

Foulkes, S.H. (1964) *Therapeutic Group Analysis.* London: George Allen and Unwin.

Holquist, M. (1990) *Dialogism, Bakhtin and His World.* London: Routledge.

Jung C.G. (1947) 'On the nature of the psyche' in *Collected Works 8,* pp.343–342. London: Routledge and Kegan Paul.

Le Bon, G. (1946) *The Crowd.* English version first published 1896.

Winnicott, D.W. (1971) *Playing and Reality.* London: Tavistock.

Zinkin, L. (1979) 'The collective and the personal.' Chapter 3 of this volume; originally published in *Journal of Analytical Psychology 24,* 3, pp.227–250.

Zinkin, L. (1989) 'A gnostic view of the therapy group.' Chapter 11 of this volume; originally published in *Group Analysis 22,* pp.201–17.

CHAPTER THIRTEEN

Three Models Are Better Than One

This chapter was presented at the Group-Analytic Society London Workshop in January 1983.

The theme of this workshop, 'Society, Culture and Personality in Group Analysis', plunges us into problems which are at the very heart of group analysis. We know that it is no easy matter to apply the psychoanalytic method to a group, but are we clear as to why this should be? Applying psychoanalysis to a group, we run into numerous difficulties which all seem to stem from the fact that although psychoanalysis is a far-reaching theory of the mind, Freud's insights essentially come from his experience of neurotic patients studied during treatment, seen singly in the setting of the consulting room; and the object of study – his key to helping his patients – was essentially the unconscious contents of the patient's mind, which Freud was engaged in 'making conscious'.

The nature of society, the world in which the patient lived and, particularly, the patient's past were of course of great interest to Freud in his understanding of the unconscious and how the patient came to think in the way he did; but the structure of these events outside the consulting room could largely be taken for granted. Certainly Freud has often been criticized for generalising too much from the middle-class neurotic Viennese of the turn of the century, but these criticisms have more force as criticisms of the application of his theory outside its observational field than of his clinical insights. Although Freud himself applied his theories to consider groups and society, these ideas seem highly speculative compared with the direct study of his patients, where the true strength of his theories lay.

Matters are quite different with the therapy group, where questions like the relationship of the individual to society, the way individuals form groups, the existence or otherwise of a group-mind or a group-unconscious become central.

Let us now clear the ground and accept that we do not yet have a very satisfactory model for group analysis. With due respect to Foulkes, he did not and could not have been expected to do much more than point the way to such a model, to indicate the need for it and to show us some of the ingredients with which we might construct it. Clearly many of the ways of thinking which he brought in are derived from psychoanalysis but others, like mirroring and social exchange, are not. It is these that significantly differentiate group analysis from psychoanalysis.

There are of course other models which we can apply to group analysis, but the same problem arises. Suppose we start from the study of social systems. Can this lead us to an understanding of a patient's neurotic symptoms, such as, for example, a fear of approaching the opposite sex?

The idea I want to put over is that it is a mistake to have any one model and then 'apply' it. It is a greater mistake to jumble up ideas from different disciplines. I suggest that out of a multitude of models there are three distinct, broadly-based models that we need to work with. Models are not quite the same as theories which we may try to show are true or false, but are rather constructions which help us to perceive and make sense of what we experience in the therapeutic group.

To make it easier to grasp, I put three simple questions:

1. What sort of mind does a person have?

2. What is Man's place in the world?

3. How does one person relate to another?

These questions can be approached in different ways. By calling them psychological questions, I mean that the psychotherapist has to concern himself with their psychological significance because the psyche is his first concern. Freud's model seems to me to be primarily designed to deal with the first question and can be applied secondarily to the other two. Question 2 is better approached by a different model of the psyche, the sort of model developed by Jung. Question 1 requires an intrapsychic model and question 3 an interpersonal model. Jung's model was neither. It was a model of the collective psyche. It gives rise to so many difficulties, so many apparently irreconcilable propositions, that it is tempting to dismiss it. I believe, however, that it is indispensable. The contradictions and obscurities are not of Jung's making but lie in habits of thought which hinder us in approaching the kinds of question he asked.

The question: 'What is Man's place in the world?' is of course over-simple. It is really one of a whole series of questions like: 'What is Man's relation to his family, to his social group, to his nation, to the world and to the Universe?' One may also ask: 'What does this word "Man" mean in relation to any particular man, woman or child?' All these questions are questions about the connection between individuality and collectivity. Jung, unlike Freud, did not begin with the individual. He noted that our highly prized notion of ourselves as separate individuals is a fairly recent one. He regarded it as an acquisition of consciousness. He saw consciousness as arising like islands out of the sea of the unconscious (Jung 1926; 1968). Essentially he saw it as an *achievement*. The collective unconscious was not for him a difficult concept. What was much more difficult to understand was individual consciousness. The discovery of the unconscious was not simply the discovery of something denied to consciousness. The discovery of the unconscious completely changed what is meant by 'consciousness'. The philosophers themselves have had to try to take this in. Paul Ricoeur has made the point very tellingly. He has remarked that: 'The encounter with psychoanalysis constitutes a considerable shock, for this discipline affects and questions not simply some particular theme within philosophical reflection but the philosophical project as a whole', and he adds: 'The question of consciousness is just as obscure as that of the unconscious' (Ricoeur 1974, p.99). Jung might have said that it was considerably more obscure. He would not, of course, have meant that we readily conceive it in this way. He knew that obscurity and darkness are associated with the unconscious and light and clarity with consciousness but he regarded the over-valuation of clarity as something of a fallacy, a human prejudice. In his model, he called Freud's unconscious, as he understood it, the personal unconscious – that which is denied, repressed, split off, or disavowed by the individual but which nevertheless belongs to him. But he saw layers and layers extending beyond this, reaching ultimately to the collective unconscious. The word 'collective', which simply means shared, was one which he also used of the psyche. The psyche itself is not an individual possession, though each of us has a personal, unique conscious and unconscious. These are like the tips of an enormous iceberg, as shown in Figure 3.3 (p.58).

I come now to the most problematic question in Jung's model. If the psyche extends beyond the individual, should one regard this extension of the individual psyche as extending inside or outside the individual? Is he part of it or is it part of him? Is he speaking of an inner or an outer world? Jung never answers this question unequivocally but appears to make contradictory statements, suggesting first one, then the other concept. I think his real answer was 'both'. The way you looked at it might depend on whether you were an introvert or an extrovert. Both were valid: the whole question was relative (a question of viewpoint) rather than absolute.

This brings me to a vital difference between Jung's and Freud's model of the psyche. Freud's unit was the single organism, so for Freud the ego was a person's central organising agent: it controlled and regulated or organised the individual and mediated between the inner and outside world. For Jung the ego was the centre of *consciousness*. The true centre of the psyche was the self. But Jung also used the word 'self' for the totality of the psyche, sometimes meaning the individual psyche and sometimes the collective psyche – the Self with a capital 'S'. He also used it to indicate an archetype of 'wholeness'. These different uses of the same word have created a sense of confusion in Jung's readers which Jung himself did not seem to feel. The confusion comes from the identification of parts and wholes. How can the same thing, the 'self', be both a part of the psyche and the whole of the psyche? I have myself only gradually learned to tolerate these apparent contradictions – to retrain my mind, to drop Aristotelian logic, and I have been enormously helped in this by reading Korzybski's *Science and Sanity* (Korzybski 1953).

Korzybski speaks of 'multi-ordinal terms'. These are terms which can be used at many different levels of abstraction. For example, in this paper I use the word 'we', but I do not always mean the same thing. Sometimes I mean 'myself and the reader', sometimes 'we Jungians', 'we therapists', 'we scientists', or even 'we human beings'. The reader as an individual may include himself in this 'we' or he may not and I do not know whether he does or not. If we all wee into the same pot we may not know whose wee is whose! When I use the word 'we' I could be precise about which group I refer to but group therapists know how useful it is not to be precise.

The 'self' too is a multi-ordinal term. It has different levels of abstraction and Jung's diagrams (see Figures 3.1 and 3.2, p.57) show how he arranges things in layers or levels hierarchically but at the same time not always clearly demarcated. Note also the reversibility of the arrangement of the three areas. The 'we' is an extension of the 'I' and 'I' is also multi-ordinal. It refers to the multi-ordinal nature of the self. I was fascinated to discover that Kohut speaks of the self in its narrower sense and also in its *superordinate* sense – apparently quite independently of Jung (Kohut 1977).

In groups the 'we' refers to a group self and I find the concept of the group-self much more useful than the idea of a group mind.

Symbolism and archetypes

To summarize what I have so far said of Jung's conception of the deepest levels of the unconscious: it is *not* restricted to individual minds but is collective or shared and it is arranged hierarchically so that as we proceed towards consciousness it becomes more individual, ultimately unique to the individual.

How can these deeply unconscious contents be known? Jung's answer to this question is somewhat different from Freud's. Freud also saw the unconscious in layers: the pre-conscious, which was accessible to consciousness, and the unconscious, which was not. Freud on the whole emphasized the *forbidden* nature of unconscious contents: they are repressed, disavowed, displaced and so on. If they appear in consciousness, it is in a *disguised* form, because they are otherwise unacceptable to consciousness. For Jung the unconscious has never been conscious and can *never* be directly known. It can be apprehended only through symbolic representation. Jung differentiated symbols from signs. A sign stands for something known; for example, a purse stands for the vagina. A symbol shows something unknowable. We can understand something about it but only through the symbol. Jung often spoke of 'the true symbol' or the living symbol and spoke of it as being inexhaustible. The idea of the collective unconscious came not from a theoretical preconception but from Jung's noticing the same symbolic motifs occurring in widely different cultures, and these motifs or recurring patterns he called the archetypes: not a new term but borrowed from Plato.

This all too brief summary of Jung's approach is not primarily meant to be a sort of introductory lecture on analytical psychology. I give it to show the value of model 2 in group analysis and it may help in understanding why I think Foulkes brought in Jung to supplement Freud in his presentation of group analysis. Let us take as an example the shadow, one of Jung's archetypes. The shadow is the dark, inferior, sinister side of the psyche. Jung distinguished the personal shadow from the collective shadow. If we understand this hierarchically in a group, we can see the individual shadow, the group shadow, the community's shadow, the society's shadow and Man's shadow. In a Group-Analytic Society workshop we can see the shadow of the small group being thrown onto the large group and the large group throwing it outside the workshop onto 'society'. What we call society can be seen as a construct or abstraction placed in this hierarchy. It, too, has no fixed place in this hierarchy: it too is a multi-ordinal term.

It will be apparent from this presentation of Jung's ideas that we have a model which cannot be called intrapsychic or interpersonal. What, in contrast, can it be called? It is tempting to call it a 'systems model': it lends itself easily to treatment by general systems theory – which, I think Jung anticipated in his thinking. I think it is important to distinguish it from the way family therapists use systems therapy. They focus on and stick to one system – the family – while Jung uses an extended concept of the psyche extending through all possible systems. Analytical psychology can be taken as a way of answering my second question: 'What is Man's place in the world', but it is equally an answer to the question: 'What is the world's place in Man?' Inner and outer are not really seen as two worlds; they are rather two different ways of seeing the same world.

Freud's model is by contrast intrapsychic. It is a study of the *inner* mental life of the individual, of *inner* conflict, hidden because of the forbidden expression of instinctual drives. It is a psychology based on a theory where the ego, not the self, is at the centre. I know that later exponents of psychoanalysis, especially object-relations theorists, have not kept to such confines. Winnicott's 'transitional area' and Bion's 'O' are good examples of this. For the purposes of my paper, what is important is not what is Freudian and what is Jungian but the co-existence of two different models of the psyche, neither of which is true or false. We need both.

We also need a third model – an interpersonal one. I am saying that two models are better than one but three models are even better than two. We may wish to be parsimonious and make do with the two models – and they can indeed be applied to interpersonal phenomena. But it seems to me that these require yet another perspective, one where persons-in-relationship are taken as a central fact: not groups, not individuals, but the I–Thou, the dialogue, the encounter between two people. The dyad, the interaction between two persons, is primary and central to this approach: both the individual and groups of more than two are peripheral and secondary to it. Having taken Freud as the exponent of the first model and Jung as the exponent of the second, I would propose Martin Buber as the exponent of the third (Buber 1947; 1970). He conveys the quality of what it feels like to be in a true relationship with another. Buber had an experience which was very important to him. He was consulted by a young man and talked with him, but the young man afterwards committed suicide. Buber knew that in some important respect he had failed to *meet* this young man and he developed the I–Thou idea out of this experience.

This model, applied to psychotherapy, is not one which regards the relationship as something which is constructed like a contract in order for psychotherapy to take place; or which is liable to happen like transference or countertransference in the course of psychotherapy; nor is it an enacted relationship or a form of play or a trial for other 'real' relationships elsewhere. In this model the relationship *is* the psychotherapy. It is perhaps the only thing that really matters. It is what gives significance to everything else. The real world is not outside the consulting room. It lies in the relationship and it *is* the real world. We all know this reality of a true meeting with another person in a group. We know when it happens. It is just that it is difficult to incorporate it within a theory because theories are always I–it.

It is essential that the model recognizes the interpersonal relationship as the primary datum. Buber says: 'In the beginning is the relation' (Buber 1970, p.69). We can see the truth of this if we watch babies, not just as babies, but as babies and mothers in interaction. It is difficult to find a suitable name for this model. It is interpersonal, of course, but it is much more than this word conveys. Its most important aspect is that a person's sense of himself derives from the interaction with another and is also sustained by interaction, enhanced by it, transfigured by it, when one person truly addresses another. I could call it an existential model with its idea of the 'significant other' but I do not wish to exclude other disciplines which recognize the same facts from different angles. I am thinking of the symbolic interactionist school of sociologists like Mead (1965), Cooley (1964) and Goffman (1959); the work of Harry Stack Sullivan (1953); those who use communications and cybernetic theory like Bateson (1972) and Harley Shands (1960) to explicate the circular nature of human interests; and finally the revolution that has taken place in infant/mother observation, in social development. What these different approaches have in common is *dialogue* – so I am calling it a dialogue model.

Martin Buber is for me the supreme exponent of dialogue because of his distinction between I–Thou and I–it. A person can relate to another as an it – indeed, it is often desirable that he should. The 'Thou' of the I–Thou need not actually be a person. It can be a horse, a tree or a stone – provided that the subject is not simply an observer who records, classifies and makes notes – not even what Buber calls an onlooker who (like Bion) is receptive to the other by emptying himself of memory, desire or the need to understand. He is 'one who is aware', who reaches out to the other, feels himself to be *addressed* by the other and *meets* the other by his response. To respond in the I–Thou is to be *responsible*. I like this notion of responsibility as being the response – the being 'answerable to' – in the dialogue of the small group. It is so much better than the woolly word 'caring'

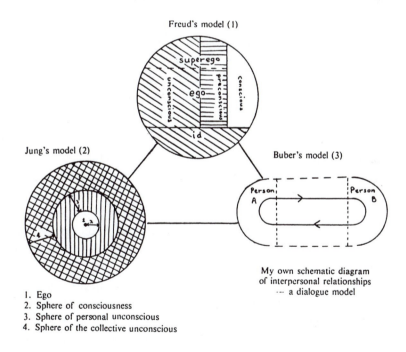

1. Ego
2. Sphere of consciousness
3. Sphere of personal unconscious
4. Sphere of the collective unconscious

Figure 13.1 The three models combined. This triangular arrangement is a way of conveying that the three models should be balanced and one should not be given preference at the expense of the other two. It happens that Freud's model is placed at the top, but the triangle could be looked at any way round. (Adapted with permission from Hampden-Turner, C. (1981) Maps of the Mind. *London: Mitchell Beazley.)*

which is so much bandied about in the helping professions. There is in this state no longer the painful separation of 'ought' and 'is' stressed by Yiannis Gabriel (1983). The best moments of a group are when people respond to the *speech* of the other, even when no words are uttered.

What I have tried to say about the best moments of a group can perhaps be better expressed by means of a Hindu story that Buber relates:

> Once upon a time, tells the Brahmana of the Hundred Paths, gods and demons were at strife. The demons said: 'To whom can we bring our offerings?' They set them all in their own mouths. But the gods set the gifts in one another's mouths. Then Prajapati, the primal spirit, gave himself to the gods. (Buber 1970, pp.10–11)

I would argue that such interaction between individuals is what leads to the evolution of the group, the development of a group culture – not the group sharing an experience, not a group listening to an individual talking about himself, but interpersonal interaction within the group. One of Bateson's great innovations was to see interaction as the unit of evolutionary change. He says:

> – in 1935. I thought that the processes of Schismogenesis were important and nontrivial because in them I seemed to see evolution at work: if interaction between persons could undergo progressive qualitative change as intensity increased, then surely this could be the very stuff of cultural evolution. It followed that all directional change, even in biological evolution and phylogeny, might or must be due to progressive interaction between organisms. (Bateson 1972, p.127)

The words 'interaction between' are the important ones for my purposes here. The unit of change is not the individual, not the group, but the interaction between individuals.

It may seem strange that I give this dyadic model such prominence in group analysis. It may seem to belong more to one-to-one psychotherapy. My own view however is quite the reverse, that it is much more applicable to the small group, though unfortunately somewhat neglected. My reasons are twofold. First, dialogue occurs much more naturally and spontaneously between group-members than between therapist and patient. Second, when dialogue takes place in a group, two people experience it but several others observe it, participate in it and evaluate it. The great difficulty with the model is that some people like Buber appeal to experience of the I–Thou and others, like infant-observers, study it from the outside; but the group can do both. The analyst relates to his patient but he cannot really see the interaction because he is in it. Nor can he ever see his patient relating to another. He can only imagine these things. In a group, two can relate and others can see and say what they have seen.

The name 'object-relations theory' is not accidental. It deals with subject-to-object. I am speaking of subject-to-subject, of *inter*-subjectivity where each enhances in the other the sense of being a unique, special and valued person.

For me, then, there are three models for group analysis, not one. There are three things that I want to happen in the course of a group. I want each individual to use the group to explore his own conflicts (model 1); I want each individual to participate in the experience of being *part* of something, to have a sense not of what belongs to him but to what he belongs (model 2); and I want each member to enter into dialogue (model 3). A 'good' group is, for me, one in which all three develop. I do not think we can yet combine these models into one great supramodel. If I try I have an unwieldy abstraction which I cannot handle.

The workshop at which this paper was given tried to relate the group to culture and to society. I hope I have shown that whether we address ourselves to the group, to culture or to society to try to find a place for the individual we need to be eclectic in the best possible sense and that three models are considerably better than one.

References

Bateson, G. (1972) *Steps to an Ecology of Mind.* London: International Textbooks, p.127.

Buber, M. (1970) *I and Thou.* Translated by W. Kaufmann. Edinburgh: T & T Clark.

Buber, M. (1947) *Between Man and Man.* London: Kegan Paul, Trench, Trubner and Co.

Cooley, C.H. (1964) *Human Nature and the Social Order.* New York: Schocken.

Gabriel, Y. (1983) 'Discontents and illusions: the inevitable costs of civilization?' *Group Analysis* XVI/2 pp.130–144.

Goffman, E. (1959) *The Presentation of Self in Everyday Life.* London: Penguin Books.

Jung, C.G. (1926) 'Two essays in analytical psychology.' *Collected Works 7.*

Jung, C.G. (1968) *Analytical Psychology: Its Theory and Practice.* London: Routledge and Kegan Paul.

Kohut, H. (1977) *The Restoration of the Self.* New York: International Universities Press Inc. p.97.

Korzybski, A. (1953) *Science and Sanity.* Lakeville: International Non-Aristotelian Library.

Mead, G.H. (1965) *Mind, Self and Society.* Chicago University Press.

Ricoeur, P. (1974) *The Conflict of Interpretations.* Evanston: Northwestern University Press, p.99.

Shands, H.C. (1960) *Thinking and Psychotherapy.* Cambridge, Mass: Harvard University Press.

Sullivan, H.S. (1953) *The Interpersonal Theory of Psychiatry.* New York: W W Norton.

CHAPTER FOURTEEN

Malignant Mirroring

When Foulkes, in his *Therapeutic Group Analysis* (1972), introduced the mirror-reaction as one of four factors which were specific for group analysis, he was using an ancient metaphor. This metaphor, like that of the shadow, indicates that knowledge comes through reflection, that is through images, through appearances which copy some absolute and universal truth. This can be seen in Western philosophy as Platonic tradition and the very words 'reflection' and 'speculation' use the metaphor of mind as mirror. The mind, according to this idea, has knowledge only through its ability to reflect or to copy something outside itself.

Foulkes' use of this metaphor to explain a cardinal therapeutic factor in group analysis has been very little developed either by him or by his followers. This paper is an attempt to develop the implications of the metaphor and to show both its richness and its paradoxical nature, so that as well as being therapeutic it can also act like a malignant growth, as a destructive force in the group. The paradox seems to me to arise from the fact that self-knowledge makes us increasingly aware of our self-knowledge; that knowing ourselves means seeing ourselves and that seeing ourselves means ourselves seeing ourselves. This very act of self-knowledge also produces self-estrangement. 'Mirroring' therefore has a terrifying, alienating and destructive quality and is not simply the benign therapeutic factor that Foulkes suggests.

Hamlet – the play within the play

Shakespeare, whose works contain a great deal of mirror imagery, calls Hamlet's cunning device to 'catch the conscience of the King' a mirror held up to nature. Hamlet alters a play to effect an uncanny likeness to a story told to him by the ghost. Then he uses it to find out if the story is true. When Claudius suddenly recognizes himself in the play, Hamlet knows that the ghost is no mere hallucination. The mirror held up to nature reveals a hitherto unseen reality. By this device, Hamlet and Claudius and the audience gain 'insight'.

The mirror as an analogic device

The play in *Hamlet*, then, acts like a mirror because an imagined reconstruction of what may have happened fits or analogically represents, through its similarity of structure, what is now seen to have 'really happened'. The now apparent distinction between analogic and digital communication can help us to conceptualize how this new insight has occurred.

If we imagine Claudius watching the play he can be seen quite suddenly to 'reframe' it. The murder of the player-King suddenly presents *himself* murdering his brother. Anthony Wilden (Wilden 1972), in a very clear explanation of the analogic–digital distinction, has suggested that reframing is the very first act of digitalization. Digital communication depends on the use of sharp distinctions, of an on–off, either–or, or one–zero kind. Counting on the fingers (digits) would be an obvious example, where arbitrary divisions between numbers are used.

Analogic communication depends on the other hand on the mapping of real, discontinuous physical qualities found in nature. It relies on similarity rather than difference. Wilden distinguishes between meaning and signification. The analogue is rich in meaning but lacks precision. Digital communication gives signification, that is precise information, but is poor in meaning. It now looks as if the predominant hemisphere of the brain specialises in digital and the non-dominant hemisphere in analogic communication. One makes use of 'meaningful' patterns which are 'like' something, the other of precise, discriminatory signification. The mirror, though an analogic device, becomes a digital one at the moment that the 'frame of reference' changes. A mysterious, mythical meaning suddenly gives way to precise significance. Claudius now knows that Hamlet knows. Hamlet now knows what he previously suspected. The new knowledge combines actual historical knowledge and the terrible 'meaning' of what has taken place.

Insight and psychotherapy

The moment in which Claudius recognizes himself is one in which Hamlet, Claudius and the audience all gain insight. Simultaneously they know something both about each other and about themselves. Hamlet says through his 'mirror': I will show you what you are. This is what you are like. The audience, watching the play, all gain this insight too in so far as they recognize themselves in the play. Later, Hamlet holds up a mirror to Gertrude, his mother, and forces *her* to see what she is like.

The psychotherapist constantly tries to show the patient what he or she is like, but, in doing so, there is an unfortunate tendency to regard the psychotherapist's view as objective. Freud regarded the analyst as an objective mirror, recommending that the analyst be opaque like a mirror. Perhaps Shakespeare's mirror metaphor is more applicable. The therapist does have a view of the patient. But only if the patient recognizes himself when shown this view does the therapist know that his view is correct, though the word 'correct' is better changed to 'significant'.

Group therapy reduces the tendency to regard the therapist's view as objectively correct because the presence of the other group members introduces several other views. Each may be distorted, a mere projection, even a 'mad' perception, just as it is an open question whether Hamlet is mad – an open question even for Hamlet himself. Insight is better thought of as a significantly new view of the self rather than the acquiring of objective new knowledge.

Self knowledge through the view of the other

The idea that we know ourselves through being mirrored by the view of another person is contrary to a second common tenet of psychotherapy (the first being the idea of the neutral objective therapist). This is the idea that self-knowledge proceeds from knowledge of others, but only by knowing one's self can one know others. This idea is also expressed in *Hamlet*. Polonius says:

> To thine own self be true,
> And it must follow, as the night the day
> Thou canst not then be false to any man.

This seemingly profound notion receives short shrift in the play, because Hamlet has no way of being true to himself until he can establish the truth of others. Indeed at the moment when Claudius gives himself away Hamlet simultaneously gains knowledge of Claudius and of himself. He knows that his perception through the ghost is not a hallucination.

Winnicott (Winnicott 1971) suggests that the baby gains self-knowledge through the mother's face. He says: 'The mother is looking at the baby and what she looks like is related to what she sees there.' Classical psychoanalytic theories of infant development tend to assume that the baby gradually has to sort out his perceptions of his own body and bodily state from his perceptions of his environment. Winnicott's idea is that the environment (mother's face) can tell him what he is. He perceives his mother's perceptions.

Winnicott's notion is amply supported by a mass of evidence from mother–infant observation and seems to occur very early, probably from the beginning of life and certainly long before the establishment of 'object-constancy'. Here I wish to draw attention to two points involved in Winnicott's observation that I have already made through Shakespeare:

1. The baby seeing himself as in a mirror reflected in his mother's face, sees not the 'objective truth' but the mother's subjective response to him (and we can add that his response to her then produces another response to him in a circular interaction or dialogue).

2. The baby's 'insight' into himself occurs at the same time as he gains knowledge of his mother.

Thus, human mirroring is both intersubjective and reciprocal. The baby reflects back the mother to himself also.

Lacan

Winnicott expresses in his paper his debt to Lacan and his *'stade du miroir'* first put forward in 1936. Although Lacan also stresses the importance of the infant's first view of his reflected self there are far-reaching differences in his formulation.

Winnicott only uses the *metaphor* of the mirror in the face of the mother while Lacan talks about the baby's first view of himself in an *actual* mirror and assumes that the mother (as Other) acts in the same way as an actual mirror. Consequently, Lacan sees the mirror perception as fundamentally a source of alienation. This is because the stage occurs (from six to 18 months) when the baby sees himself for the first time as a whole – but 'out there'. In his body, he can at this stage only experience himself to be in pieces (*le corps morcelé*). His jubilation is therefore a response to finding himself in control of the specular image – outside himself.

According to Lacan, it is only with the acquisition of language that this integrated self is called 'I' but there remains a permanent split between the *moi* out there and the *je* referred to by the word. Winnicott does refer to the unfortunate fact that the mother may respond in a distorted way to her baby (graphically illustrating this distorted perception by alluding to the paintings of Francis Bacon) but Lacan is speaking of a fundamental source of distortion which is universal and part of the human condition.

Benign and malignant mirroring

Winnicott and Lacan seem to me to be expressing two opposing ideas of mirroring. Winnicott is speaking of a benign, integrative process leading to the development of a healthy sense of self (but which can go wrong with early maternal failure) and Lacan of a disturbing sense of alienation resulting from the very fact of our ability to see ourselves as a whole; we can only see ourselves outside ourselves (though language can help us to deal with this frightening perception).

Foulkes, like Winnicott, sees mirroring in the group as benign, indeed as a therapeutic factor. Yalom, however, draws attention to the pathological and destructive aspects in his description of the 'double-mirror reaction' (Frank 1957). This can be observed in groups as an 'uncanny attraction–repulsion' between two individuals who partly resemble each other. Yalom (Yalom 1975) attempts to explain this phenomenon in terms of mutual projective identification. In my view, this goes only part of the way, because it relies on a psychoanalytic concept in which one individual is seen to be projecting a part of himself into the other. Such formulations always assume the analyst to be the objective judge of his patients, that he can recognize what 'really' belongs to the other.

Although it is helpful, up to a point, to think in terms of distortions being due to projections, what needs exploration is what I am calling the *malignancy* of the process. This requires an interactional standpoint. The double-mirror is a metaphor for a process in which both partners are caught up. Projective identification as described by Melanie Klein is a one-way process, an activity of the baby, although there may be some recognition by later theorists in object-relations that the object, that is, the mother, has to participate before this can take place. The shift from an analytic intrapsychic model to an interpersonal one involving more than one person needs to be made explicit when dealing with group analysis.

Winnicott, as we have seen, showed how the child's view of himself is essentially dependent on the view of another. Here he was following Lacan who sees more clearly the terrifying implications of this fact, that what is unconsciously desired is the desire of the other, that because no sense of wholeness can come primarily from within ourselves we can only see ourselves as the object of others and are thus essentially alienated from ourselves.

Kohut (Kohut 1971) also uses 'mirroring' in a benign sense; he speaks of 'mirror-hungry' patients, of the narcissistic patient's need to have his grandiosity emphatically mirrored by the analyst. This advice, whatever its value, should not be properly called 'mirroring' because the analyst, if he is a mirror, will reflect what he sees. If what he sees is hateful, he will respond with hate. Such a reaction is not encouraged by Kohut although it is, in a sense, truly empathic. However, Kohut uses the word empathic in a rather special way to indicate only those reactions which he regards as therapeutic in helping to build up self-esteem. My view of this malignant mirroring process is that, like a cancer, its destructiveness lies in its uncontrolled taking-over. It is a growth gone wrong. It takes place not only when a negative response is elicited. Loving can be just as malignant as hating, as we may see in a brief look at the Narcissus myth.

Narcissus

Narcissus is so beautiful that according to Ovid everyone on seeing him, whether male or female, instantly falls in love with him. Instant falling in love is perhaps not the same as loving. It is a response not to a person who is known but to an image of that person. In the figure of Echo, an extreme problem is reached because she cannot contribute anything of herself to which Narcissus can relate. She can only meaninglessly mimic his words and the ends of his sentences. He rightly rejects all this admiration and spurns Echo's love. He can thus be seen not as mirror-hungry but as persecuted by a surfeit of mirroring.

Unfortunately, he comes upon a mirror which he cannot escape: he is trapped by the beauty with which he is cursed. At this point he fulfils the very first prophesy of the blind Tiresias that Narcissus will reach a ripe old age only if he does not see 'or know' himself. Narcissus, as he gazes at the pool, cannot survive because of epistemological errors. In most versions of the myth he does not recognize himself: it is his twin sister, another beautiful youth, or the nymph Echo herself. Only in Ovid's version does he finally see himself, but even so there is a profound error. He mistakes the map for the territory, the copy for the original. If he could see that what he sees is not himself but just his reflection he could surely leave it.

So we are looking here at the Narcissus myth not as Freud did, as self-love or libido directed inward, but as libido mistakenly directed outward, as an epistemological problem arising from the very nature of the mirror.

The tragedy of Narcissus is that he unknowingly does the one thing he must not do. Like Oedipus, he meets the very fate he tried to avoid. Seeing himself is forbidden and therefore the mirror is taboo.

Mirrors

The idea that to see one's self in a mirror is prohibited is almost universally found in primitive folklore. This universality and the bipolarity of the mirror image, its magical powers for good and evil, suggest that an archetype is at work. We find in Frazer's *The Golden Bough* that in ancient Greece and India and also among the Zulus, the Basutos and in the Saddle Island of Melanesia it is regarded as dangerous to look at one's own image. In the latter case, there is a pool into which if anyone looks he dies. This is also noted by Roheim (Roheim 1919) in his seminal work on the mirror and he points out that the prohibition is particularly directed towards children.

Human mirrors and ordinary mirrors

Perhaps there is an ancient wisdom in the mirror taboo. Mirrors are now such commonplace objects and everyone is so familiar with the image they present, which people think is what they look like. It is easy to forget that the modern silvering process which makes possible what we regard as an accurate mirror-image is a recent technological advance and that until recently mirrors, which were largely a matter of 'looking into a glass darkly', were highly prized and, being expensive, available only to the few – and indeed regarded by most as sacred objects (Spencer n.d.). The face, and every face as Winnicott points out is different, is the most expressive part of the human body and is not normally visible to its owner, only to others. The best mirror, says George Herbert, is 'an old friend'. This expresses the idea that in some sense the human response is more reliable, gives more true knowledge of what we look like than this now commonplace artificial device.

The group-analytic group makes great use of the human mirror as helping members to see themselves better but the mirroring phenomena that occur are far more complex than those described by Foulkes' mirror-reaction. For the most part, as the members of the group become old friends they become good mirrors. Nevertheless, if things do go wrong they may go very wrong indeed. The malignant processes can be very destructive to group endeavour. I suggest that these processes can all be understood by consideration of the possible evil effects of actual mirrors. I have already indicated some of the reasons for this but will try to give a more systematic explanation in summary after looking at the clinical material.

Some clinical considerations

First of all, mirror-imagery frequently arises in the group. The mirror metaphor is readily used by group members in such phrases as, 'Your problems seem to mirror mine,' or even, 'This group is like a mirror that I can see myself in.' Such imagery seems to arise naturally out of a common preoccupation with how people are coming across or are being 'seen' by others. Very often people are attracted or fascinated by this particular feedback, which has been compared with a hall of mirrors.

Why does mirroring occur in group analysis? We place patients in a small circle facing each other. We tell them that the idea is to understand themselves better. We encourage them to react freely and spontaneously to each other. We discourage them from being too intellectual in this process and from making the detached interpretations we expect of a psychoanalyst; and as therapists we place ourselves in the background, mostly engaged in facilitating this process. Thus each member can use the other members like mirrors, although in general he will not be conscious of this.

As I mentioned earlier, it is not necessary to invoke the mechanisms of projection and introjection. Jack may look at John and say to himself: 'He is acting, or reacting, or looking, just like me.' This is a process of recognizing oneself in the other. Alternatively, Jack may use John's reactions to him as providing information about himself; for example, if John is amused Jack knows he is amusing, though this may or may not be intentional. Now let us suppose that Jack sees John looking at him with an expression of hatred or contempt. This may not bother Jack, but let us suppose that it does. He feels convinced that he *is* hateful or contemptible. Again there need be no projection or introjection. It is possible that Jack had been looked at in this way before. He may not know when or by whom. Perhaps it was his father when he was small. Perhaps it took years for him to shake off this concept of himself which is now revived.

This situation actually occurred in one of my groups. When I was selecting patients for the group I had already interviewed and accepted Jack and when I later saw John I thought he too would fit in very well in the group and, particularly, that he would get on well with Jack. This was not the first time that I had made the mistake of assuming that two people who resemble each other will get on well together. To begin with, all went well. They seemed to take to each other. I had thought of both of them as being highly intelligent, charming and amusing but schizoid personalities. Both were highly successful in their academic careers but both had a sense of futility about this and in both cases I sensed that there were very primitive and chaotic feelings hidden behind the smooth exterior.

It was perhaps for this reason that Jack very soon began to get on John's nerves. 'Why do you smile all the time?' John asked. He had noticed, as I had, Jack's falsely smooth exterior but, unlike me, he reacted to this with a mixture of anxiety and anger. Now why was John the only person in the group to react to Jack in this specific way? The usual answer would be to say that he had projected something on to him, but this explanation is not sufficient. I suggest that the very similarity between John and Jack which I had noticed led to Jack acting as John's double. This meant that John's own habitual defence – the supercilious sardonic smile – could now be seen as in a mirror. He was unlikely to have seen this in a real mirror because he could not have looked at himself with this expression, but nevertheless he recognized it without being able to identify it as his own. After all it was Jack who was smiling in this way.

Gradually at the next few sessions the situation grew worse, until on one occasion John exploded with rage in a way that surprised and frightened the whole group. John had been explaining to the group that he felt so futile that he was thinking of suicide. His rage was because he once again saw the smile on Jack's face mocking him. This time Jack denied that he was smiling but John swore that he had been. Very soon after this Jack left the group quite suddenly and I never received an explanation from him for this. He had previously appeared to be a well-motivated member, and had attended without missing a session. My own conviction is that he had not been able to deal with equally strong persecutory anxiety induced by John, who was in turn acting as a mirror for him. Before this happened there had been some attempt by them to understand the strength of their negative reactions to each other and it had emerged that each reminded the other of his father. They had both experienced their fathers as aloof, highly demanding of academic success and contemptuous towards them. It could be said that in each case there had been an experience of similar mirroring with the father.

To explain the way in which this reaction had gradually built up to an explosion, leading to Jack's drop-out from the group, the notion of positive feedback is helpful. John's sense of emptiness and futility might have aroused Jack's sympathy and concern. This concern would have reduced John's feelings of futility and the situation between them would have become more stable, so that the more John talked the more concerned Jack would have become, until John would have felt so relieved that he need talk no further. Instead of the stabilizing effect of this negative feedback, the opposite occurred. The more John talked, the more Jack smiled and the more Jack smiled the more futile John felt. This is positive feedback leading to runaway, a breakdown in the system. This explanation, derived from cybernetics, would also explain the persecutory effect of the mirror and this malignant kind of mirroring is what is found in so many stories of the double.

I have seen other examples of this phenomenon in groups in which one member acts as the double for the other. It seems to be one variety of the well known phenomenon of pairing. It is often more subtle than in the example that I have given and it may be the explanation for many dropouts which occur in group therapy which are otherwise difficult to explain.

I think there are certain individuals who are more susceptible to this double effect and who induce it readily in others. In one group, I had such a member. This was a man who told the group that as a child he had a recurrent nightmare. He was standing on the front of a sort of train and he saw another train approaching him on the same track. On the front of the other train was another boy who had a dagger in his hand intending to kill him. He realized that he too had a dagger in his hand and suddenly he realized that the other boy was himself. When the train collided he would either have to kill the other boy or be killed by him, but it made no difference because in either case he would be killing himself and with this terrifying discovery he awoke screaming. He told this dream to the group in a way which evoked, to the full, the uncanny atmosphere of the sinister Double, the duplicated self, the mirror image which you cannot destroy without destroying yourself, but which will destroy you unless you destroy it (Rank 1971). He also made me aware of a deep-rooted existential dilemma which helped me to understand a number of strange events which had occurred in the group.

This man, whom I shall call Peter, seemed to have a strange effect on the other members. The first instance occurred with a girl who was (like him) bisexual and who presented an unprepossessing and rather masculine appearance and who had made it clear that she felt herself to be unacceptable because she was so unattractive. She said she had come from a family where all the other members were beautiful and referred particularly to her handsome father and brother. Peter said to her that she *was* attractive – even beautiful. She appeared to respond with some pleasure although she denied that it was true. At the very next session she arrived surprising us all by an absolute transformation. For the first time she looked attractive and feminine and was wearing a dress instead of dirty trousers, but the striking thing was that although several people commented on the change, Peter, who had previously given her much attention, appeared not to notice her. This proved to be her last appearance in the group. It was as though she had looked into a mirror and not seen herself there or what she saw was not herself.

I filled her place with a man, William, whose problem was that he was timid and frightened of people and most of his first session was taken up by Peter trying to make him feel comfortable in the group. Towards the end of the session, however, Peter suddenly said with much feeling that William provoked a strange sense of fear: he felt that William was looking at him with a hostile stare which he found most unsettling. William denied any feeling of hostility towards Peter but did say he knew about the stare (which neither I nor the rest of the group had noticed) because others had commented on it in the past. He also did not appear again in the group and Peter felt that he had somehow driven William away as well as the girl.

I was struck by the sudden reversal effect: how William, who was frightened, had suddenly become frightening to Peter and how Peter's fear had then frightened William off. Each had acted as a frightening mirror to the other. Although one could say that Peter had projected his hostility to William, it is also true that he had picked up William's hostility as none of the rest of us had been able to do, showing a remarkable perceptiveness not uncommon in borderline personalities.

I next introduced another new member to the group, not without some anxiety, and by this time we were all apprehensive as to what would happen. Joseph seemed much tougher. He was an older man who had had quite a long experience of being in another group. Nevertheless he appeared surprisingly nervous and shy and Peter seemed careful not to pay him too much attention. What developed was a kind of feud, an attraction–repulsion such as Jerome Frank has described. There was a strong rivalry, each wanting to be the group therapist, and by a strange coincidence they found they had a friend in common outside the group. Peter betrayed Joseph's confidence to this friend and a terrible row developed in which both offered to leave the group. This was one of many rows, but there were times of great intuitive understanding and intimacy between the two men. Both survived in the group and gradually the intensity of their ambivalent relationship diminished. I made a number of interpretations which included sibling rivalry, unconscious homosexuality and projection in each case of an unsatisfactory father–son relationship. All this may have helped but something is left unexplained in these familiar ways of interpreting – the sense of the uncanny and the extraordinary power of the attraction–repulsion.

One incident occurred which illustrates what I mean. Peter told the group that, on leaving after the previous session, walking out through a dimly lit hospital corridor, he had seen a sinister figure standing in the shadows. He was sure it was Joseph lying in wait for him ready to knife him. Indeed it was Joseph, although, of course this was not his purpose. Joseph could be seen to represent an archetype, the Shadow in its menacing aspect, but also as in Peter's dream he was a *Doppelganger,* his own mirror-image. This figure represents Death and it pursues its victim relentlessly.

Perhaps it can be better understood if I explain the problem that brought Peter into the group. He had become obsessed with a young man, a beautiful youth whom he recognized as being similar to himself at the same age. His fascination for this young man was such that it made his whole life feel futile by comparison and at the same time threatened to destroy everything he had: his wife and children, his work, his house and everything that he had achieved, all of which he now saw as valueless compared with this vision of beauty. Unless he could tear himself away from this image he was doomed; and this of course is the fate of Narcissus gazing at his own mirror-image in the pool.

Some preliminary conclusions

I have called this final section of my paper 'Some Preliminary Conclusions' because having tried to extend and develop Foulkes' notion of the mirror reaction, I have uncovered a hornet's nest which raises as yet unsolved problems going beyond group analysis into the nature of knowledge, insight, self-consciousness, identity and how we relate to others. Conclusions at this stage raise a host of new questions and must therefore be quite preliminary.

First of all, it seems that we all need feedback from others, probably throughout life, not only to maintain a self-image but also to change. Group analysis has the potential to make use of this fact, more than any other kind of therapy. The mirror provides an ancient and universal metaphor based on the connection between seeing and knowing for the modern technical and abstract concept of feedback in the language of cybernetic theory.

At the same time, the mirror, as well as being endowed with beneficient magical properties, has always been regarded as a source of great danger and is associated with death. My clinical material illustrates what I call 'malignant mirroring'. Understanding of this phenomenon can be facilitated by understanding the dangers inherent in actual mirrors. These dangers, apprehended in myth and superstition, are manifold but they all seem to result from deception.

Some of the forces of deception are:

1. The mirror can never show us as others see us because it reflects back either ourselves looking in a mirror or caught unawares, never ourselves relating to another person.

2. The feedback, whether complementary or symmetrical (to use Bateson's (1972) distinction), is positive feedback which, in cybernetic terms, if uncontrolled leads to runaway and breakdown of the system.

3. It gives rise to epistemological errors, the most fundamental of which is to say, 'That's me': identifying with an image, or mistaking map and territory.

4. If the image is seen as separate, as 'out there', it produces a sense of alienation, as Lacan has suggested: a sense of the 'uncanny', a combination of familiarity and strangeness, as Freud (1919) has suggested; and a sense of fear of loss of soul, as Roheim (1919) and Otto Rank (1971) have amply demonstrated from anthropological studies.

5. The mirror cannot take part in a true dialogue. Winnicott's idea of the early mirroring by the mother's face has been supported by more recent work on infant–mother observation but this all points to early non-verbal dialogue or proto-conversations; for example, the mother may smile, but this is a response to the baby. If the baby smiles back it is not a mechanical mimicry but a response to the mother's smile. These responses take place over time as in an exchange. Furthermore, they are not just responses. Unlike the mirror, each brings his or her own self into the interaction.

6. It makes no difference whether the image in the mirror is regarded as good or bad for malignant mirroring to occur, as the Narcissus myth shows.

7. The mirror does not truly 'meta-communicate'. The obvious example is the horror people feel as they see themselves ageing in the mirror. The 'old friend' in contrast may reflect the ageing but also meta-communicates that this is acceptable or even lovable. In looking at a mirror the unacceptability of ageing may be projected onto it and wrongly be felt to come from outside (again giving rise to an escalating spiral of positive feedback).

All these points are preliminary and need a great deal of amplification. At this stage I simply want to draw attention to the dangers and provide the beginnings of a conceptual framework for understanding them.

On the whole, then, 'mirroring' is part of the group process and a cardinal therapeutic factor. It can largely be left to itself or quietly encouraged by the conductor. On the other hand, it can turn malignant. Such a development needs prompt and radical measures from the conductor. It is one of the few indications for him to be very active and determined in the group. Very often it takes place between two individuals and the rest of the group become paralysed onlookers. The therapist may be struck by the uncanny atmosphere which is generated. On such occasions, seeing two participants locked in a mutually destructive battle, the conductor may, like a referee at a boxing match, have to part the combatants before too much damage is done. His sensitivity to the strange uncanny atmosphere may alert him to the presence of an unseen mirror in the room. Indeed he must endeavour to take the evil mirror away.

References

Bateson, G. (1972) *Steps to an Ecology of Mind*. London: Intertext Books.

Foulkes, S.H. (1972) *Therapeutic Group Analysis*. London: George Allen and Unwin.

Frank, J.D. (1957) 'Some determinants, manifestations and effects of cohesiveness in group psychotherapy.' *International Journal of Group Psychotherapy 7*, pp.53–63.

Freud, S. (1919) 'The uncanny.' *Standard Edition 17*. London: Hogarth Press.

Kohut, H. (1971) *The Analysis of the Self.* London: Hogarth Press.

Rank, O. (1941) 'The double as immortal self.' In *Beyond Psychology*. New York: Dover Publications.

Rank, O. (1971) *The Double. A Psychoanalytic Study*. New American Library.

Roheim, G. (1919) *Spiegelzanken*. Leipzig.

Spencer, M.J. (n.d.) *Mirror as Metaphor and Symbol*. Cassette tape. C G Jung Institute: Los Angeles.

Wilden, A. (1972) *System and Structure*, Ch VII. London: Tavistock Publications Ltd.

Winnicott, D.W. (1971) 'Mirror rôle of the mother and family in child development.' *Playing and Reality*. London: Tavistock Publications.

Yalom, I.D. (1975) *Theory and Practice of Group Psychotherapy*. New York: Basic Books.

CHAPTER FIFTEEN

Loss of Self in Envy and Jealousy

My contribution to this workshop is the result of some reflections which began with an observation of myself. It has always seemed to me that my own envy as well as jealousy gave rise to a feeling which was quite different from what is usually described. In order to clarify the difference I began to recall situations in the past in which I had been envious or jealous. The experience, for me, was invariably a painful one and the pain had a specific quality in which I had a specific bodily sensation. It consisted of a sinking feeling in the stomach. This was accompanied by a perception that my value had gone down and that I was not who I thought I was but rather some diminished remnant of what I had been even a moment before. Usually the onset was a sudden one. By beholding or just hearing about another's good fortune, I had an intense sense of loss but it was not the loss of anything which I had previously been aware of having. It was like losing something which I had previously taken for granted. There was a sense, too, that this loss could never be made good. I can best describe it as being like a scene in a film where one sees a man opening a safe deposit box. One knows that he has put in the box a vast amount of cash which represents the proceeds of a bank robbery but that someone has cleverly gained access to the box and taken all the money. The man opens the box, now empty, and immediately closes it again. He closes his eyes and then brings himself to open the box again. The box is really empty and he cannot believe it. One can imagine what he is feeling and it is just the feeling I am trying to describe – a sense of disbelief. One's sense of reality is profoundly altered. Then one has to readjust, to accept the new reality and one is immeasurably the poorer.

What has happened? I think there are two things. There is both a painful reappraisal of the self and, as a corollary, a re-evaluation of the world in which one lives. It amounts to a discovery that one's own life is not as good as others' lives. It goes beyond the wish for any particular thing that would put it right. Somehow one had accepted the inequalities of life but this *particular* inequality is too much. One can only deal with it by lowering one's sights, so to speak, but in doing so one has to redefine oneself.

I found I could recall many experiences of this sort. One which stood out was a younger colleague telling me that he had been approached and offered a job which I would have loved to have and wouldn't have dared to apply for. What upset me was not just his getting the job, but his being asked to apply for it by a much admired older colleague and I think it was not so much the job but the relationship which I envied, a father–son relationship such as I had never had.

On self-analysis, I could see that I must have had an unconscious hope that such a thing would happen to me and that what had now disappeared was this hope. I now lived in a world where such things could and did happen to others but never to me. My safe deposit box was empty. The sense of emptiness, of impoverishment of the self, was immediate and the sickening physical sensation took hold and was quite outside my control. It is not sufficient to indulge in reminiscence; in the end our effectiveness as therapists depends on what we can understand of our own experience. There are a number of theoretical and clinical points which I would now like to make which arise from these introspective reflections.

First, there is the problem of distinguishing envy and jealousy. In my example, there is a great deal of overlap. Clearly I was envious of my friend's good fortune but I was also jealous of his relationship with a father-figure, or at least with an imagined and idealised relationship from which I was excluded. This kind of overlap is so common that the distinction between them may not appear clinically very useful. It seems to me that it is for good reasons that the two words are used interchangeably in common speech. But, particularly in group situations, it is useful to distinguish between wanting something that someone else has got and wanting to destroy a relationship that exists between other people.

The experience of loss of self is described in the analytic literature, but not as being a primary one. Envy and jealousy are usually described as situations giving rise to fantasy rather than as affects in themselves, and the fantasies are of violence, whether one thinks of Klein's notion of the infant's violent rage towards the good breast, of Freud's association of the lack of a penis with castration or of the violence of the intercourse imagined in the parental couple in the primal scene. Both envy and jealousy then come to be thought of as feelings in themselves, a violent and destructive rage, and other feelings are thought of as being secondary, constituting the wide variety of defences against intolerable anxiety. It is true that feelings of loss of self are described, but they are never primary. For example, in *Envy and Gratitude* devaluation of the self is listed as one of the defences against envy, which Klein sees as an expression of a basic drive, the death instinct (Klein 1957), and in penis envy the little girl is said to resign herself to her loss of the penis. Anna Freud speaks of a restriction in the ego (Freud 1968). Loss of self generally is thought of as resulting from anger directed inwards. My suggestion is that loss of self, which may be threatened but may have already happened, is primary. It may or may not give rise to anger and destructive fantasies. If it does, it is because the envying or jealous person feels he or she has rights which have been or are about to be violated. But this is a more advanced state than the sense of loss I have described. Here there are no rights. One is entitled to nothing.

Although one can call this state of mind 'depression', it is not the more mature depression which implies concern for the object one wishes to destroy. The object, in this state, is totally outside one's reach. One is immediately reduced to impotence. I prefer to refer to a 'state of mind' rather than a feeling. The feeling is resultant of a particular construction of the reality of one's situation. Of course, it can always be argued that this state is simply the fantasied result of repressed destructive wishes, and undoubtedly envy and jealousy do give rise to a malicious pleasure in the ill fortune of others. This malice does impair one's future chances of good relationships and this sequence does very commonly occur clinically. It is also true to say that the destructive wishes are commonly denied and that there are various defences against their becoming conscious. Nevertheless, I believe that such destructive wishes should be seen not as constituting envy but as ways, albeit primitive ways, of trying to put things to rights. 'Getting even' means not just getting revenge but regaining an even keel, restoring a harmonious universe and a harmonious sense of one's self and one's place in it, to which one feels one has a right.

It is time that I introduce the word 'narcissism' but I do so with reluctance. Certainly what I have been describing as loss of self is often referred to as narcissistic injury or a blow to one's self-esteem. My reluctance is because the word usually implies a self-reflective state which I am not wishing to impute. Self-esteem usually is taken to mean that I esteem myself in the same way that I esteem others. Narcissism is taken to mean self-reflection. But I am speaking of a state which precedes self-awareness or indeed any relationship with one's own self. There is now a good deal of infant research which suggests that a sense of self begins to emerge from the beginning of life through the mother's entering into a relationship with the baby which the baby must experience long before it can know that it is experiencing it. The absence of this sense of self can therefore result from a deficit in relationship rather than from a frustrated drive. In the actual myth of Narcissus, Narcissus dies because the image he tries to reach, which he does not know is his own, is something he has never before experienced. It is because he experiences it as outside himself that he dies in his attempts to reach it. He can neither be it nor have it. What I am describing as loss of self is a discontinuous change in that direction. It is a loss of what one is rather than of what one has. People who are afflicted with envy and jealousy would, in this formulation, be those who are deficient in their primary relationships of loving and being loved. If they do become angry, spiteful or scheming there is hope for them. At least they have rights. But others do not feel angry. They simply diminish. Clinically when such patients begin to feel angry, even if they become paranoid, it is an achievement.

If this is so, the distinction is by no means academic. It makes a good deal of difference to the sort of interpretation which is helpful. Although some patients express relief when their destructive envious wishes are verbalised (and Melanie Klein gives several examples of this (Klein 1957)), others are not helped at all because they have not reached the stage of being angry or destructive. Their emptiness is also hopelessness and helplessness. In fact their emptiness, their hopelessness and their helplessness *is* them and if one tries to uncover an underlying anger one tries in vain. Interpretations have then to be based on an understanding of this. The negative transference is not then negative in the sense of unconscious hostility to the analyst but is negative in the sense of a loss of self. This can also be understood as a loss of meaning and the difficulty is to restore a meaning to the analysis.

A further consideration is that there is a loss of vitality. The loss of a sense of self means the loss of creativity and of liveliness. In this connection, Daniel Stern's notion of vitality affects in the newborn infant is helpful because the quality of vitality as compared with feelings of deadness can be seen to be very early in origin and to depend on the quality of the mother–infant interaction (Stern 1985). The anger and rage of envy and jealousy do have great vitality but this is deceptive. They are the *only* signs of life in a restricted field. This is most clearly seen in pathological jealousy, where all the intense energy is encapsulated in the delusion which protects the subject from the sense of impoverishment I have described.

In the group, the therapist is in the position of being able to observe how envy and jealousy affect people differently when faced with the same situation, e.g. when the therapist or one member becomes pregnant, goes on a holiday or becomes successful. It is easy to take up the anger and spite which some members may be expressing. It is often less easy to pick up those who silently withdraw or who become less themselves. One sees how envy is stimulated by others, more clearly than in individual work. The defence against envy is often to be enviable. It is important, though often difficult, to give support to group members who gloat and boast and triumph at the expense of others. Essentially their situation is no different from that of their victims who are provoked into envy. Even when they win they lose.

Often the group analyst feels pulled between two positions with regard to justice or fair play. Does one try to be fair or get people to accept that the world is not fair? In the long run, it seems to me that neither outrage nor resignation are mature responses to inequality. As the group matures it grows in the understanding that if what is missing is the vitality and creativity which comes from a sense of self, then there are no winners and no losers. If the sense of being nobody, which is at the root of envy and jealousy, can be enhanced or restored in each member of the group, then all benefit.

Nevertheless, there is some convenience in distinguishing between wanting something that somebody else has got and wanting to destroy a relationship that exists between other people. Jealousy is often thought to be restricted to triangular situations; and though this is by far the commonest form, the notorious 'eternal triangle', it also happens that an individual can feel excluded from a *group* of people who are felt to be in a relationship with each other. This situation is often found in the therapy group. Nor is it restricted to one individual. One commonly finds that the group divides into two sub-groups. Sometimes, as in what I have called 'malignant mirroring', two people in the group become preoccupied with each other and the rest of the group is jealous (Zinkin 1983). Both envy and jealousy, however, can take one of two forms in the group: either the member withdraws, with the loss of self I described earlier, or he or she becomes destructive and actively tries to break up or at least to devalue what is going on between the others. It may be a matter of fine judgement in these situations for the group conductor to decide how to weight an interpretation, whether to emphasize that members of the group are being excluded or whether to draw attention to how destructive the jealous members are being, either to themselves, if they withdraw, or to the others, if they cannot tolerate the creative relating they are enjoying.

There remains an important difference between envy and jealousy which is worth bearing in mind in group therapy, though it plays an important part in individual therapy as well. That is that in every society or social group, jealousy is sanctioned in ways in which envy is not. Jealousy is more usually thought of as holding on to a right, while envy is the illegitimate longing for something one feels one lacks. The jealous husband, though often the subject of ridicule and contempt, at least has the right to a faithful wife, a right which is usually defensible in law. In fact the jealous husband is obliged by some societies to seek justice against the dishonour he would otherwise incur. In societies characterised by honour and shame, a father might have to kill his daughter who has been raped, in order to save the family name. But envy is kept private and secret and has no social sanction.

What I am emphasising here is the group culture. Every group has its own implicit rules, its own idiosyncratic ways of dealing with breaches of its sense of what is fair. Whatever one's personal feelings may be, it is always necessary to exercise a fine judgement, bearing in mind the group culture. Both envy and jealousy should be regarded not only as potentially destructive to the group process, but as emerging signals that the rights of certain members may legitimately need to be protected and that the group will have its own means of restoring the balance.

At the same time, with both envy and jealousy, it is helpful to think in terms of injured narcissism rather than drive theory. If using drive theory, one may be over-inclined to think of some sort of basic instinctual process requiring discharge, with all the defences associated with the erotic and death instincts. I think Melanie Klein has been largely responsible for this emphasis in the case of what she believed to be a primary envy of the breast (Klein 1957). By emphasising the destructive nature of envious impulses, she has reinforced a long cultural tradition of treating envy as not only evil but sinful. I think this leaves out of consideration the fact that people often become quite good at controlling or containing their envious or jealous feelings, but that in doing so they pay a high price in terms of personal misery and loss of important parts of the self.

Unfortunately, it is difficult to like someone who is riddled with these feelings. This is particularly true when the feeling seems to be unjustified by observed reality. It is hard to remember that the envious or jealous person who is not deluded may be all too painfully aware that what she is feeling so acutely is not at all what she should be feeling. Such a person is afflicted, rather than evil, and afflicted not by malice but in discovering within herself a terrible choice. She can either relieve her feelings at the expense of others or do her best to give up wanting so desperately what other people seem so effortlessly to have.

My main hope in this paper has been to draw attention to the plight of these sufferers. Telling them they are envious or jealous is unhelpful. It is important first to recognize their pain, then ascertain what it is they feel they lack, then to see whether there are ways in which they might have what they want or else accept that they cannot, in which case they may have to be helped in the slow process of mourning their loss.

I believe that the therapy group is by far the best medium in which these problems can be recognized and also worked through. It is not a task for the group conductor alone and it is often better understood by other group members who may more easily be able to identify with the envious or jealous person. Even if nothing else can be done, nothing is worse than feeling isolated. My view is that there is nothing more therapeutic in group analysis than the sense of being accepted by the whole group. Change is another matter, but it is acceptance which makes change possible.

References

Freud, A. (1968) *The Ego and the Mechanisms of Defence.* London: Hogarth Press and Institute of Psycho-Analysis.

Klein, M. (1957) *Envy and Gratitude.* London: Tavistock Publications. New York: Basic Books.

Stern, D. (1985) *The Interpersonal World of the Infant.* New York: Basic Books.

Zinkin, L. (1983) 'Malignant mirroring.' Chapter 14 of this volume, originally published in *Group Analysis* XVI/2, pp.113–126.

CHAPTER SIXTEEN

All's Well that Ends Well – or is it?

This is Louis Zinkin's last paper. Shortly after presenting it at the Institute of Group Analysis, London, March 1993 at a joint IGA/Society of Analytical Psychology workshop entitled 'Ending or Stopping', he collapsed and died.

I should like to begin by explaining that I shall be using the word 'analysis' a great deal and that, when I do, I am speaking equally of individual and group analysis. I am, however, not concerned with forms of therapy, such as short-term focal analytic therapy or with closed groups, even though these approaches can teach us much about ending therapy.

Last year we had a joint Institute of Group Analysis and Society of Analytical Psychology workshop on 'The Art of Assessment'. I said then that I thought it was the second most difficult topic in psychotherapy. When pressed to say what I thought was the most difficult, I said: 'Termination'. With much encouragement from Liza Glenn, I then gave some thought to the present workshop, because it seemed an excellent topic on which Jungian and group analysts could exchange views. But last year we encountered a difficulty. This was that we had engaged a number of experts on assessment and some people complained that there had not been enough time given to them and that the conference was expensive and they didn't think they got enough back for their money. Though I felt sympathetic to this complaint, my own feeling was that it is no good expecting answers from the experts. It is true that experienced assessors can give their conclusions on the best way *they* have found to do it. But people complained that this did not help them because they didn't work under the same conditions and in any case they didn't agree with what was being suggested.

I think when we talk about 'termination' the same problems may arise. As we gain experience we may learn more about how to end therapy but all patients are different and every analysis is different, even with the same analyst, so that it becomes very difficult to argue from one patient to another. The fact is that there simply is no agreed way of doing it, nor when it is right to end. There are various maxims and bits of advice but if you look at the literature you will find a great deal of conflicting opinions as to detail. Nearly everybody is agreed that you have to end sometime and that it is most undesirable to go on for ever, but when it comes to establishing criteria for when to end, there is not only no agreement but the criteria given are not easy to apply to any particular patient. They depend heavily on the theoretical orientation of the analyst. For example, a Kleinian might look for the achievement of the depressive position, others will talk of neurotic symptoms having been satisfactorily worked through, acting out having ceased, a strong ego having been established, or they might fall back on Freud's twin criteria, such as the ability to work and to love or the replacement of neurosis by common unhappiness. Jungians have even greater difficulty if they use the concept of individuation, where the goal is completeness, or, as Jung said, becoming more what one truly is. Unfortunately Jung also considered these goals to be unattainable, and the process to continue throughout life. So there is always further to go.

Sometimes the analyst will take up the position that it is not a question of the process of analysis ever ending: it is simply an assessment of the point where the patient doesn't need the analyst any longer. This is often regarded as the ability to internalise the analyst and at this stage the patient is considered able to continue the dialogue with the internal analyst. This was, I think, Jung's view. He in any case regarded the process as primarily one between the patient and the unconscious. It was essentially self-analysis. This was why he did not like seeing patients more than about twice a week. He expected them to work on themselves in the meantime and the analyst was only there to facilitate the process. He does not seem to have worked with patients for very long himself, and like Freud would probably be horrified at the length of present day analyses.

But even if we could all agree on when to end, there is still the problem of how. Should one give a definite ending date? How long should one give? Should one postpone it if necessary (and most analysts have agreed that patients have an awkward way of going back to where they started once the ending date has been agreed)?

Another source of disagreement is whether the analyst should go on analysing until the patient finally leaves the room for the last time or, on the contrary, should try to 'dissolve the transference' by becoming more real, giving more personal information, for example revealing more feelings about the patient than is considered desirable while analysing, and so on. Should the ending be regarded as final? Should it be made explicit that patients can come back if they feel the need or should this be discouraged? It is very frustrating for the analyst not to follow up but would he or she be just gratifying personal needs if he or she suggested seeing the patient again, say annually? Or would this defeat the whole purpose of ending?

These are just a few problems besetting the analyst, and I want to leave open the questions of the 'how' of ending and concentrate on the 'when' question. We embark on a form of therapy which has no built-in ending and no clear-cut unchanging goal. It is an approach which differs from all others in that it is an exploration of the unconscious and though we can know more and more about the unconscious, replacing it with ego, making the unconscious conscious, as Freud said, we know that there will always be an unconscious. However many numbers we subtract from infinity, we are always left with infinity. And, by definition, what remains unconscious will continue to be unknown, or anyhow very hard to get at, or at the very least, hard to get at by oneself. And the whole beauty of the process is the continuous discovery that when one thought one was getting somewhere, one realizes that either it is a blind end or a false trail, or a new possibility opens up. So each new insight requires a change of direction and new insights are quite endless, thank goodness. This being so, ending, just like assessment, cannot, it seems to me, be part of analysis, cannot be itself an act of interpreting the unconscious. In some way the analyst has to stop analysing and have a different sort of conversation, one which will review the work done and speculate as to the work which could be done if the analysis were to continue. And, of course, the analyst and the patient might disagree. I would even suggest that if the analysis has gone well, there will not be too easy an agreement to end, even if both do agree finally to do so.

Perhaps a sign of being ready to leave analysis is the ability to disagree, to think for oneself and not to comply automatically. A lot will depend on the therapist's attitude, the extent to which he or she puts it as a suggestion and is ready to consider the patient's different point of view, that one wants to end and the other does not. This raises very searching questions for the therapist. One has to ask, if wanting to continue: am I wanting to hold on to the patient for my own needs (including financial needs)? Am I taking too pessimistic or too optimistic a view of the patient's capacity for further change? Am I wanting this patient to go and make room for a better one? The patient has similar problems and may well suspect the analyst's motives, either for ending or not ending.

Perhaps the greatest difficulty for the analyst can be stated thus: in order to consider the question of ending analysis, one has to stop being an analyst. If for example the patient talks about ending and all the analyst does is to interpret this as the wish to avoid some painful confrontation, in other words, to think of the patient's wish to end as a form of acting out, then the patient may rightly feel let down. On the other hand, one can imagine the situation where the analyst fails to interpret in this way, seizing on the patient's wanting to end to avoid some problem which really one should try to overcome.

There are of course all sorts of possible endings. Sometimes one has to end for reasons which are external to the analytic process, but one always hopes that the end will have some coherent significance, a sort of natural conclusion. Michael Fordham makes a contrast between ending and stopping, the title of our workshop. There is a great difference between bringing something to an end and just stopping. An end always implies a goal or purpose having been achieved, as when we say the end justifies the means. But is the end of therapy, in this sense what is achieved in the course of the work, necessarily expressed at the time the therapy actually stops? Does the way it ends, the understanding expressed at the end, the things that are said in the very last session, represent a true understanding of what has taken place, of the value of the work? This is like asking whether a man's life can be evaluated at the time of his death. We all know how mundane the last words of the dying may be, the inadequacies of obituaries, the falseness of the funeral oration or the inanities we offer at parting, as we wait for the train to pull out. So does a good ending reflect a good analysis? There may be cases where the patient leaves for quite the wrong reasons, perhaps in a dissatisfied state, but where a great deal of good work has nevertheless been done. If one cannot reliably assess the value of the analysis at the time of ending, is there a better time to do so, say six months later? Certainly looking back on one's analysis can be like looking back on one's parentage. One goes on assessing it all one's life, sometimes realising where it has failed and sometimes appreciating it in a new way.

All patients in analysis have separation problems, and even if they don't think they do, the analyst will draw their attention to the forthcoming break, and be interested in how the anxiety about this is handled. If the patient denies any such problem, the analysis may not be of much value anyway. Some analysts pay much more attention to this than others, and some, I think, overdo it. But there is a general maxim that the way the final ending is negotiated depends on the way all the other partings have been treated, including the endings of sessions. In other words, the implication is that there is a gradual working-through of lesser separations which is the most important criterion of when and how to end the analysis, and will determine the quality of the parting. Again, we may want to question this. Although it may have some bearing in patients who, having suffered early traumatic separations, have problems with later ones, there surely must be a fundamental difference between handling what is known to be a temporary separation and one where one expects never to meet again.

All these questions are questions of which analogy seems the most apt. One can think about a doctor ending a course of treatment when he thinks the illness is cured, or he can do no more, and I suppose this is the most usual model. But in many ways this crude picture of the medical model is the worst possible one. Even doctors go on being around for their patients in a way that analysts are often not prepared to be. But more importantly, the relationship with the doctor does not come close to the intimacy of an analytic relationship where the analysis has been even moderately successful. Nor is this relationship incidental to the work. I would be inclined to say it *is* the work. There is a paradox here. The longer the analysis, the more difficult it ought to be to end it, and the more likely it is that it will get even longer.

The same objections can be raised to the other analogies that can be used, such as weaning a baby from the breast, or children leaving home. In these cases also the relationship continues in a new way, and the ending is only one aspect of the relationship. Admittedly, a process of mourning is needed in these other situations, because something is indeed lost for ever, even though the relationship continues and may be better than it was before. When psychotherapy ends, one mourns alone. The therapist or the group is no longer available and nobody else can understand why you are not simply relieved not to have to go any more or pay out any more.

Mourning is of course necessary where there is a death or at least an unalterable loss. But the end of therapy should be a new life beginning and if it is true that the analyst can be successfully internalised, there is nothing to mourn. Ideally, of course, a great deal of mourning is anticipatory and can be shared by both patient and analyst long before they actually separate (and in the case of the group, the whole group can share in this process). The most difficult case is the sudden and unanticipated death of the analyst or of the patient and in both cases one has little support in mourning. Should the patient or the analyst go to the funeral of the other?

The Jungian idea of individuation is, as I have said, a life journey and may even continue beyond death, so clearly there is no question of this being completed within a therapeutic framework. Jung appears to be quite silent on the subject of our workshop; at least 'termination' is not listed in the General Index to his vast *Collected Works*. I imagine this was because there was no question in his mind of the patients finishing when he said 'goodbye' to them.

The situation for group analysis is very similar. S.H. Foulkes took it for granted that one did not stay in a group for ever but he gave no clear guidelines for when and how to end. In the slow-open group, the group goes on indefinitely and there may be groups which have gone on for twenty-five years or longer. It is understood that group members will leave when they are ready; it is not uncommon for people not to feel ready for many years. The situation differs, of course, from individual therapy in that the group will go on after the individual member has left and this is often a painful thought, as is the thought of being replaced by a new member, often immediately. Also the tradition is that after giving notice a member should attend the group until the end of the notice, usually for a month, and is reminded that leaving is not a purely individual matter as the whole group is affected.

The question of leaving is considered not to matter for the member alone or for the therapist, who may not have a strong opinion one way or the other. Sometimes the group goes through stages when it is considered very wrong for anyone to leave. At other times people ask each other why they are staying so long and sometimes there are epidemics of leaving. No sooner does one member say he or she is thinking of leaving than others pipe up to say they have the same idea, to the dismay of the group conductor, and there ensues a quarrel as to who should be given precedence. As with individual analysis, there is considerable controversy as to when one is outstaying one's welcome and there is the same problem of excessive dependency, of analysis interminable and of therapy becoming a way of life. On the one hand, it is difficult to justify asking anyone to leave a group who is continuing to benefit from it and, on the other, one does see people encouraging a member to stay on in order to solve their own problems. It is true, too, that the member who benefited most from the group is the one who has the most to give back, to help the group function well and be of the most help to others. At the other end of the spectrum there is the difficult patient whom one might be quite relieved to see leave. It is hard to be objective and impartial in such cases and the group conductor often relies on trusting the group to come to the right decision. Although 'trusting the group' is a group-analytic technical maxim, it may sometimes be a byword for the easy way out.

In spite of all these difficulties, there are a certain number of cases where one has little real doubt that the patient, whether in a group or in individual analysis, is ready to leave, where it feels absolutely right and where the manner of ending feels as good as it might be. A classic description of the way analysis should end is given by Michael Balint:

> If this process can develop in an undisturbed way, a surprisingly uniform experience dominates the very last period of the treatment. The patient feels that he is going through a kind of re-birth into a new life, that he has arrived at the end of a dark tunnel, that he sees light again at the end of a long journey, that he has been given a new life, he experiences a sense of great freedom, as if a heavy burden had dropped from him, etc. It is a deeply moving experience; the general atmosphere is of taking leave for ever of something very dear, very precious – with all the corresponding grief and mourning – that this sincere and deeply felt grief is mitigated by the feeling of security, originating from the newly-won possibilities for real happiness. Usually the patient leaves after the last session happy but with tears in his eyes and – I think I may admit – the analyst is in a very similar mood. (Balint 1950, pp.196–199)

Balint here describes a combination of deep grief and a newly-won possibility of what he calls 'real happiness'. His description is quite touching. It is how every analysis ought to end, but I can only recall one which ended like this. The circumstances were unusual in that the analysis began with the ending of a marriage and ended when a new relationship was found. In this new relationship my patient had found true happiness and she had also, in the course of the analysis, given up one successful career to begin a new and more creative one. With her new partner and her new career, she was happier than she had ever been. Both survived a honeymoon period and I was very happy with the idea of ending and felt we had achieved a great deal. There was also grief at ending which I felt too, so we ended with the mixture of grief and joy which Balint described. The fact remains that this is the only ending I can recall which fulfilled this ideal.

What perhaps we might all agree is that a good and successful ending is never without pain. If there is no pain, the work and the relationship cannot have been of much value. Where we might differ is in the question of how much pain, what the pain should be about and what compensates adequately, short of newly-won real happiness, for this pain.

It is sometimes said that ending is part of analysis; that it is built in to it, part of its essential structure. The sentiment here would be that all good things have to come to an end and that all's well that ends well. The analogy would be that of a story with a good plot, and we can think of tragedy or comedy, each of which has a logical and coherent end which is integral to its genre. Whether it ends sadly or happily, there is a deep sense of resolution which feels right as the story draws to a conclusion which seems inevitable. Of course, in our postmodernist age most stories do not end like this – they often just stop, quite arbitrarily. How often, nowadays, do we see a film in which just when it's getting interesting the cast list goes up? It used to say 'The End'. Now it just tells who was in it and who made it. Often there is deliberate ambiguity in the ending and we can go on discussing what happens afterwards. It is worth reminding ourselves that artists frequently have difficulty in knowing when they have finished. A painting can always be added to, improved or altered and often an artist stops not because the painting is finished but because he or she wants to start another.

I want to mention briefly the special case of training analysis because I think it highlights all the problems of ending. Should training bodies have the right to insist on continuing analysis until the training is over? Do analysts who continue to meet their own analysts professionally or socially ever know what it is like to end? Is the wish to train a way of avoiding this loss? Should the analyst ever agree to end the analysis just because the training is over, or is this stopping rather than ending? I simply ask these questions so that we can try to find answers. I do have views, of course, but I have to say that I am not very sure about any of them.

If the ideal ending is rare, we should consider whether we are perhaps persecuting ourselves unnecessarily in seeking it. We might agree that a good ending is never abrupt and unpredictable, nor when we are 'stuck and can go no further', nor again is it a case of grinding to a halt. Should one then agree to end when the analysis is going well and continuing to be productive? Is the best time to leave a party when we are most enjoying ourselves, like Cinderella, or like the gambler's maxim to quit when you are ahead? My paper originally ended with this question and you might think this is a rather arbitrary point at which to end. If I stopped now, it might be read as an admission of failure to answer my own questions, or it might be to make the point that all endings, including the ending of analysis, is in the last resort arbitrary.

But this would be a premature closure and I wanted my introductory talk to give us food for thought. So I have decided to continue just a little longer, and you will notice that I am now like the analyst who believes in becoming more transparent towards the end.

I believe that all human relationships depend on a tension between opposites. The opposition is as follows: on the one hand, we value mutuality, dialogue, equality, empathy, sharing of understanding. On the other we value conflict, encounter, recognition of irresolvable differences, 'bumping up against the other person', and the differences in the direction in which each of us must go. 'Parting is such sweet sorrow.' We need therefore some rituals for ending any meeting with another person and all societies have such rituals at every stage of life. Though I cannot solve the problem, perhaps I can at least limit its scope. Let us acknowledge that we need ritual endings to therapy. This will never be a natural endpoint, always an artificial one and the question then is reduced to that of looking at the rituals we have. We should not enact them unthinkingly. A committee, for example, has evolved ways of ending its own deliberations which continue to be most unsatisfactory, like putting it to the vote, passing on to the next item on the agenda, guillotining, or just leaving an issue.

So I will not bring this talk to an end but to a stop. I will stop with the thought that, in the end, we end in an arbitrary way. Even in the most favourable cases we should not pretend that the possible work is ever finished. Ending and stopping are never totally distinct and nor are the 'when' and 'how' of ending separate. If everybody agrees to end, then how to end is not too difficult, and conversely, if we are unsure how to end, we should probably not be ending at all.

Finally, I am sure we will, in this workshop, need to discuss how we understand the nature of time. Most of the controversy on this subject might be less contentious if we recognized that there is more than one kind of analytic time. It is convenient to distinguish two. One is linear and historical, like a narrative with a beginning, an end and a duration which can be measured; the other is circular or cyclical, never begun and never ending.

And with this thought I will now stop.

Reference

Balint, M. (1950). 'On the termination of analysis.' *International Journal of Psycho-Analysis 31*, 3, pp.166–9.

Subject Index

Author Index